SIEGE
THOR

WRITER: **KIERON GILLEN**

THOR #607-609
ART: **BILLY TAN** & **BATT** AND **RICH ELSON**
COLORISTS: **CHRISTINA STRAIN, PAUL MOUNTS, MATT HOLLINGSWORTH**
& **JUNE CHUNG**
LETTERER: **VIRTUAL CALLIGRAPHY'S JOE SABINO**
COVER ART: **MICO SUAYAN** & **LAURA MARTIN**

THOR #610
ART: **DOUG BRAITHWAITE**
COLORISTS: **ANDY TROY, DOUG BRAITHWAITE** & **PAUL MOUNTS**
LETTERER: **VIRTUAL CALLIGRAPHY'S JOE SABINO**
COVER ART: **MICO SUAYAN** & **LAURA MARTIN**

SIEGE: LOKI
ART: **JAMIE MCKELVIE**
COLORIST: **NATHAN FAIRBAIRN**
LETTERER: **VIRTUAL CALLIGRAPHY'S JOE CARAMAGNA**
COVER ART: **MARKO DJURDJEVIC**

ASSISTANT EDITOR: **ALEJANDRO ARBONA**
EDITOR: **RALPH MACCHIO**

NEW MUTANTS #11
ART: **NIKO HENRICHON**
LETTERER: **VIRTUAL CALLIGRAPHY'S JOE CARAMAGNA**
COVER ART: **TERRY DODSON** & **RACHEL DODSON**
ASSOCIATE EDITOR: **DANIEL KETCHUM**
EDITOR: **NICK LOWE**

COLLECTION EDITOR: **JENNIFER GRÜNWALD**
EDITORIAL ASSISTANTS: **JAMES EMMETT** & **JOE HOCHSTEIN**
ASSISTANT EDITORS: **ALEX STARBUCK** & **NELSON RIBEIRO**
EDITOR, SPECIAL PROJECTS: **MARK D. BEAZLEY**
SENIOR EDITOR, SPECIAL PROJECTS: **JEFF YOUNGQUIST**
SENIOR VICE PRESIDENT OF SALES: **DAVID GABRIEL**
BOOK DESIGNER: **RODOLFO MURAGUCHI**

EDITOR IN CHIEF: **JOE QUESADA**
PUBLISHER: **DAN BUCKLEY**
EXECUTIVE PRODUCER: **ALAN FINE**

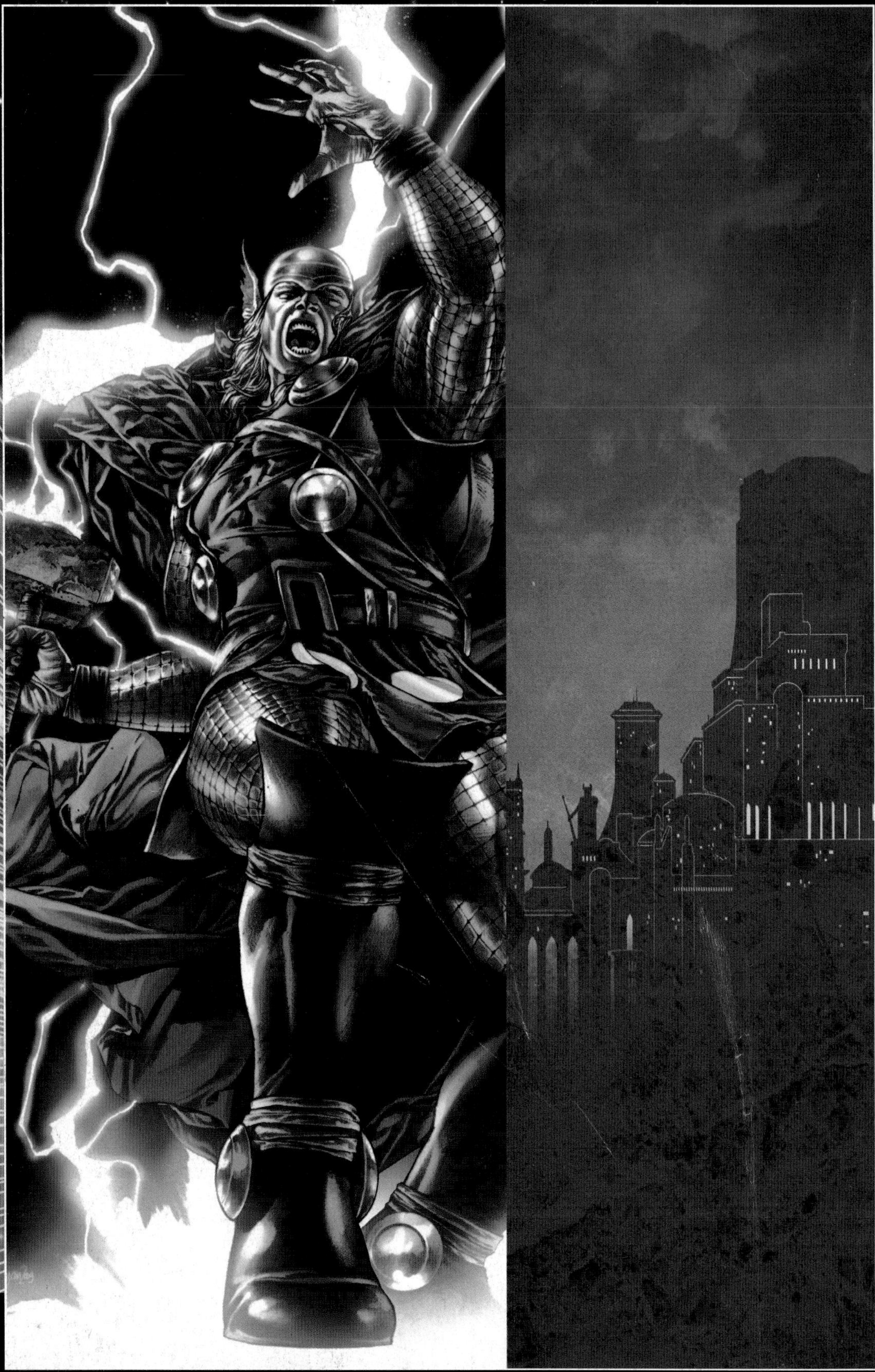

THOR #607

THOR #607 DEADPOOL VARIANT

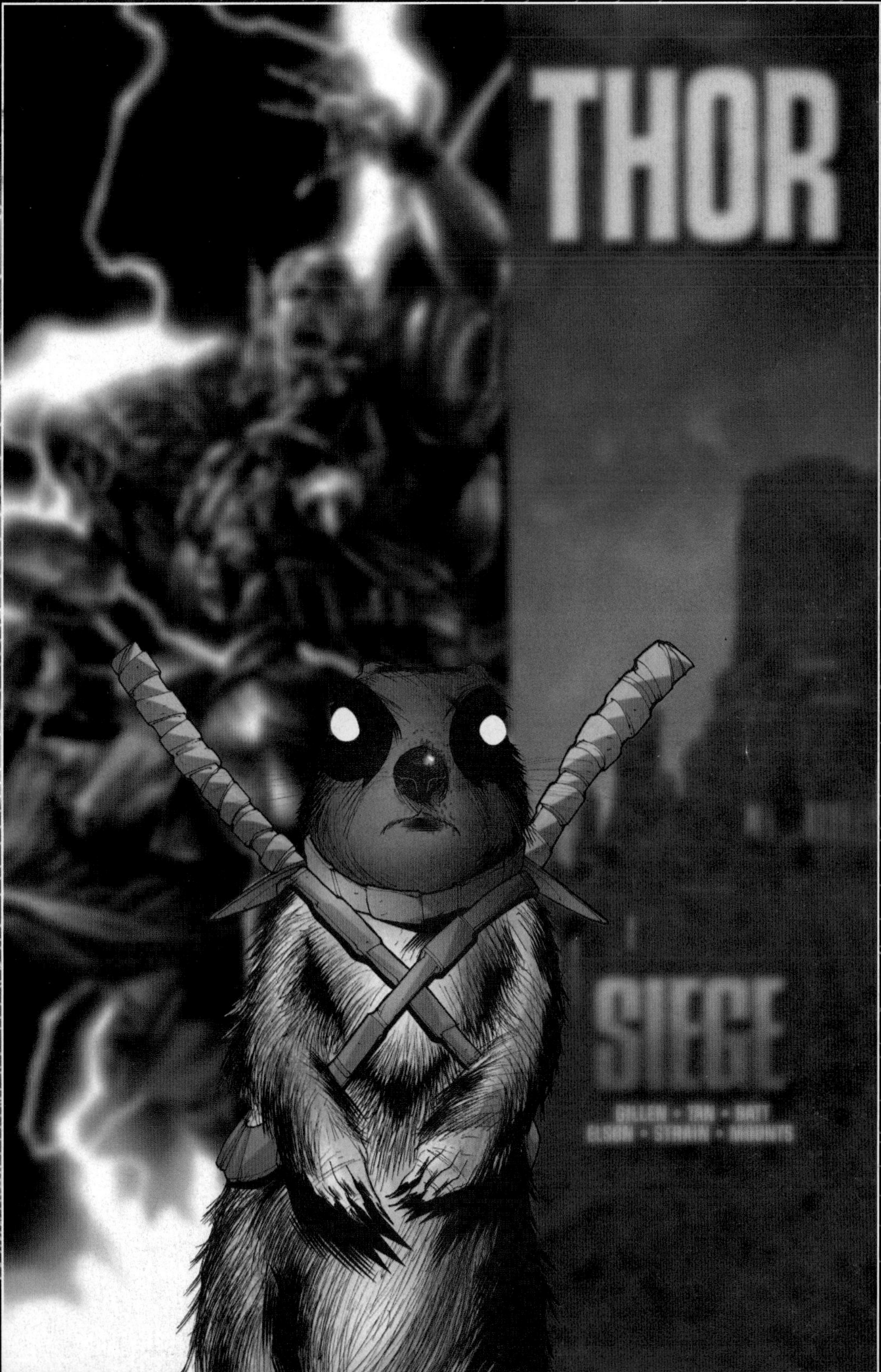
THOR
SIEGE

BY **JUAN DOE**

THOR

PREVIOUSLY...

DARK TIMES HAVE COME FOR THE GOD OF THUNDER.

THROUGH THE MANIPULATIONS OF HIS WICKED BROTHER, LOKI, THOR WAS CAST INTO EXILE. IN HIS ABSENC[E]
THEIR BROTHER BALDER WAS PLACED ON THE THRONE OF ASGARD...WITH LOKI AS ADVISER, WHISPERIN[G]
POISON IN THE KING'S EAR.

BUT IT ISN'T MERELY BALDER WHO'S FALLEN UNDER LOKI'S INFLUENCE. AS A MEMBER OF NORMAN OSBORN[']
CABAL OF SUPER VILLAINS, LOKI HAS MANAGED TO CONVINCE THE POWER-MAD OSBORN THAT ASGARD HA[S]
NO PLACE BEING ON EARTH, IN ITS NEW HOME OUTSIDE THE SMALL TOWN OF BROXTON, OKLAHOMA...TH[AT]
ASGARD MUST BE REMOVED...

FABRICATING AN INCIDENT, OSBORN CAUSED A CATASTROPHE IN CHICAGO, KILLING HUNDREDS – AND MA[DE]
IT APPEAR AS THOUGH THE ASGARDIAN WARRIOR VOLSTAGG WAS RESPONSIBLE. AND AS DIRECTOR OF T[HE]
LAW ENFORCEMENT AGENCY H.A.M.M.E.R. AND LEADER OF A VILLAINOUS TEAM OF AVENGERS, IT'S OSBORN[']
JOB TO LAY SIEGE TO ASGARD...

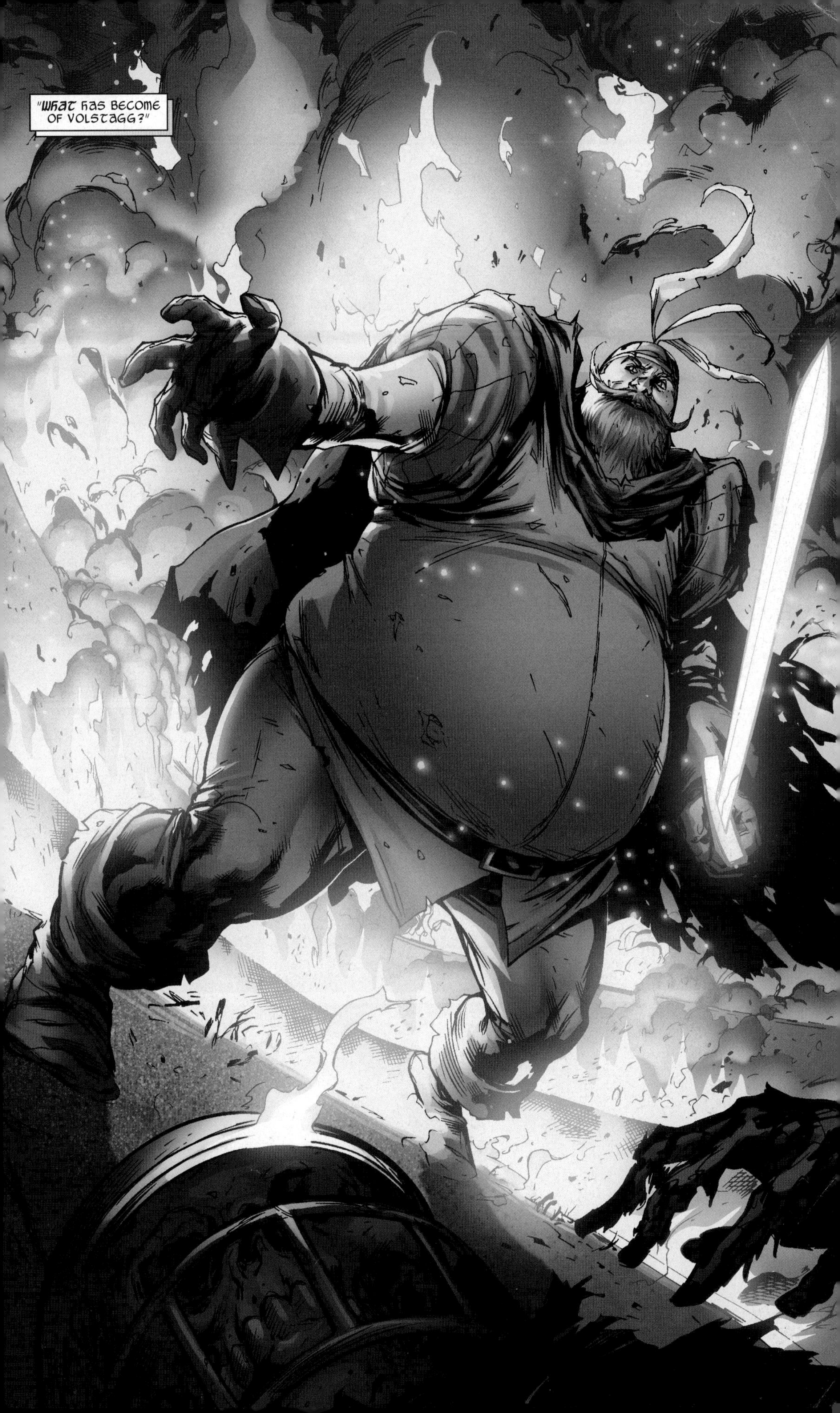
"WHAT HAS BECOME OF VOLSTAGG?"

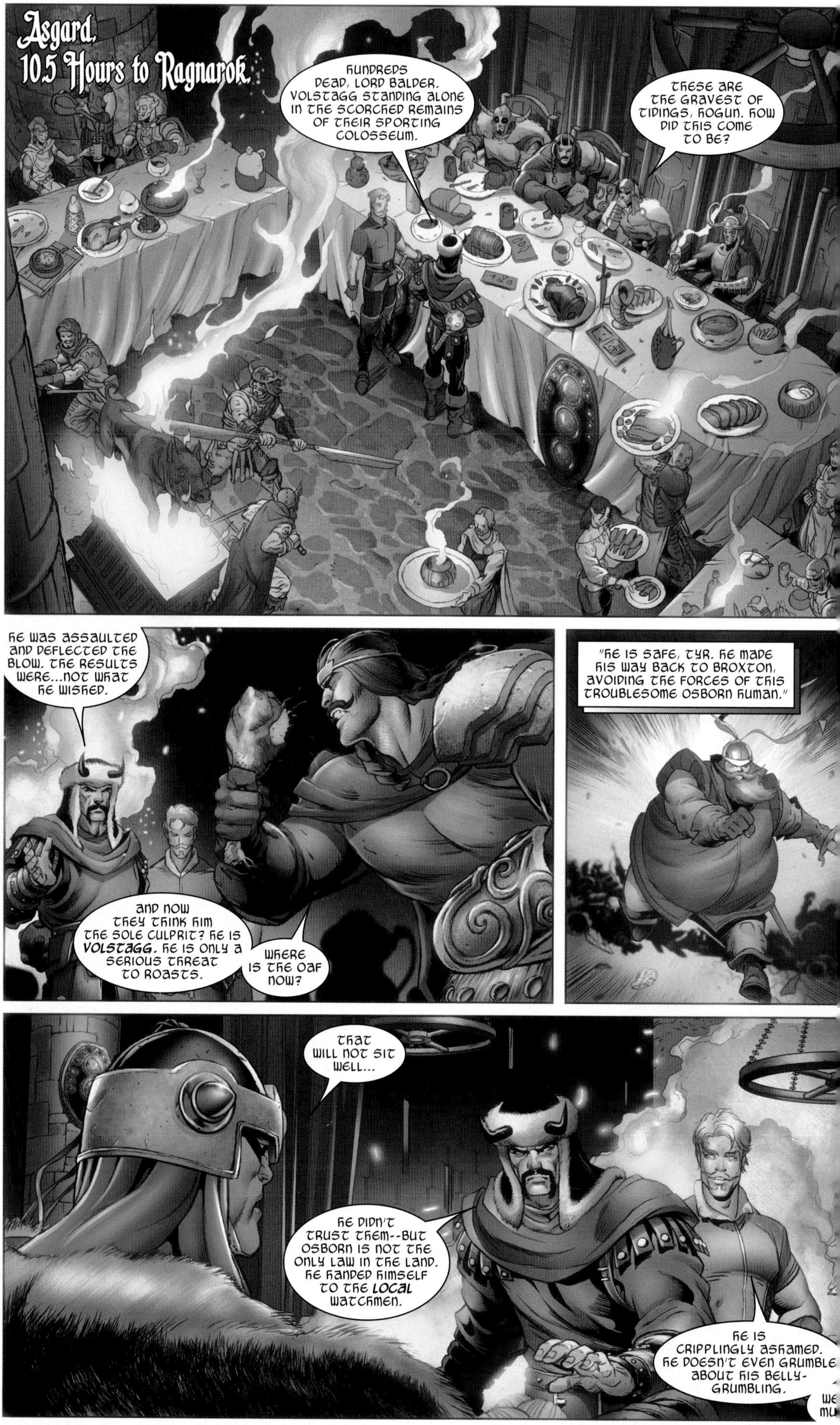

Asgard, 10.5 Hours to Ragnarok.
HUNDREDS DEAD, LORD BALDER. VOLSTAGG STANDING ALONE IN THE SCORCHED REMAINS OF THEIR SPORTING COLOSSEUM.
THESE ARE THE GRAVEST OF TIDINGS, HOGUN. HOW DID THIS COME TO BE?
HE WAS ASSAULTED AND DEFLECTED THE BLOW. THE RESULTS WERE...NOT WHAT HE WISHED.
AND NOW THEY THINK HIM THE SOLE CULPRIT? HE IS **VOLSTAGG.** HE IS ONLY A SERIOUS THREAT TO ROASTS.
WHERE IS THE OAF NOW?
"HE IS SAFE, TYR. HE MADE HIS WAY BACK TO BROXTON, AVOIDING THE FORCES OF THIS TROUBLESOME OSBORN HUMAN."
THAT WILL NOT SIT WELL...
HE DIDN'T TRUST THEM--BUT OSBORN IS NOT THE ONLY LAW IN THE LAND. HE HANDED HIMSELF TO THE **LOCAL** WATCHMEN.
HE IS CRIPPLINGLY ASHAMED. HE DOESN'T EVEN GRUMBLE ABOUT HIS BELLY-GRUMBLING.

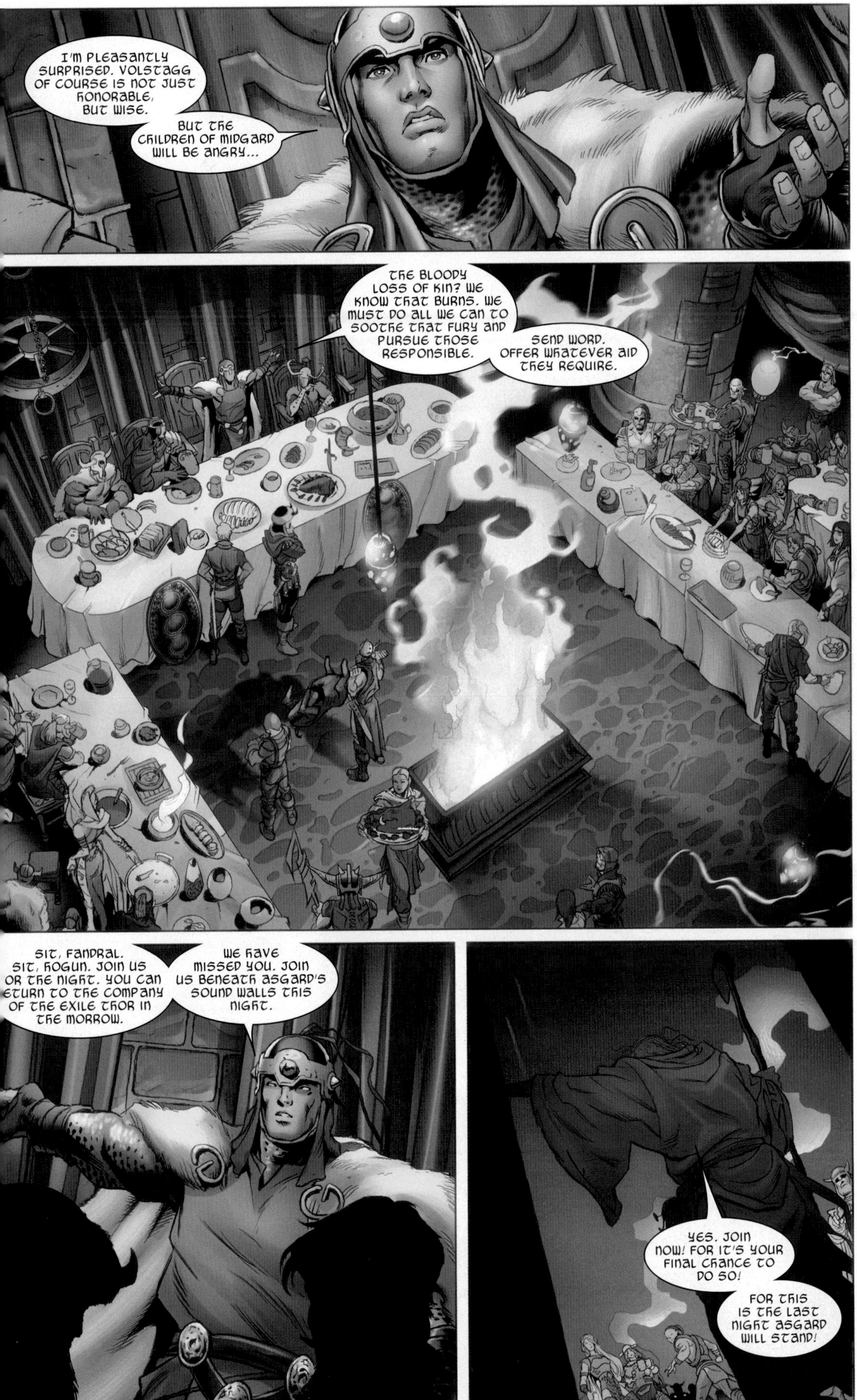
I'M PLEASANTLY SURPRISED. VOLSTAGG OF COURSE IS NOT JUST HONORABLE, BUT WISE.
BUT THE CHILDREN OF MIDGARD WILL BE ANGRY...
THE BLOODY LOSS OF KIN? WE KNOW THAT BURNS. WE MUST DO ALL WE CAN TO SOOTHE THAT FURY AND PURSUE THOSE RESPONSIBLE.
SEND WORD. OFFER WHATEVER AID THEY REQUIRE.
SIT, FANDRAL. SIT, HOGUN. JOIN US OR THE NIGHT. YOU CAN ETURN TO THE COMPANY OF THE EXILE THOR IN THE MORROW.
WE HAVE MISSED YOU. JOIN US BENEATH ASGARD'S SOUND WALLS THIS NIGHT.
YES. JOIN NOW! FOR IT'S YOUR FINAL CHANCE TO DO SO!
FOR THIS IS THE LAST NIGHT ASGARD WILL STAND!

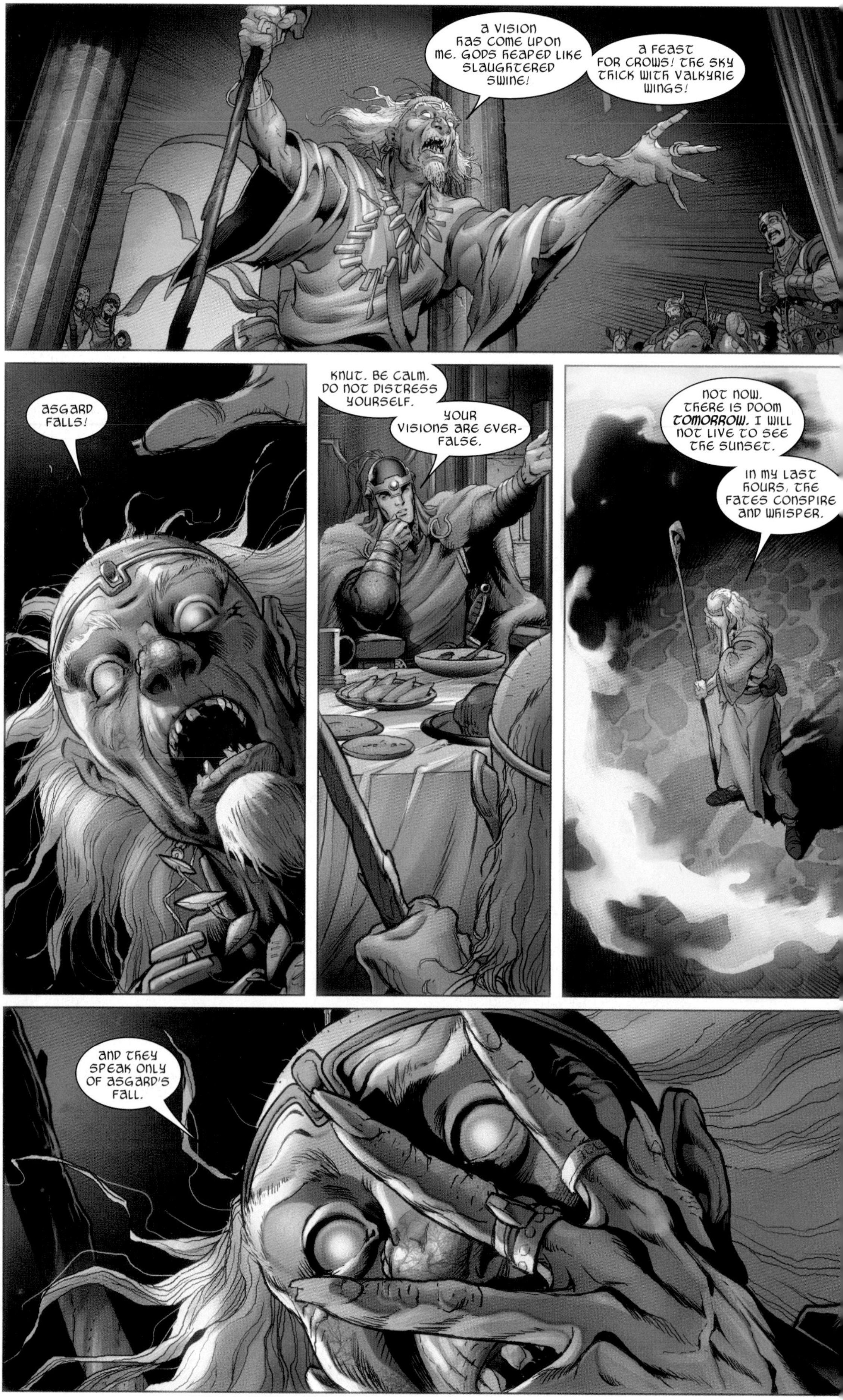
A VISION HAS COME UPON ME. GODS HEAPED LIKE SLAUGHTERED SWINE!
A FEAST FOR CROWS! THE SKY THICK WITH VALKYRIE WINGS!
ASGARD FALLS!
KNUT. BE CALM. DO NOT DISTRESS YOURSELF.
YOUR VISIONS ARE EVER-FALSE.
NOT NOW. THERE IS DOOM TOMORROW. I WILL NOT LIVE TO SEE THE SUNSET.
IN MY LAST HOURS, THE FATES CONSPIRE AND WHISPER.
AND THEY SPEAK ONLY OF ASGARD'S FALL.

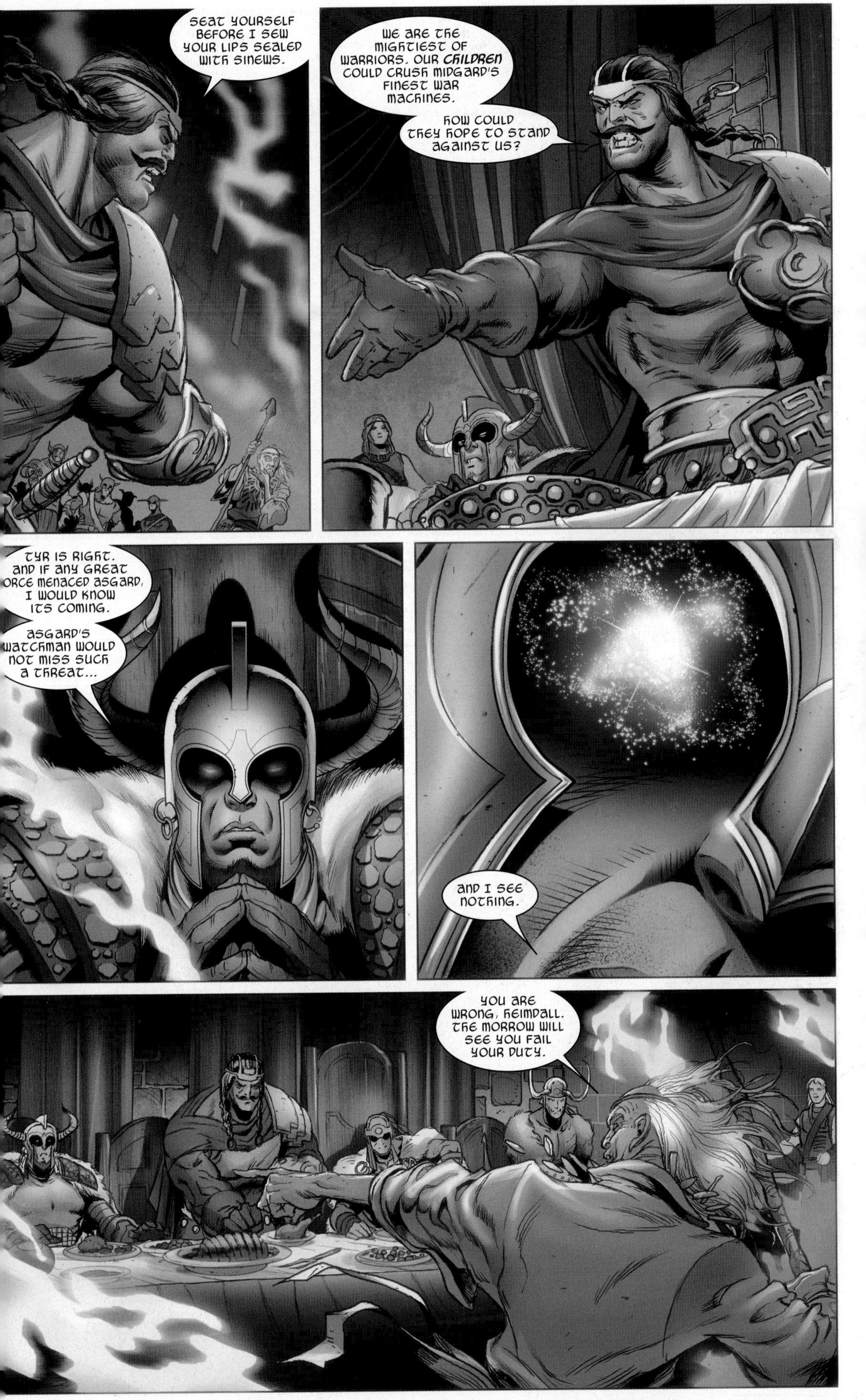

SEAT YOURSELF BEFORE I SEW YOUR LIPS SEALED WITH SINEWS.
WE ARE THE MIGHTIEST OF WARRIORS. OUR **CHILDREN** COULD CRUSH MIDGARD'S FINEST WAR MACHINES.
HOW COULD THEY HOPE TO STAND AGAINST US?
TYR IS RIGHT. AND IF ANY GREAT ORCE MENACED ASGARD, I WOULD KNOW ITS COMING.
ASGARD'S WATCHMAN WOULD NOT MISS SUCH A THREAT...
AND I SEE NOTHING.
YOU ARE WRONG, HEIMDALL. THE MORROW WILL SEE YOU FAIL YOUR DUTY.

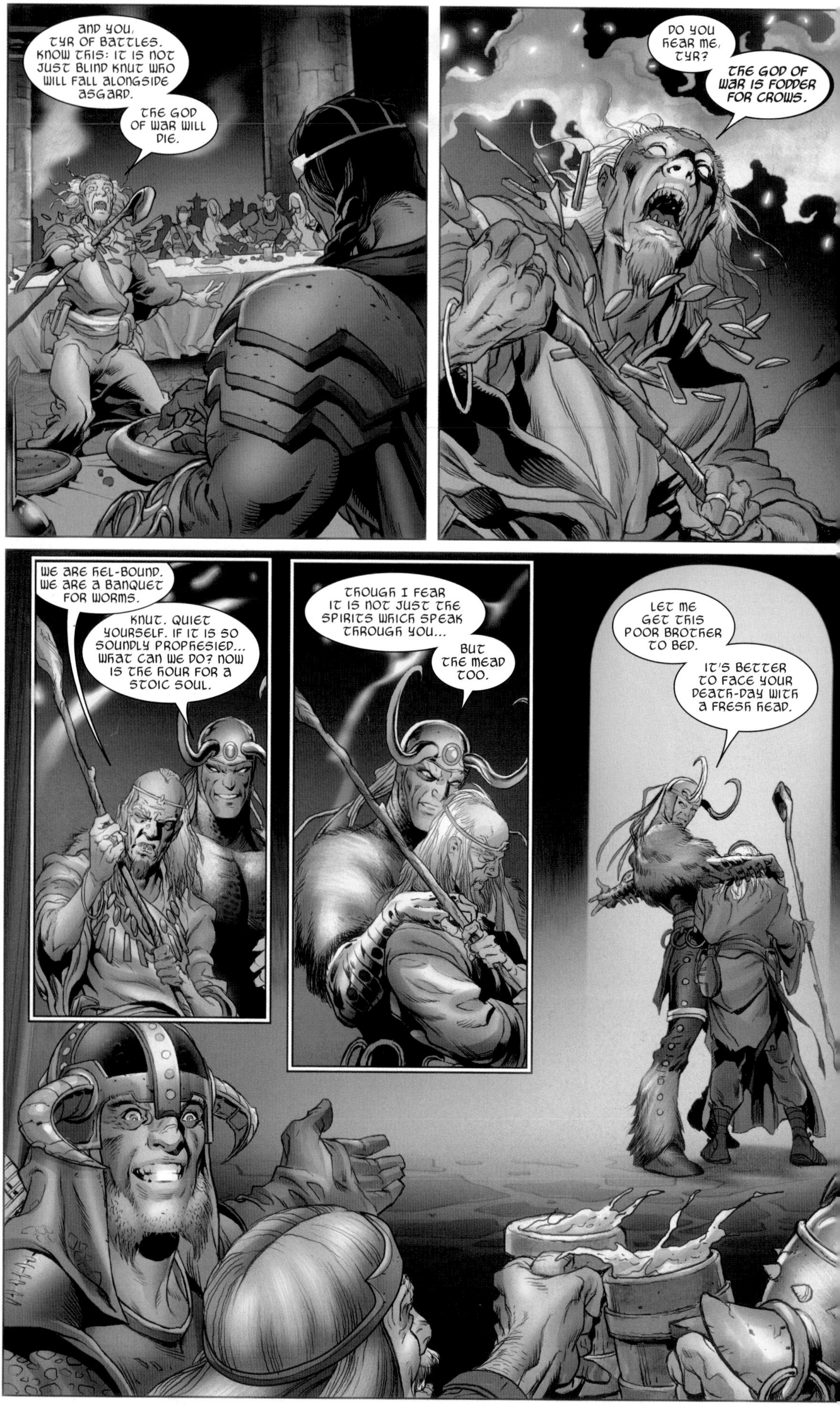

AND YOU, TYR OF BATTLES. KNOW THIS: IT IS NOT JUST BLIND KNUT WHO WILL FALL ALONGSIDE ASGARD.
THE GOD OF WAR WILL DIE.
DO YOU HEAR ME, TYR?
THE GOD OF WAR IS FODDER FOR CROWS.
WE ARE HEL-BOUND. WE ARE A BANQUET FOR WORMS.
KNUT. QUIET YOURSELF. IF IT IS SO SOUNDLY PROPHESIED... WHAT CAN WE DO? NOW IS THE HOUR FOR A STOIC SOUL.
THOUGH I FEAR IT IS NOT JUST THE SPIRITS WHICH SPEAK THROUGH YOU...
BUT THE MEAD TOO.
LET ME GET THIS POOR BROTHER TO BED.
IT'S BETTER TO FACE YOUR DEATH-DAY WITH A FRESH HEAD.

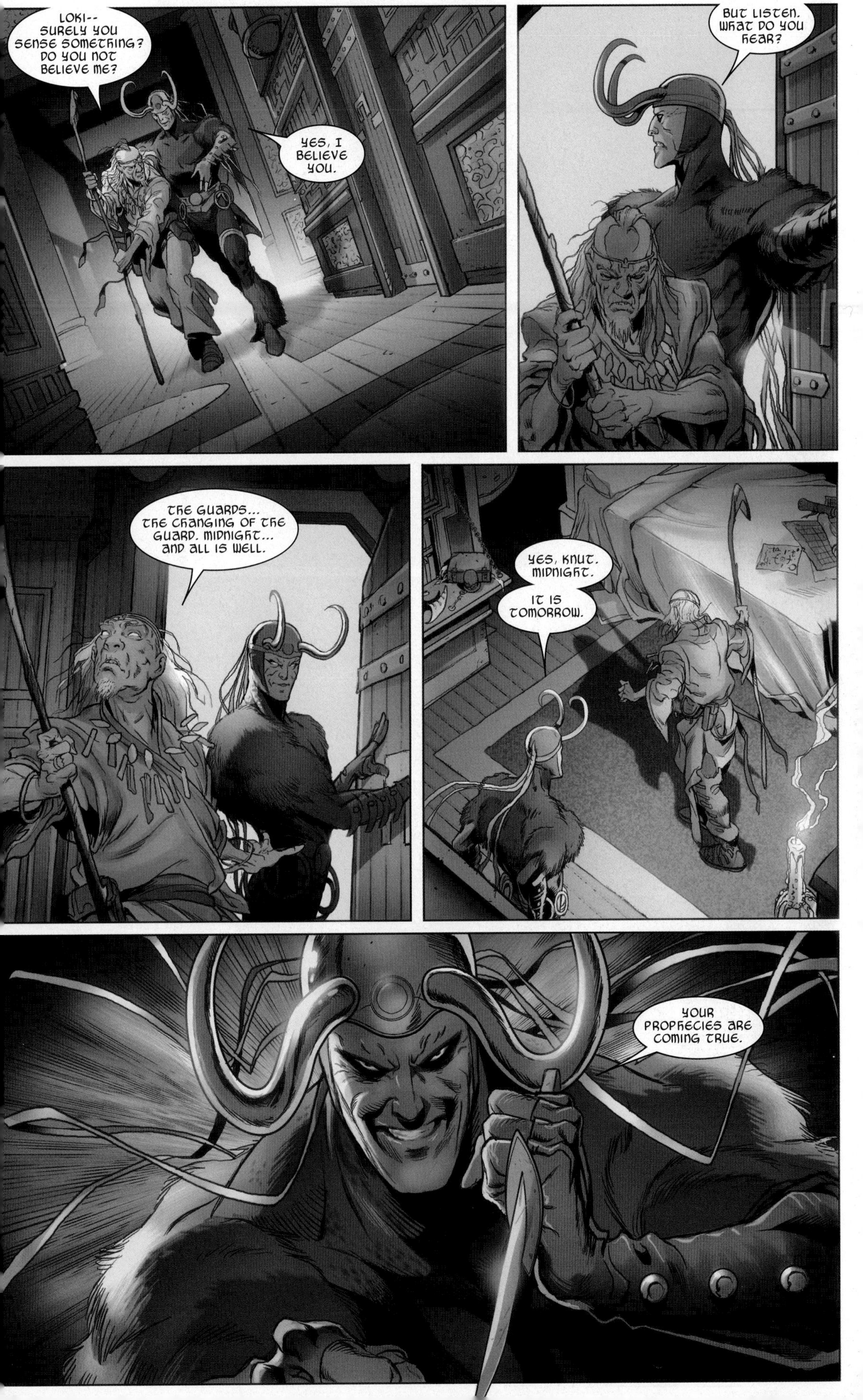
LOKI-- SURELY YOU SENSE SOMETHING? DO YOU NOT BELIEVE ME?
YES, I BELIEVE YOU.
BUT LISTEN. WHAT DO YOU HEAR?
THE GUARDS... THE CHANGING OF THE GUARD. MIDNIGHT... AND ALL IS WELL.
YES, KNUT. MIDNIGHT.
IT IS TOMORROW.
YOUR PROPHECIES ARE COMING TRUE.

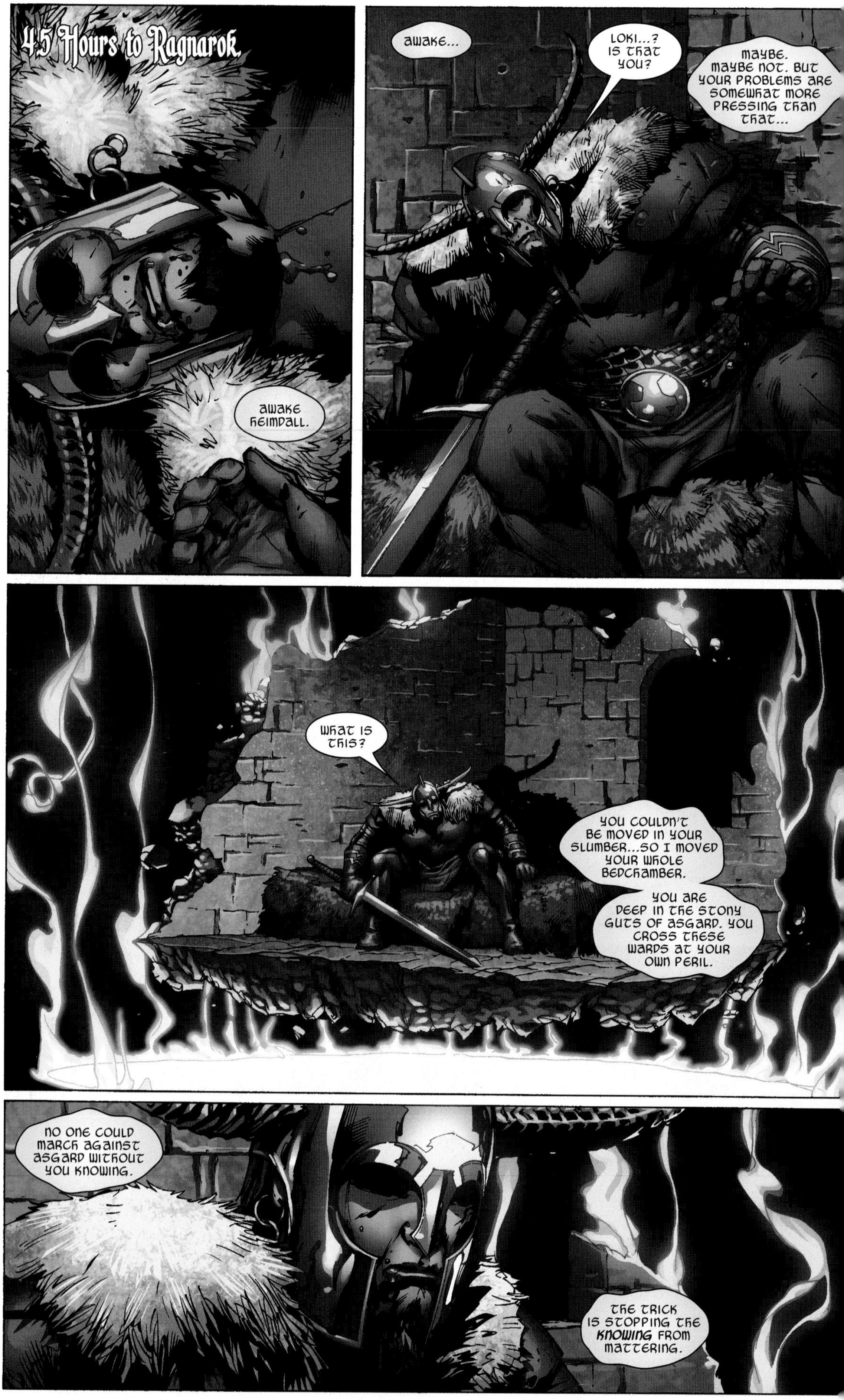
4.5 Hours to Ragnarok.
AWAKE HEIMDALL.
AWAKE...
LOKI...? IS THAT YOU?
MAYBE. MAYBE NOT. BUT YOUR PROBLEMS ARE SOMEWHAT MORE PRESSING THAN THAT...
WHAT IS THIS?
YOU COULDN'T BE MOVED IN YOUR SLUMBER...SO I MOVED YOUR WHOLE BEDCHAMBER.
YOU ARE DEEP IN THE STONY GUTS OF ASGARD. YOU CROSS THESE WARDS AT YOUR OWN PERIL.
NO ONE COULD MARCH AGAINST ASGARD WITHOUT YOU KNOWING.
THE TRICK IS STOPPING THE KNOWING FROM MATTERING.

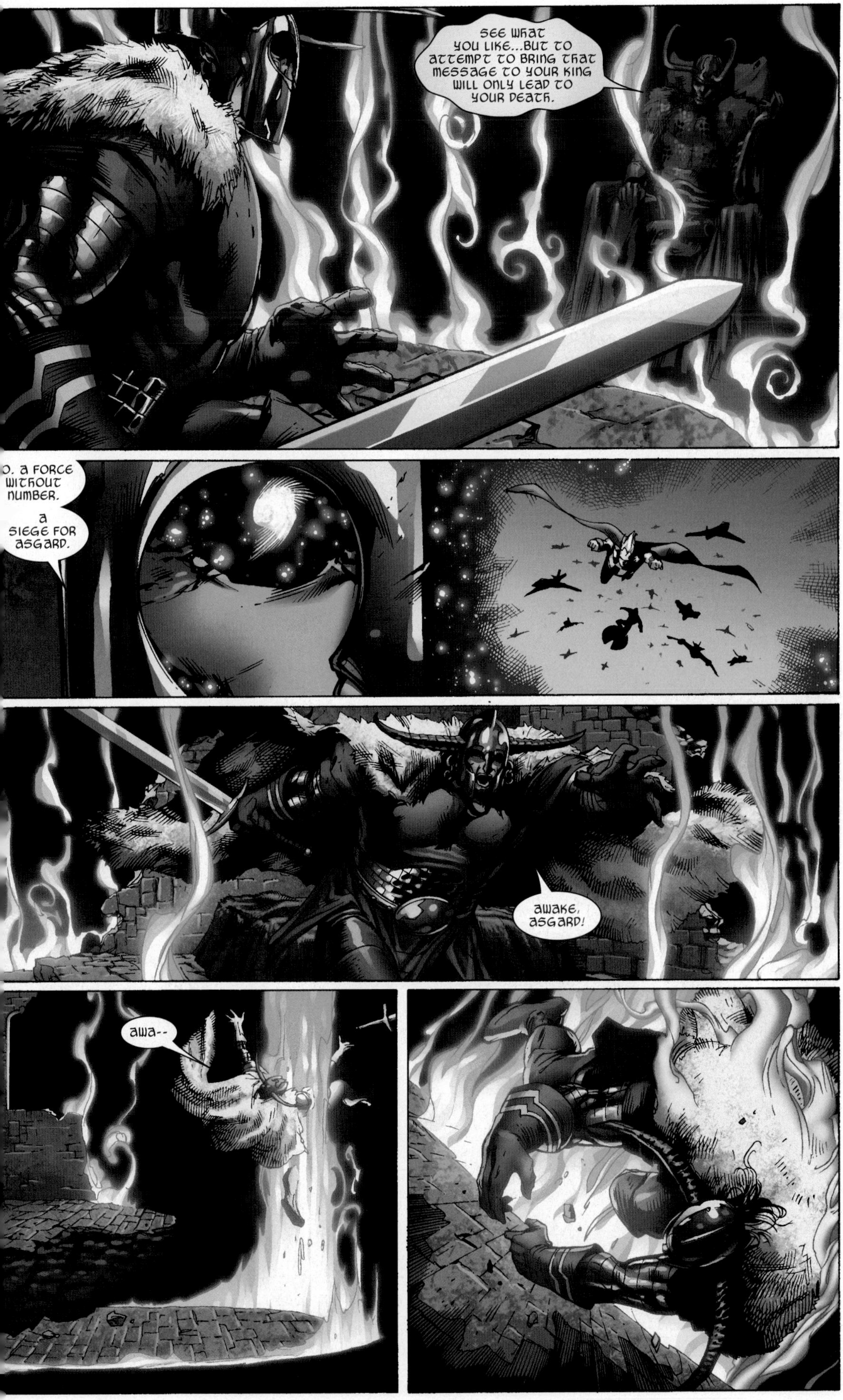
SEE WHAT YOU LIKE...BUT TO ATTEMPT TO BRING THAT MESSAGE TO YOUR KING WILL ONLY LEAD TO YOUR DEATH.
O. A FORCE WITHOUT NUMBER.
A SIEGE FOR ASGARD.
AWAKE, ASGARD!
AWA--

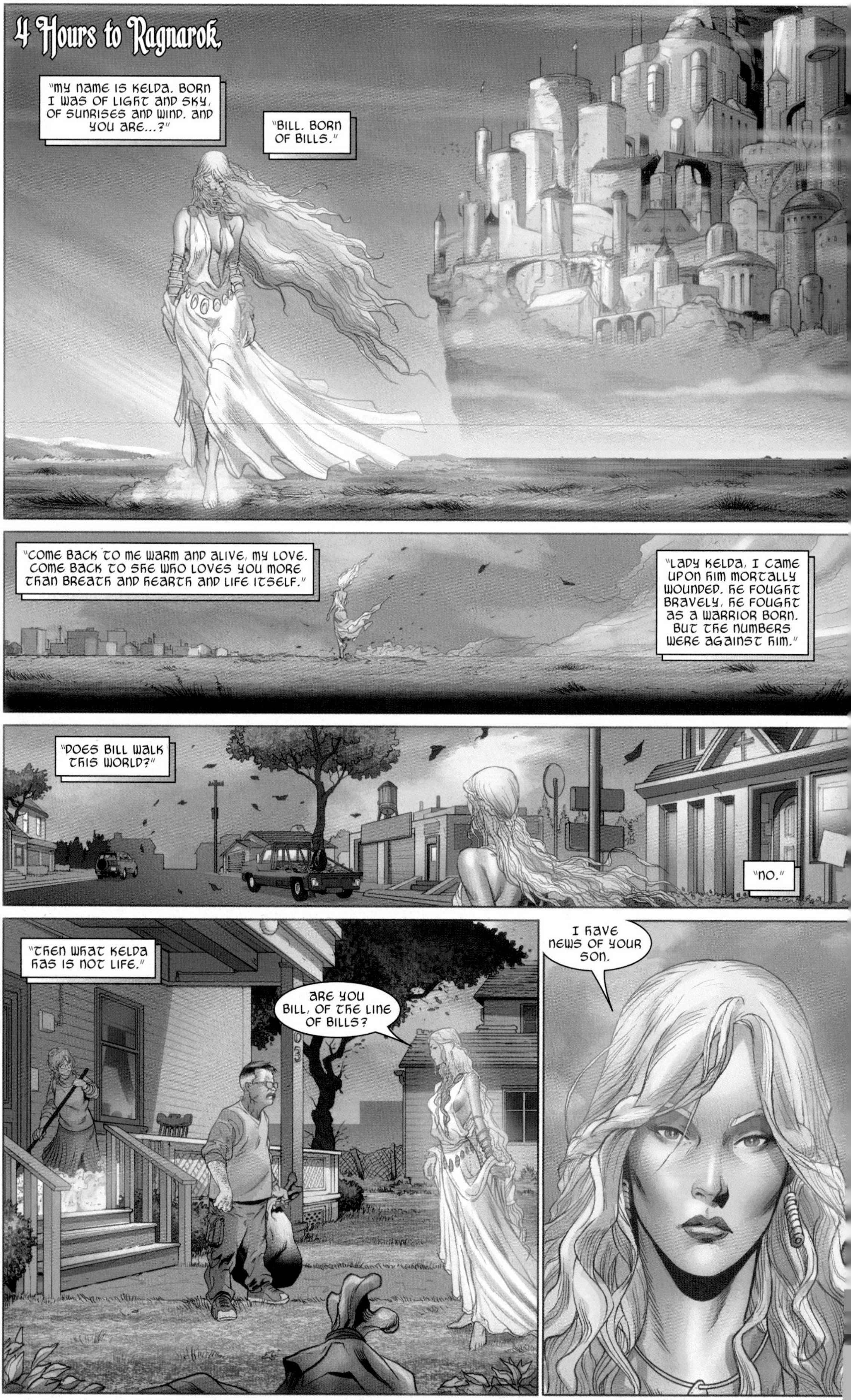
4 Hours to Ragnarok,
"MY NAME IS KELDA. BORN I WAS OF LIGHT AND SKY, OF SUNRISES AND WIND. AND YOU ARE...?"
"BILL. BORN OF BILLS."
"COME BACK TO ME WARM AND ALIVE, MY LOVE. COME BACK TO SHE WHO LOVES YOU MORE THAN BREATH AND HEARTH AND LIFE ITSELF."
"LADY KELDA, I CAME UPON HIM MORTALLY WOUNDED. HE FOUGHT BRAVELY, HE FOUGHT AS A WARRIOR BORN. BUT THE NUMBERS WERE AGAINST HIM."
"DOES BILL WALK THIS WORLD?"
"NO."
"THEN WHAT KELDA HAS IS NOT LIFE."
ARE YOU BILL, OF THE LINE OF BILLS?
I HAVE NEWS OF YOUR SON.

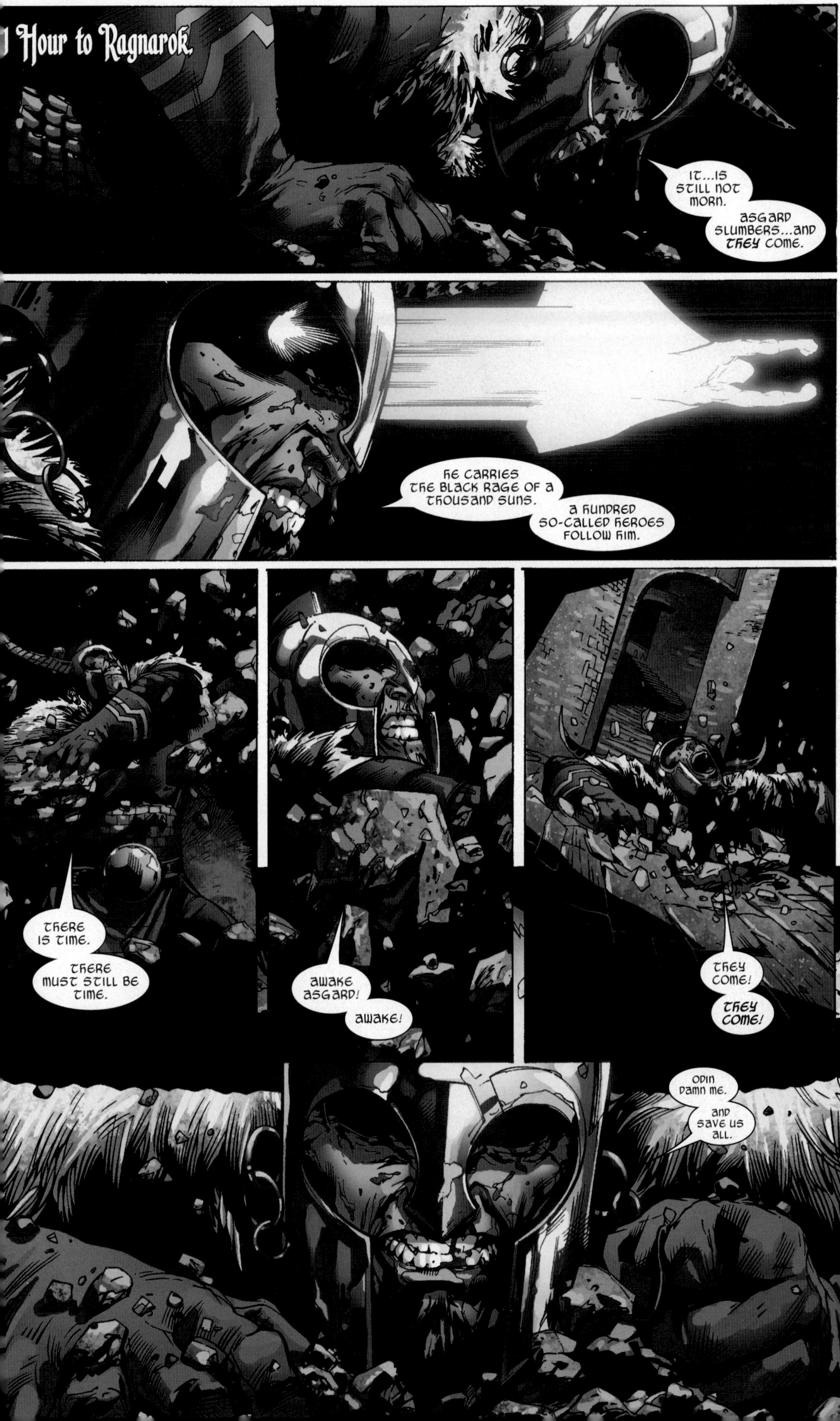
1 Hour to Ragnarok.
IT...IS STILL NOT MORN.
ASGARD SLUMBERS...AND THEY COME.
HE CARRIES THE BLACK RAGE OF A THOUSAND SUNS.
A HUNDRED SO-CALLED HEROES FOLLOW HIM.
THERE IS TIME.
THERE MUST STILL BE TIME.
AWAKE ASGARD!
AWAKE!
THEY COME!
THEY COME!
ODIN DAMN ME.
AND SAVE US ALL.

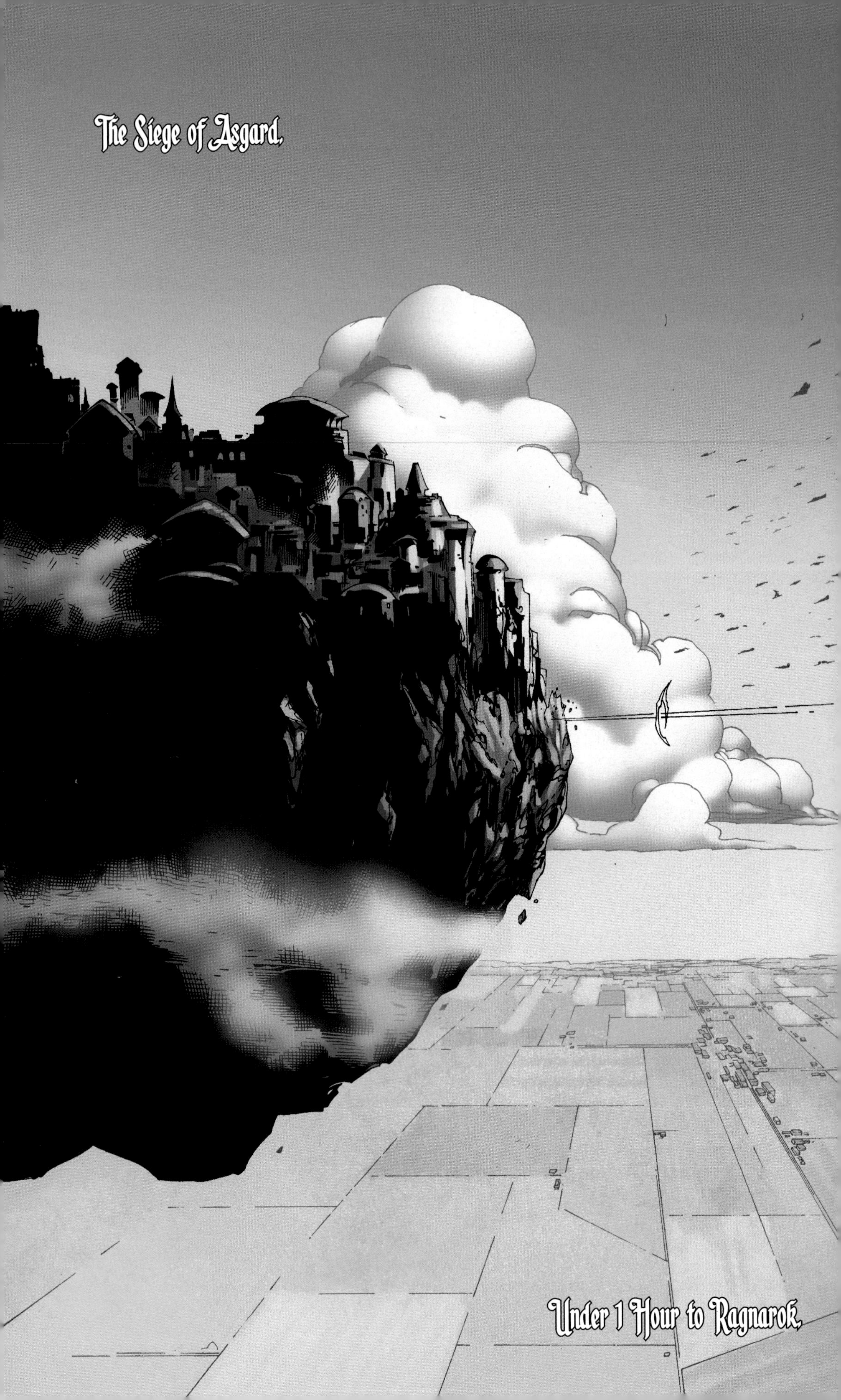
The Siege of Asgard.
Under 1 Hour to Ragnarok.

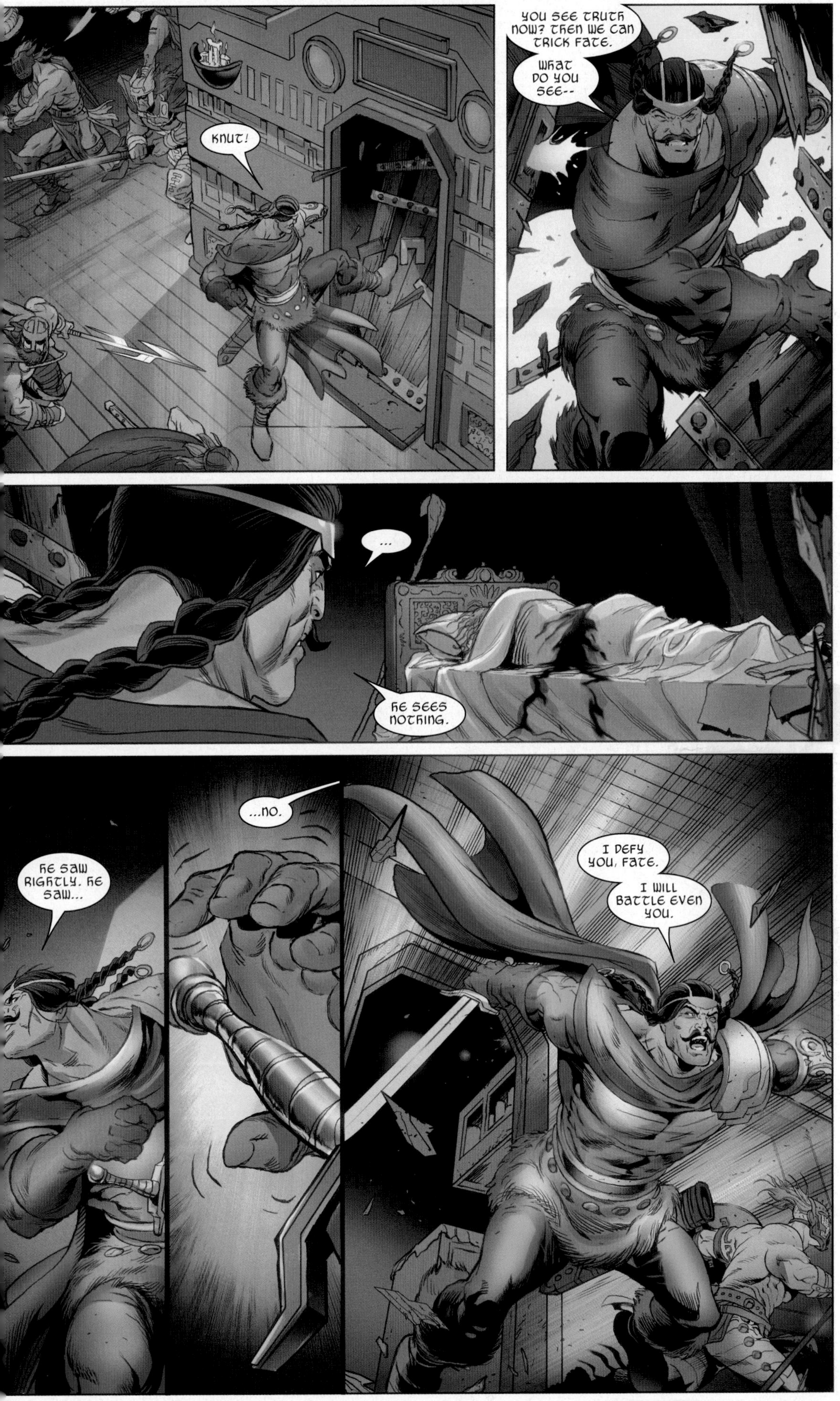
KNUT!
YOU SEE TRUTH NOW? THEN WE CAN TRICK FATE.
WHAT DO YOU SEE--
...
HE SEES NOTHING.
HE SAW RIGHTLY. HE SAW...
...NO.
I DEFY YOU, FATE.
I WILL BATTLE EVEN YOU.

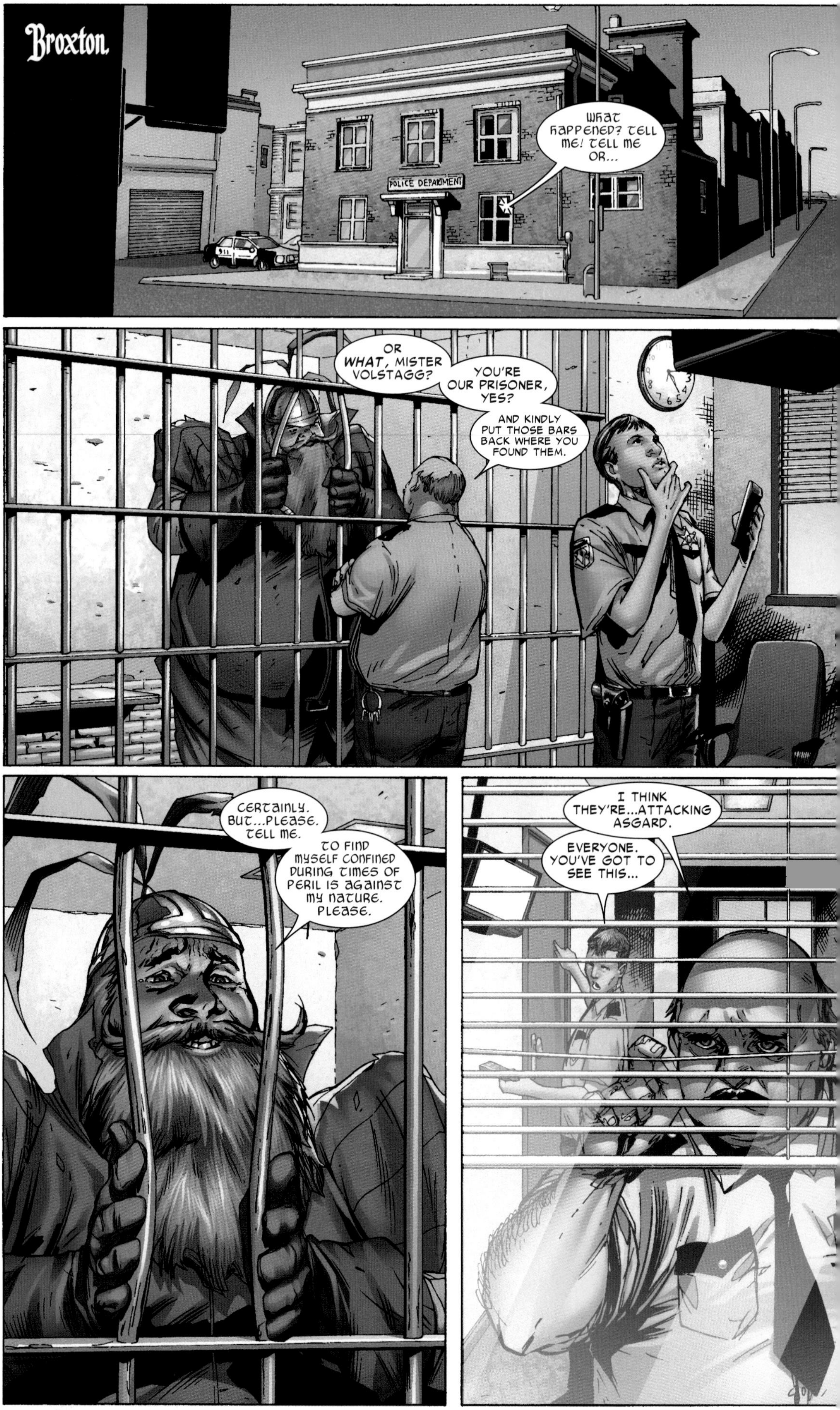
Broxton
POLICE DEPARTMENT
WHAT HAPPENED? TELL ME! TELL ME OR...
OR WHAT, MISTER VOLSTAGG?
YOU'RE OUR PRISONER, YES?
AND KINDLY PUT THOSE BARS BACK WHERE YOU FOUND THEM.
CERTAINLY. BUT...PLEASE. TELL ME.
TO FIND MYSELF CONFINED DURING TIMES OF PERIL IS AGAINST MY NATURE. PLEASE.
I THINK THEY'RE...ATTACKING ASGARD.
EVERYONE. YOU'VE GOT TO SEE THIS...

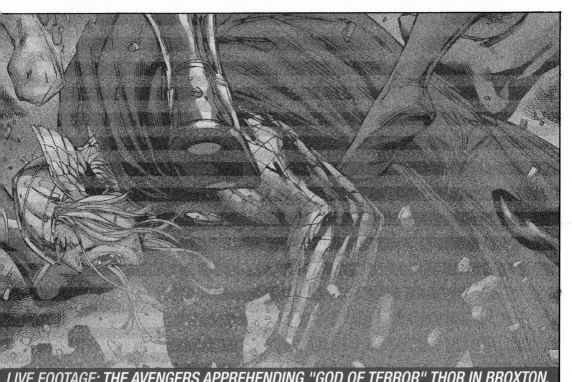

LIVE FOOTAGE: THE AVENGERS APPREHENDING "GOD OF TERROR" THOR IN BROXTON.

THIS. ALL THIS.

THE FAULT IS MINE.

NOTHING WE CAN DO, YEAH?

YEAH. NOTHING *WE* CAN DO.

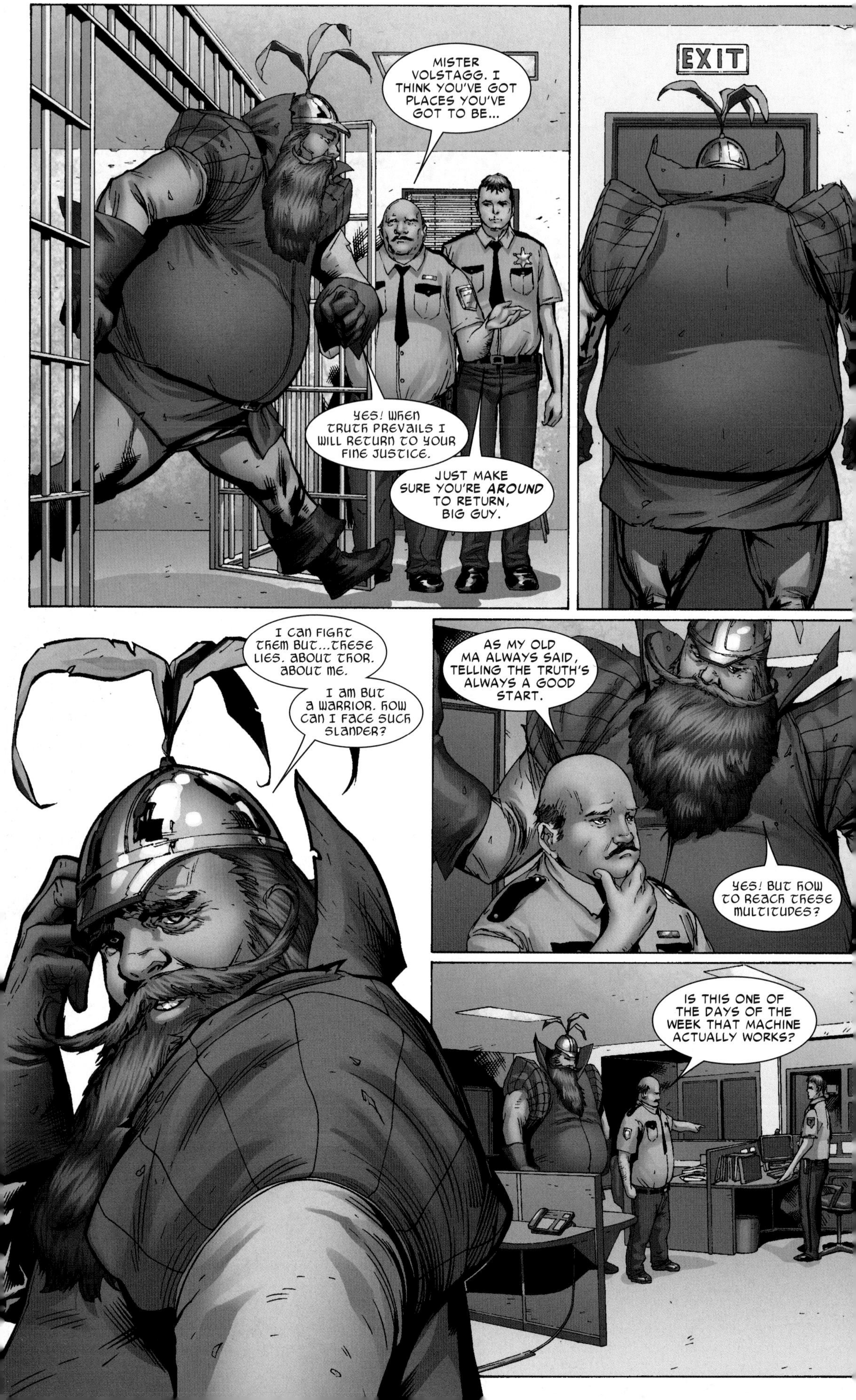

MISTER VOLSTAGG. I THINK YOU'VE GOT PLACES YOU'VE GOT TO BE...
YES! WHEN TRUTH PREVAILS I WILL RETURN TO YOUR FINE JUSTICE.
JUST MAKE SURE YOU'RE *AROUND* TO RETURN, BIG GUY.
EXIT
I CAN FIGHT THEM BUT...THESE LIES. ABOUT THOR. ABOUT ME.
I AM BUT A WARRIOR. HOW CAN I FACE SUCH SLANDER?
AS MY OLD MA ALWAYS SAID, TELLING THE TRUTH'S ALWAYS A GOOD START.
YES! BUT HOW TO REACH THESE MULTITUDES?
IS THIS ONE OF THE DAYS OF THE WEEK THAT MACHINE ACTUALLY WORKS?

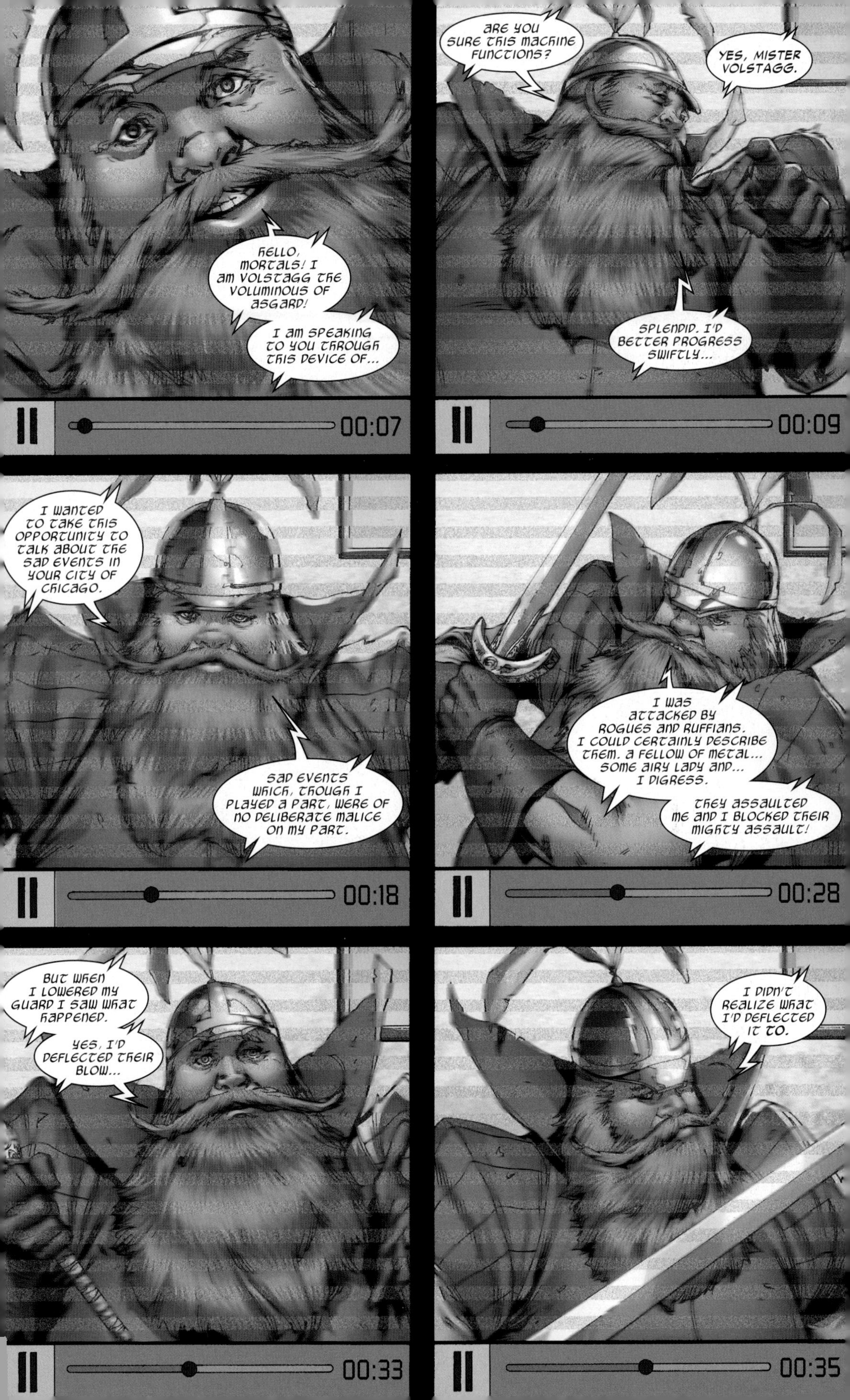
HELLO, MORTALS! I AM VOLSTAGG THE VOLUMINOUS OF ASGARD!
I AM SPEAKING TO YOU THROUGH THIS DEVICE OF...
00:07
ARE YOU SURE THIS MACHINE FUNCTIONS?
YES, MISTER VOLSTAGG.
SPLENDID. I'D BETTER PROGRESS SWIFTLY...
00:09
I WANTED TO TAKE THIS OPPORTUNITY TO TALK ABOUT THE SAD EVENTS IN YOUR CITY OF CHICAGO.
SAD EVENTS WHICH, THOUGH I PLAYED A PART, WERE OF NO DELIBERATE MALICE ON MY PART.
00:18
I WAS ATTACKED BY ROGUES AND RUFFIANS. I COULD CERTAINLY DESCRIBE THEM. A FELLOW OF METAL... SOME AIRY LADY AND... I DIGRESS.
THEY ASSAULTED ME AND I BLOCKED THEIR MIGHTY ASSAULT!
00:28
BUT WHEN I LOWERED MY GUARD I SAW WHAT HAPPENED.
YES, I'D DEFLECTED THEIR BLOW...
00:33
I DIDN'T REALIZE WHAT I'D DEFLECTED IT TO.
00:35

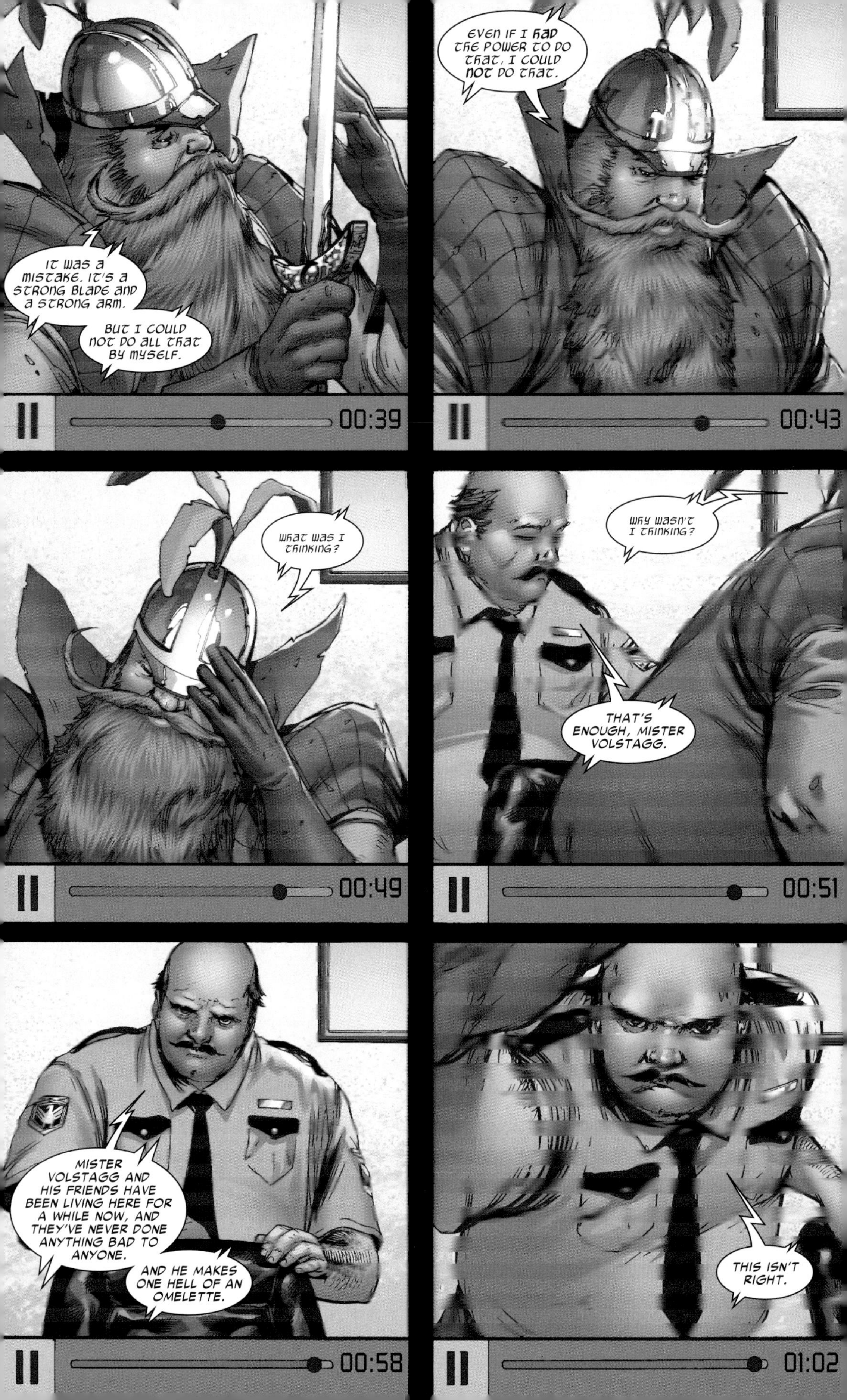
IT WAS A MISTAKE. IT'S A STRONG BLADE AND A STRONG ARM.
BUT I COULD NOT DO ALL THAT BY MYSELF.
00:39
EVEN IF I HAD THE POWER TO DO THAT, I COULD NOT DO THAT.
00:43
WHAT WAS I THINKING?
00:49
WHY WASN'T I THINKING?
THAT'S ENOUGH, MISTER VOLSTAGG.
00:51
MISTER VOLSTAGG AND HIS FRIENDS HAVE BEEN LIVING HERE FOR A WHILE NOW, AND THEY'VE NEVER DONE ANYTHING BAD TO ANYONE.
AND HE MAKES ONE HELL OF AN OMELETTE.
00:58
THIS ISN'T RIGHT.
01:02

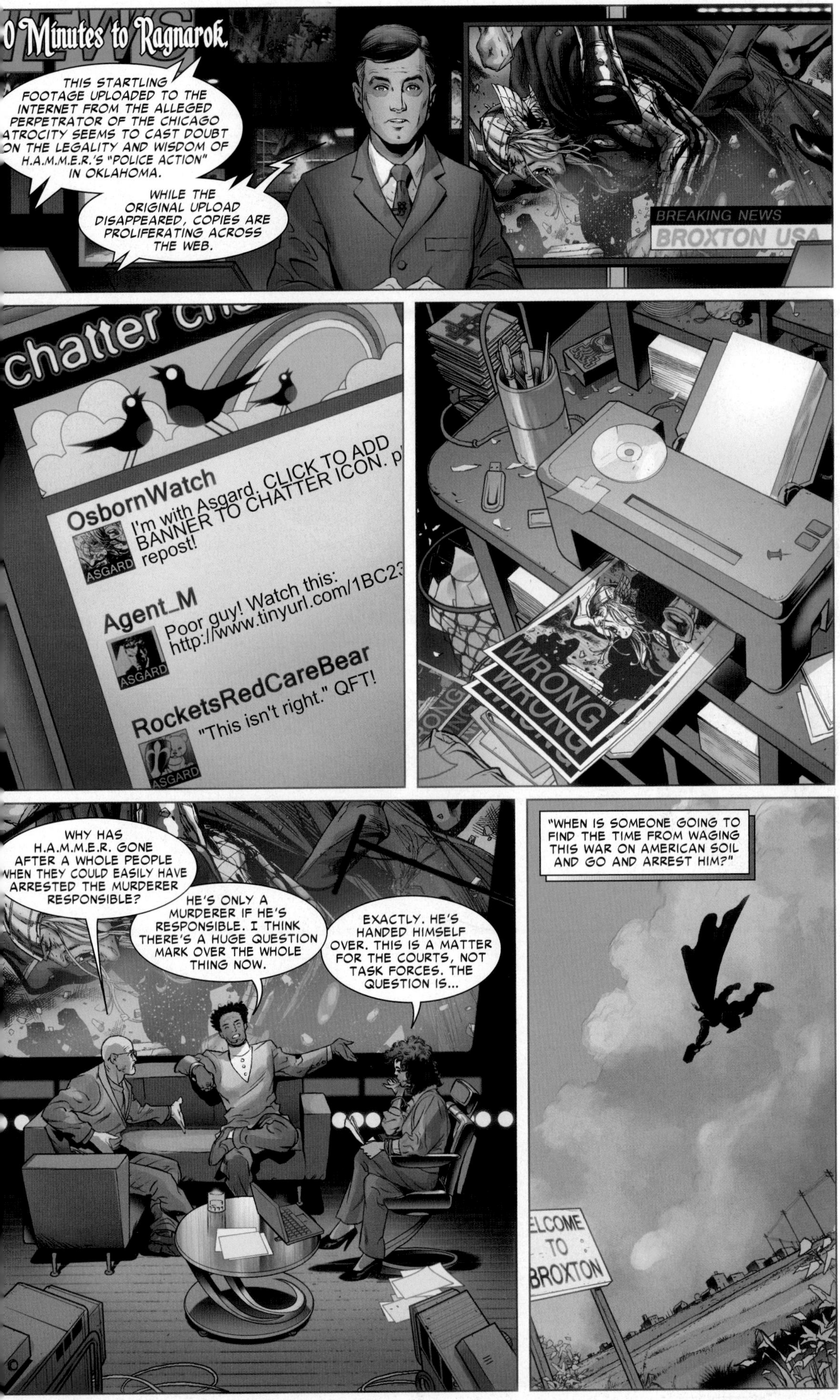

0 Minutes to Ragnarok.
THIS STARTLING FOOTAGE UPLOADED TO THE INTERNET FROM THE ALLEGED PERPETRATOR OF THE CHICAGO ATROCITY SEEMS TO CAST DOUBT ON THE LEGALITY AND WISDOM OF H.A.M.M.E.R.'S "POLICE ACTION" IN OKLAHOMA.
WHILE THE ORIGINAL UPLOAD DISAPPEARED, COPIES ARE PROLIFERATING ACROSS THE WEB.
BREAKING NEWS
BROXTON USA
chatter
OsbornWatch
I'm with Asgard. CLICK TO ADD BANNER TO CHATTER ICON. p
repost!
ASGARD
Agent_M
Poor guy! Watch this: http://www.tinyurl.com/1BC23
ASGARD
RocketsRedCareBear
"This isn't right." QFT!
ASGARD
WRONG
WRONG
WHY HAS H.A.M.M.E.R. GONE AFTER A WHOLE PEOPLE WHEN THEY COULD EASILY HAVE ARRESTED THE MURDERER RESPONSIBLE?
HE'S ONLY A MURDERER IF HE'S RESPONSIBLE. I THINK THERE'S A HUGE QUESTION MARK OVER THE WHOLE THING NOW.
EXACTLY. HE'S HANDED HIMSELF OVER. THIS IS A MATTER FOR THE COURTS, NOT TASK FORCES. THE QUESTION IS...
"WHEN IS SOMEONE GOING TO FIND THE TIME FROM WAGING THIS WAR ON AMERICAN SOIL AND GO AND ARREST HIM?"
ELCOME TO BROXTON

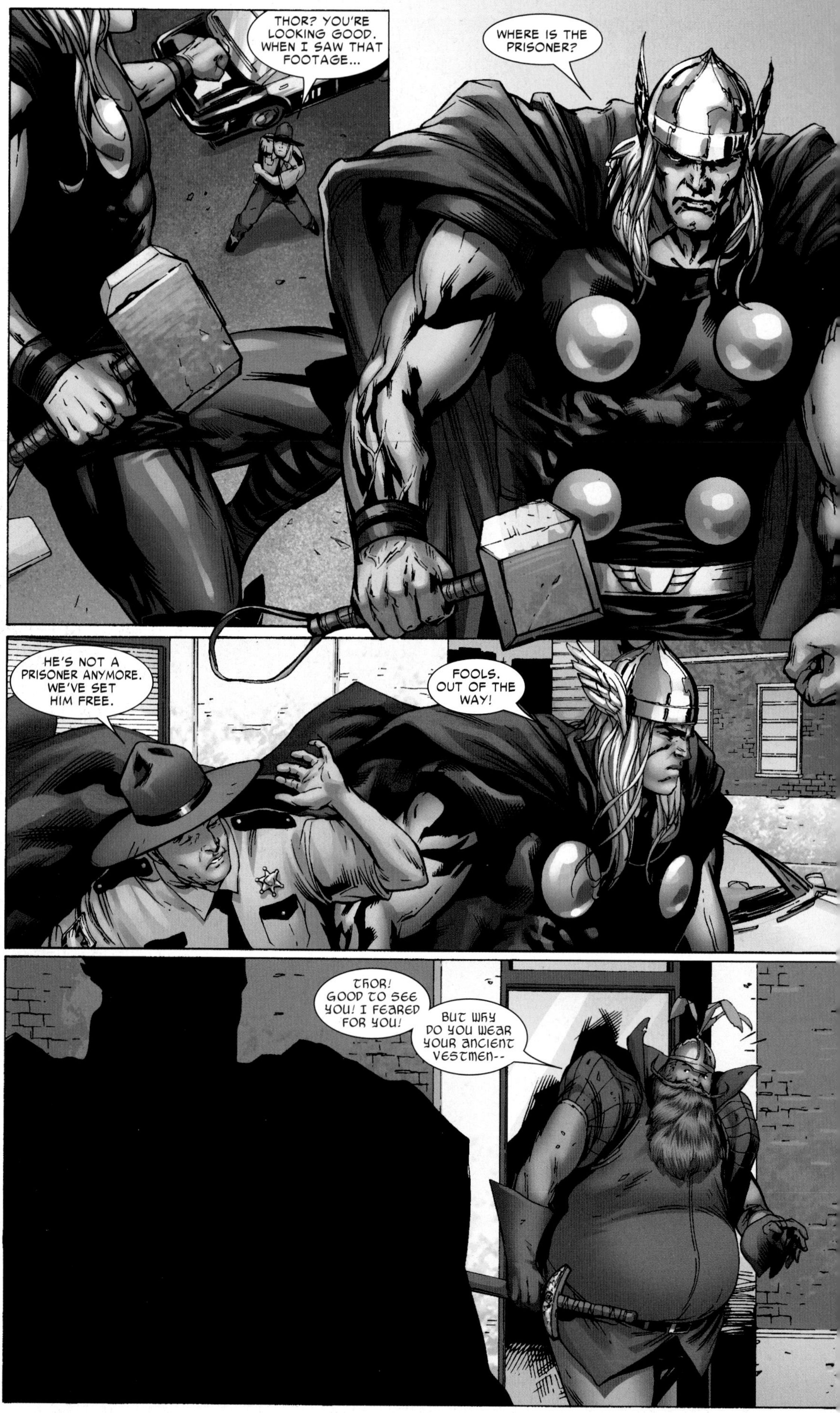
THOR? YOU'RE LOOKING GOOD. WHEN I SAW THAT FOOTAGE...
WHERE IS THE PRISONER?
HE'S NOT A PRISONER ANYMORE. WE'VE SET HIM FREE.
FOOLS. OUT OF THE WAY!
THOR! GOOD TO SEE YOU! I FEARED FOR YOU!
BUT WHY DO YOU WEAR YOUR ANCIENT VESTMEN--

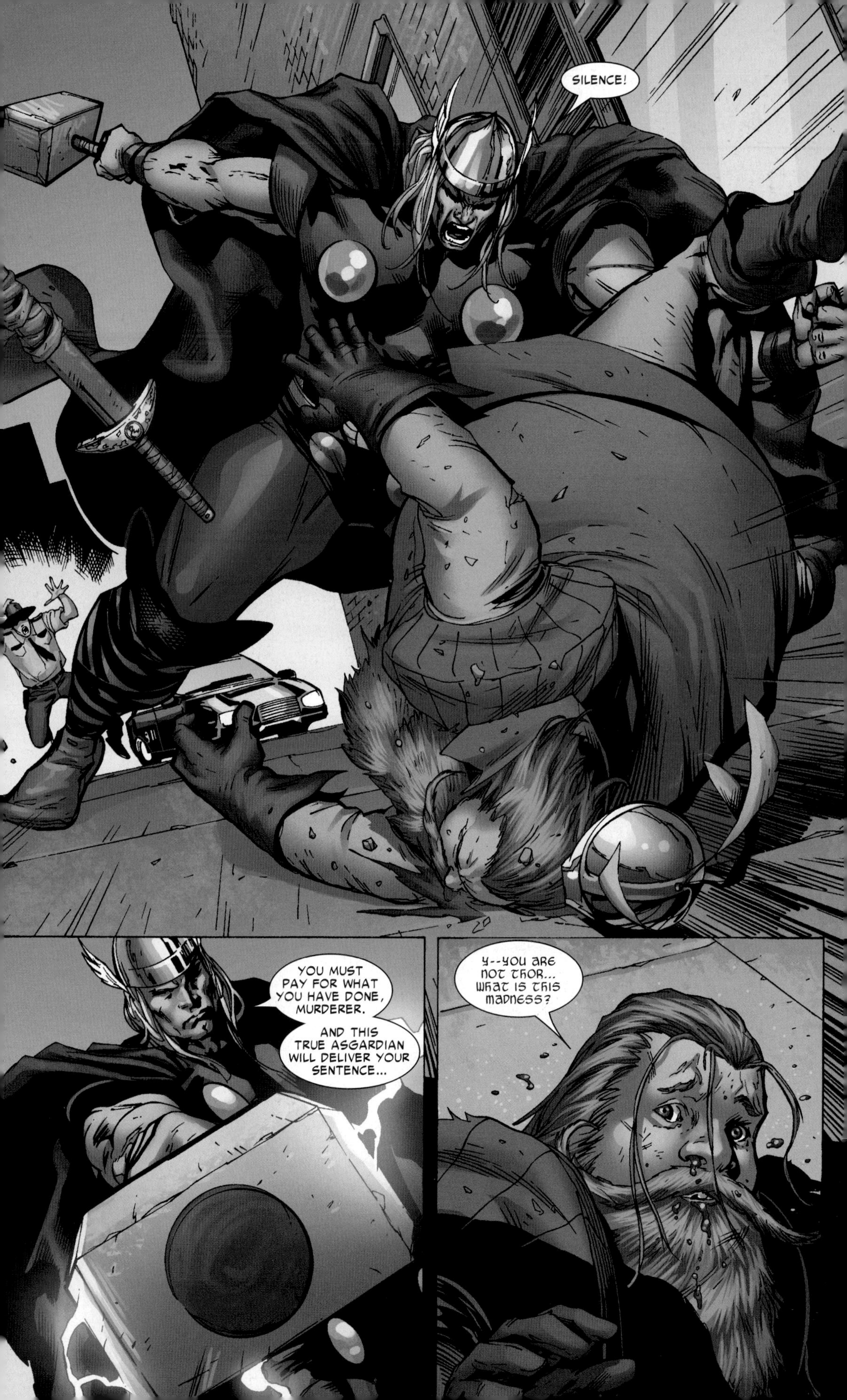
SILENCE!
YOU MUST PAY FOR WHAT YOU HAVE DONE, MURDERER.
AND THIS TRUE ASGARDIAN WILL DELIVER YOUR SENTENCE...
Y--YOU ARE NOT THOR... WHAT IS THIS MADNESS?

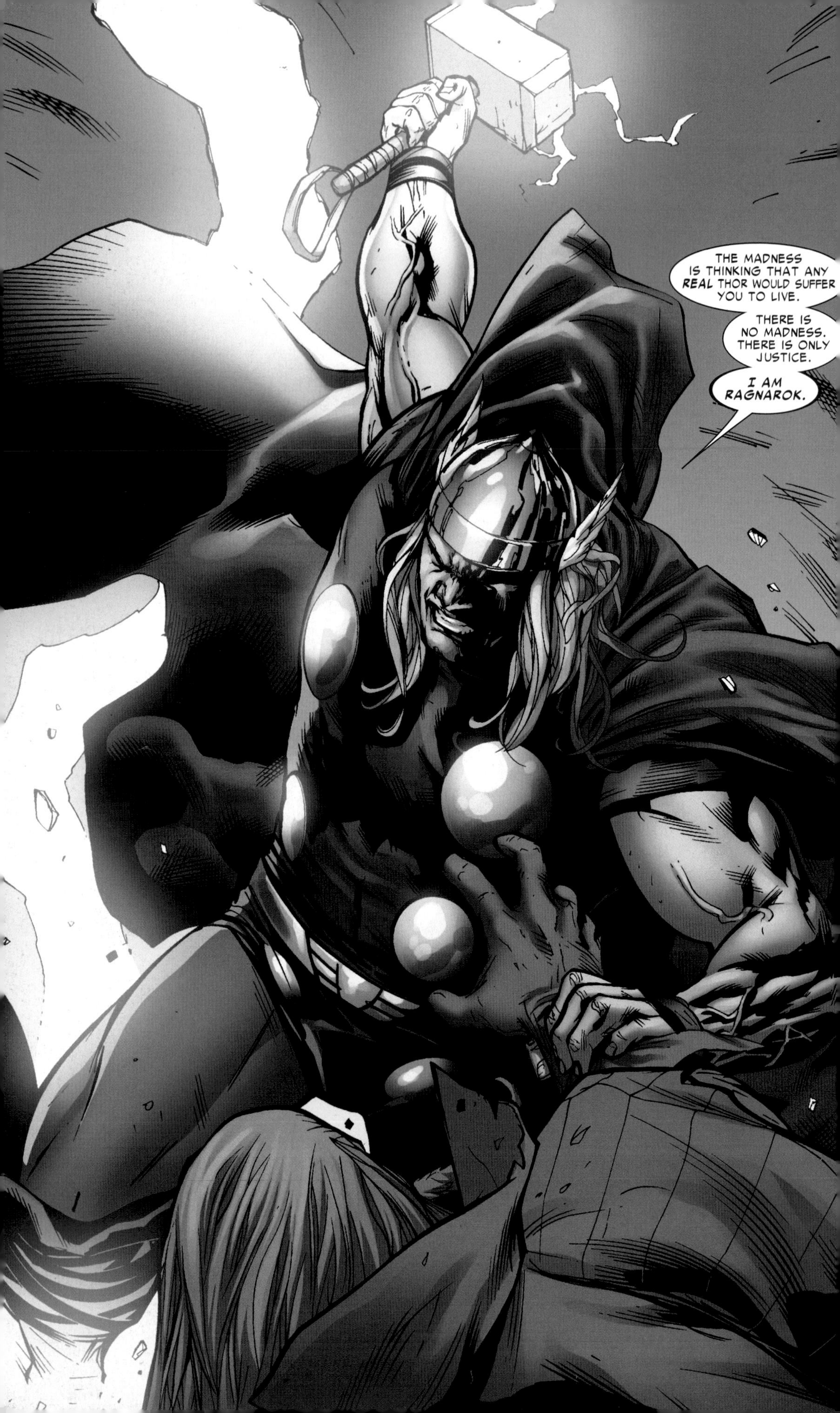
THE MADNESS IS THINKING THAT ANY REAL THOR WOULD SUFFER YOU TO LIVE.
THERE IS NO MADNESS. THERE IS ONLY JUSTICE.
I AM RAGNAROK.

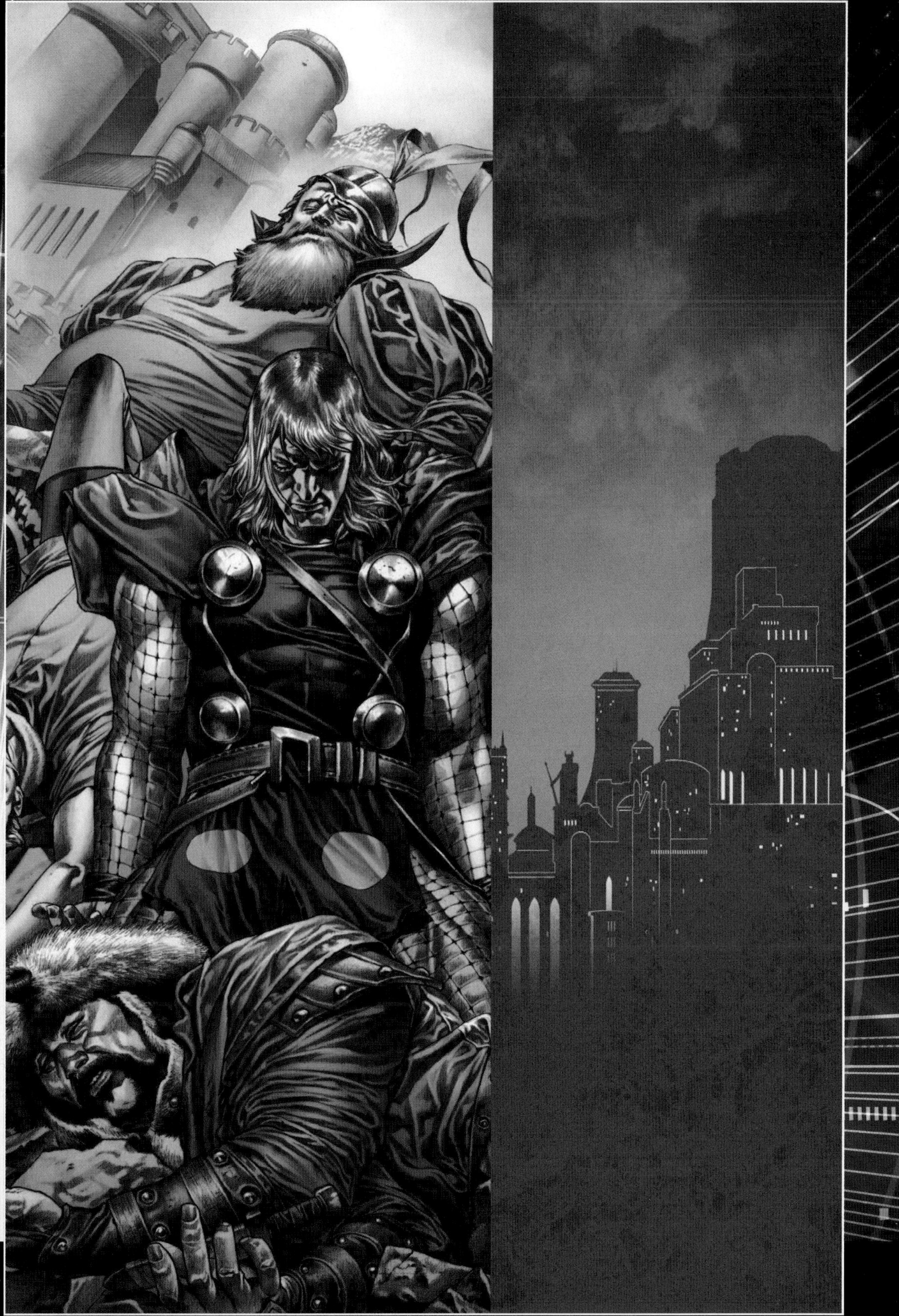

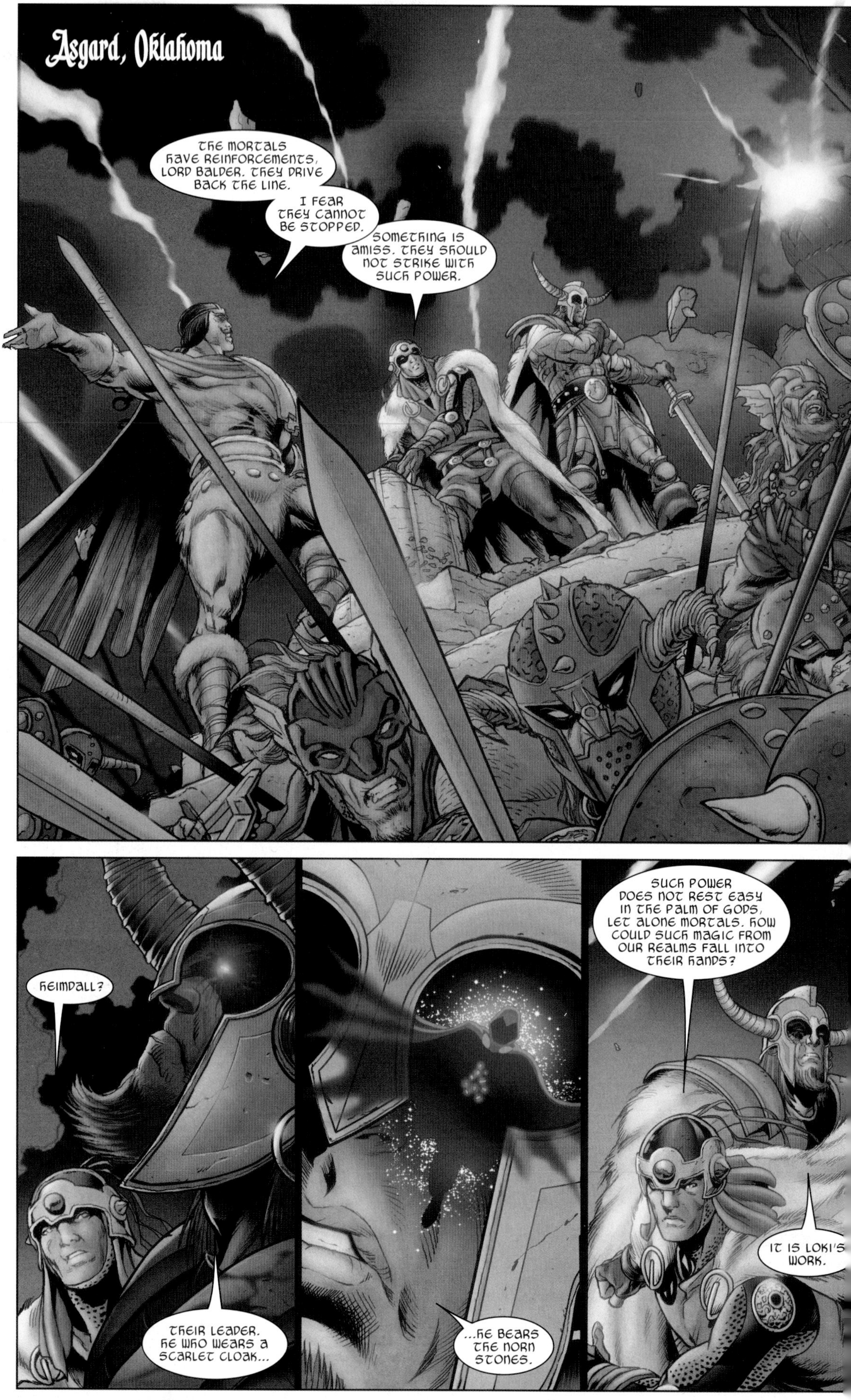
Asgard, Oklahoma
THE MORTALS HAVE REINFORCEMENTS, LORD BALDER. THEY DRIVE BACK THE LINE.
I FEAR THEY CANNOT BE STOPPED.
SOMETHING IS AMISS. THEY SHOULD NOT STRIKE WITH SUCH POWER.
HEIMDALL?
THEIR LEADER. HE WHO WEARS A SCARLET CLOAK...
...HE BEARS THE NORN STONES.
SUCH POWER DOES NOT REST EASY IN THE PALM OF GODS, LET ALONE MORTALS. HOW COULD SUCH MAGIC FROM OUR REALMS FALL INTO THEIR HANDS?
IT IS LOKI'S WORK.

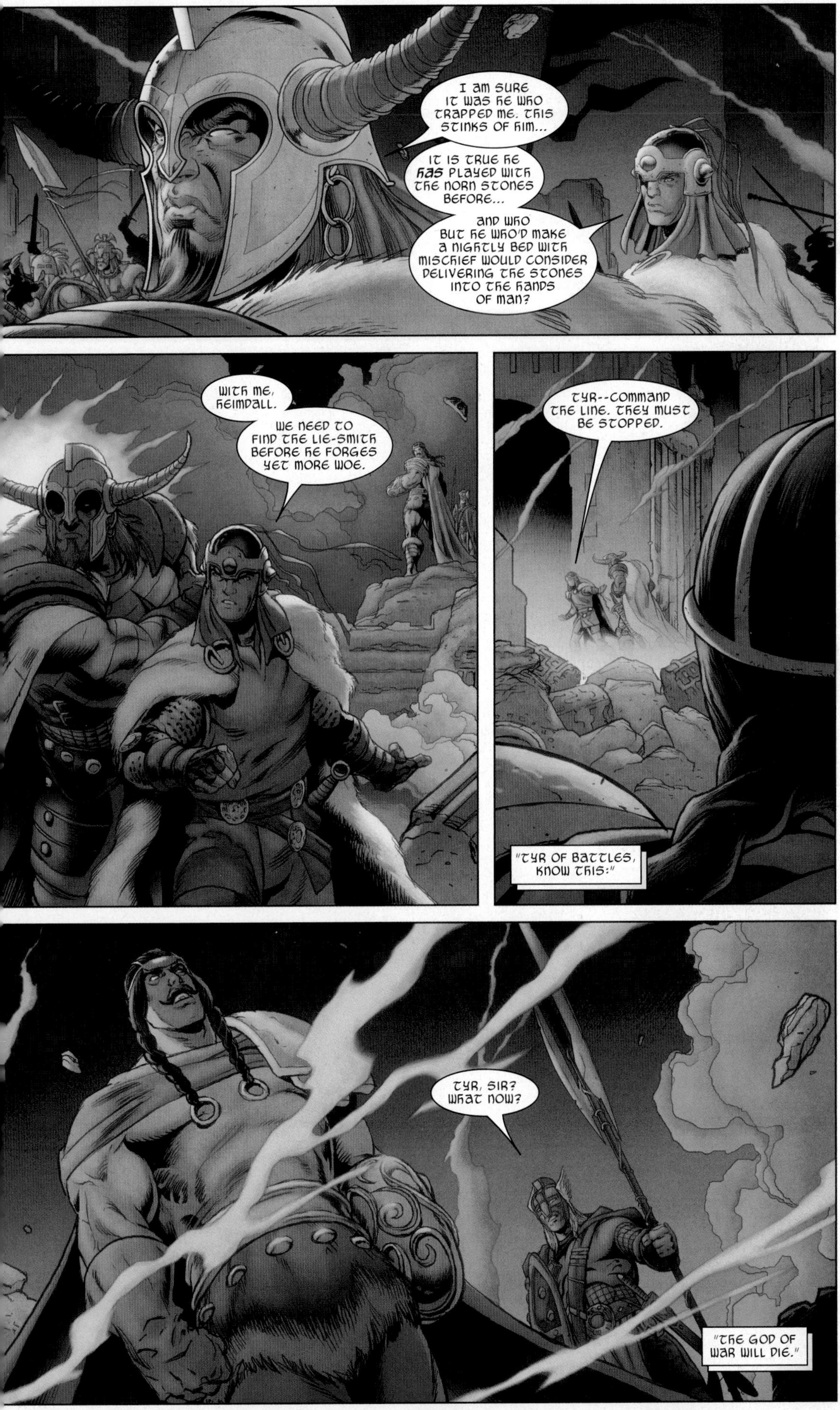
I AM SURE IT WAS HE WHO TRAPPED ME. THIS STINKS OF HIM...
IT IS TRUE HE HAS PLAYED WITH THE NORN STONES BEFORE...
AND WHO BUT HE WHO'D MAKE A NIGHTLY BED WITH MISCHIEF WOULD CONSIDER DELIVERING THE STONES INTO THE HANDS OF MAN?
WITH ME, HEIMDALL.
WE NEED TO FIND THE LIE-SMITH BEFORE HE FORGES YET MORE WOE.
TYR--COMMAND THE LINE. THEY MUST BE STOPPED.
"TYR OF BATTLES, KNOW THIS:"
TYR, SIR? WHAT NOW?
"THE GOD OF WAR WILL DIE."

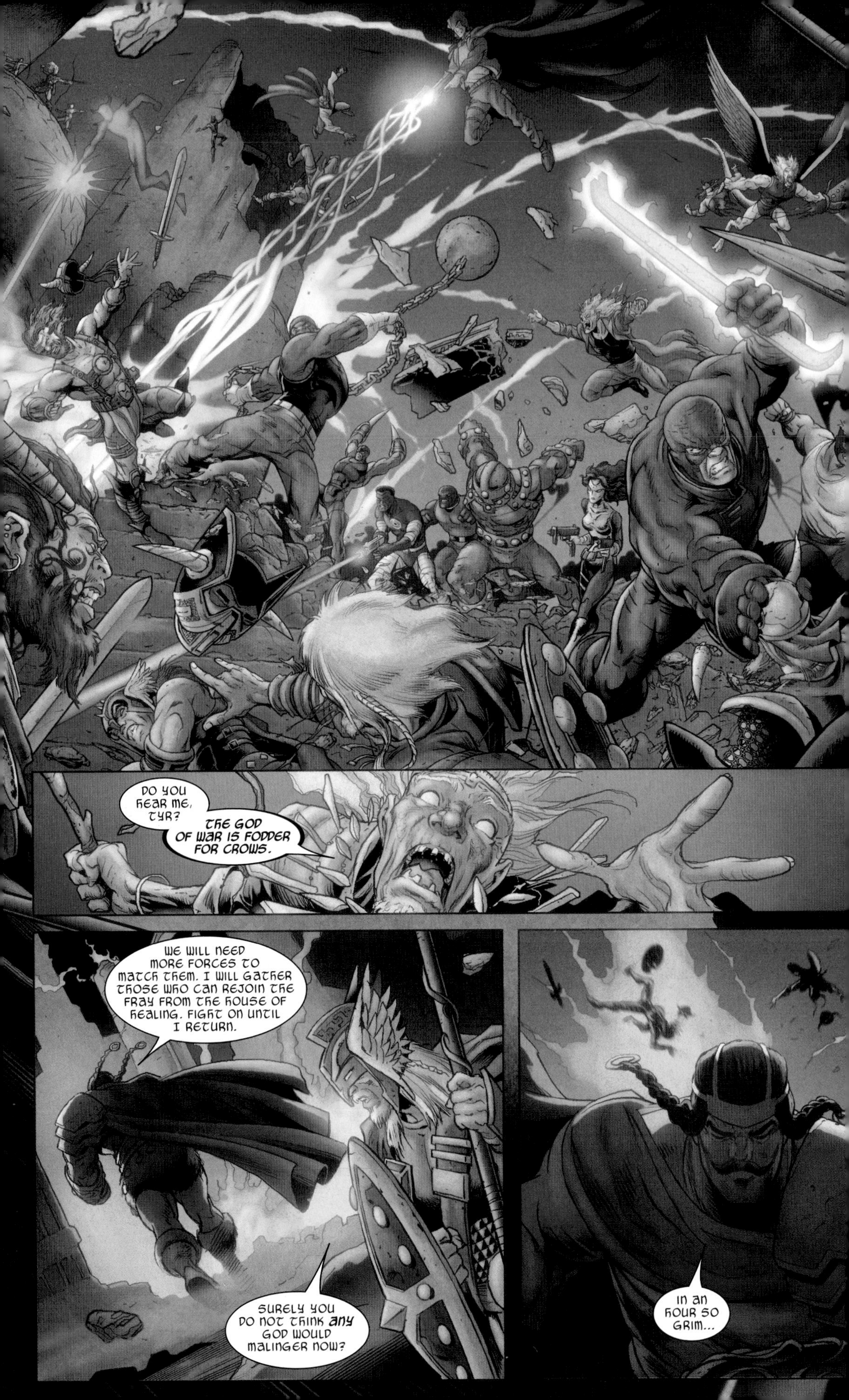
DO YOU HEAR ME, TYR?
THE GOD OF WAR IS FODDER FOR CROWS.
WE WILL NEED MORE FORCES TO MATCH THEM. I WILL GATHER THOSE WHO CAN REJOIN THE FRAY FROM THE HOUSE OF HEALING. FIGHT ON UNTIL I RETURN.
SURELY YOU DO NOT THINK ANY GOD WOULD MALINGER NOW?
IN AN HOUR SO GRIM...

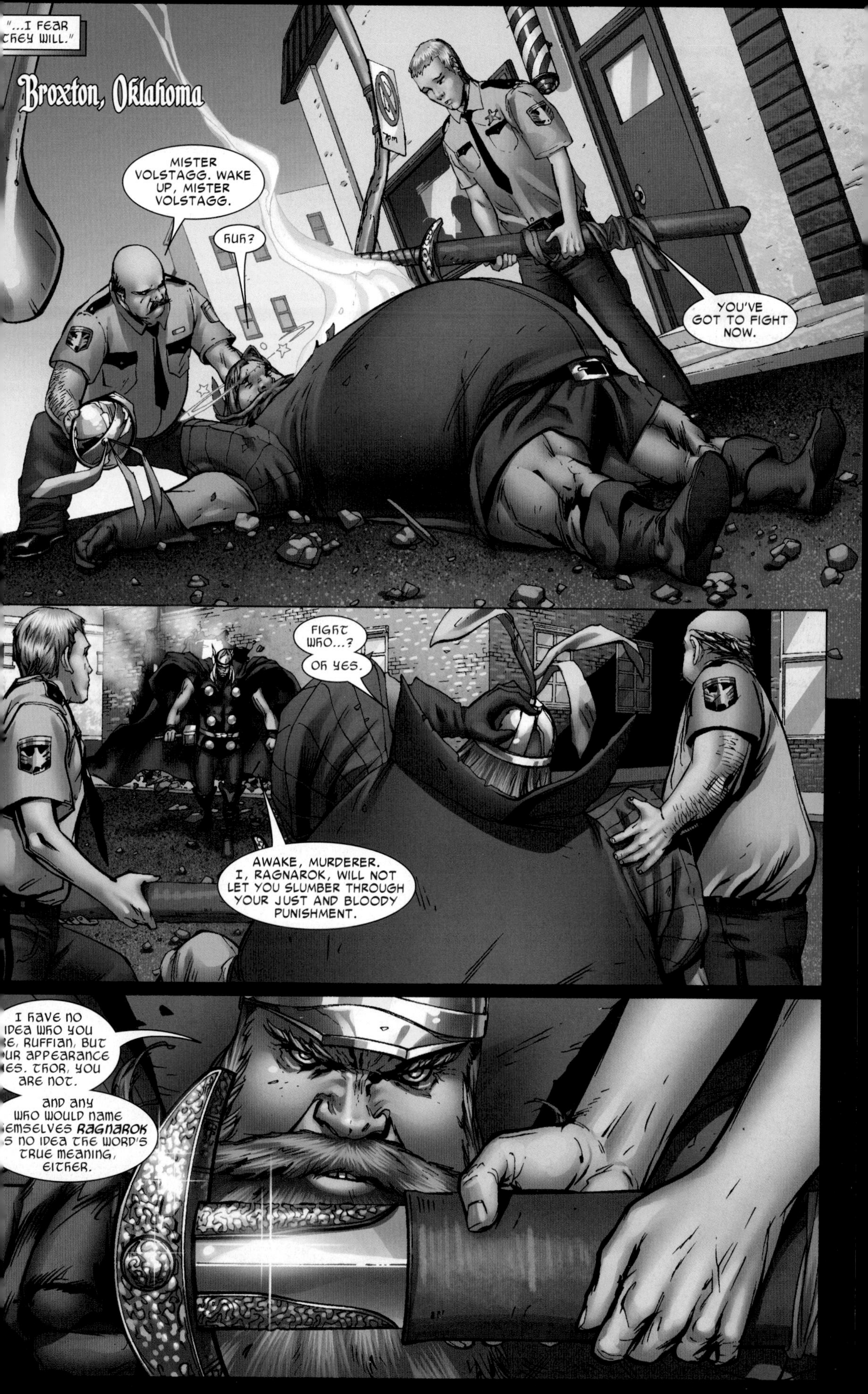
"...I FEAR
THEY WILL."
Broxton, Oklahoma
MISTER VOLSTAGG. WAKE UP, MISTER VOLSTAGG.
HUH?
YOU'VE GOT TO FIGHT NOW.
FIGHT WHO...?
OH YES.
AWAKE, MURDERER. I, RAGNAROK, WILL NOT LET YOU SLUMBER THROUGH YOUR JUST AND BLOODY PUNISHMENT.
I HAVE NO IDEA WHO YOU ARE, RUFFIAN, BUT YOUR APPEARANCE ...ES. THOR, YOU ARE NOT.
AND ANY WHO WOULD NAME THEMSELVES RAGNAROK ...S NO IDEA THE WORD'S TRUE MEANING, EITHER.

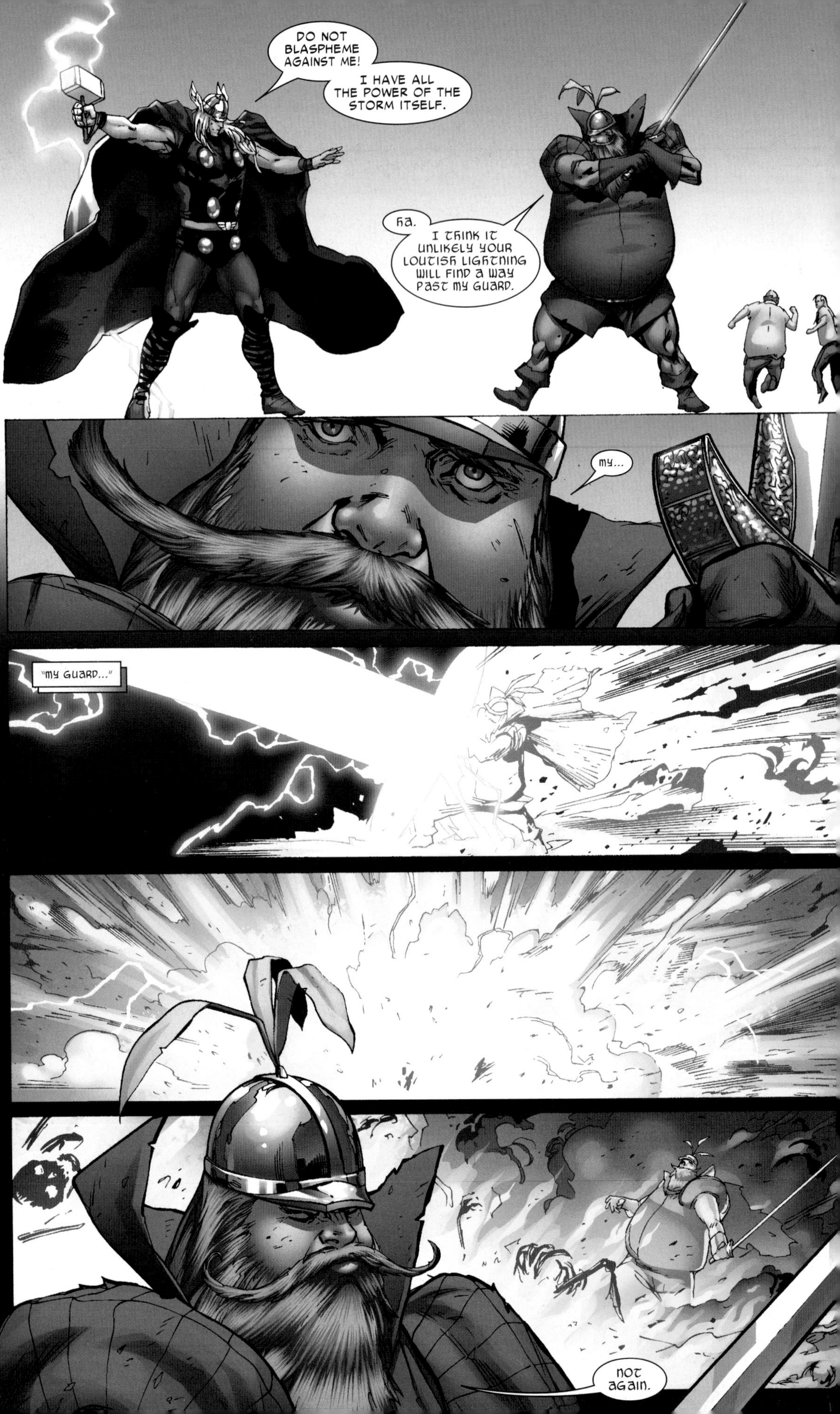
DO NOT BLASPHEME AGAINST ME!
I HAVE ALL THE POWER OF THE STORM ITSELF.
HA.
I THINK IT UNLIKELY YOUR LOUTISH LIGHTNING WILL FIND A WAY PAST MY GUARD.
MY...
"MY GUARD..."
NOT AGAIN.

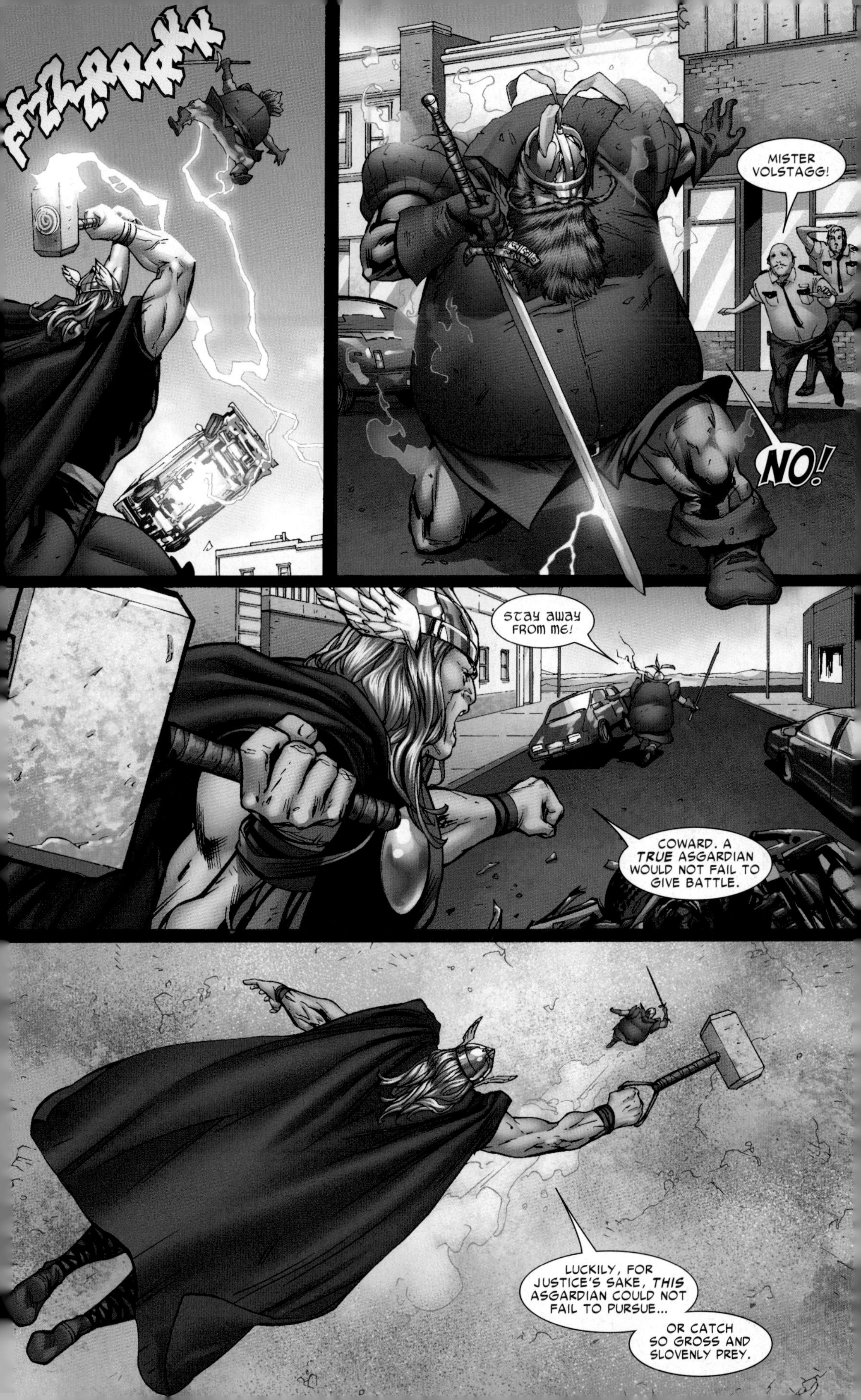
FFZZRRAKK
MISTER VOLSTAGG!
NO!
STAY AWAY FROM ME!
COWARD. A *TRUE* ASGARDIAN WOULD NOT FAIL TO GIVE BATTLE.
LUCKILY, FOR JUSTICE'S SAKE, *THIS* ASGARDIAN COULD NOT FAIL TO PURSUE...
OR CATCH SO GROSS AND SLOVENLY PREY.

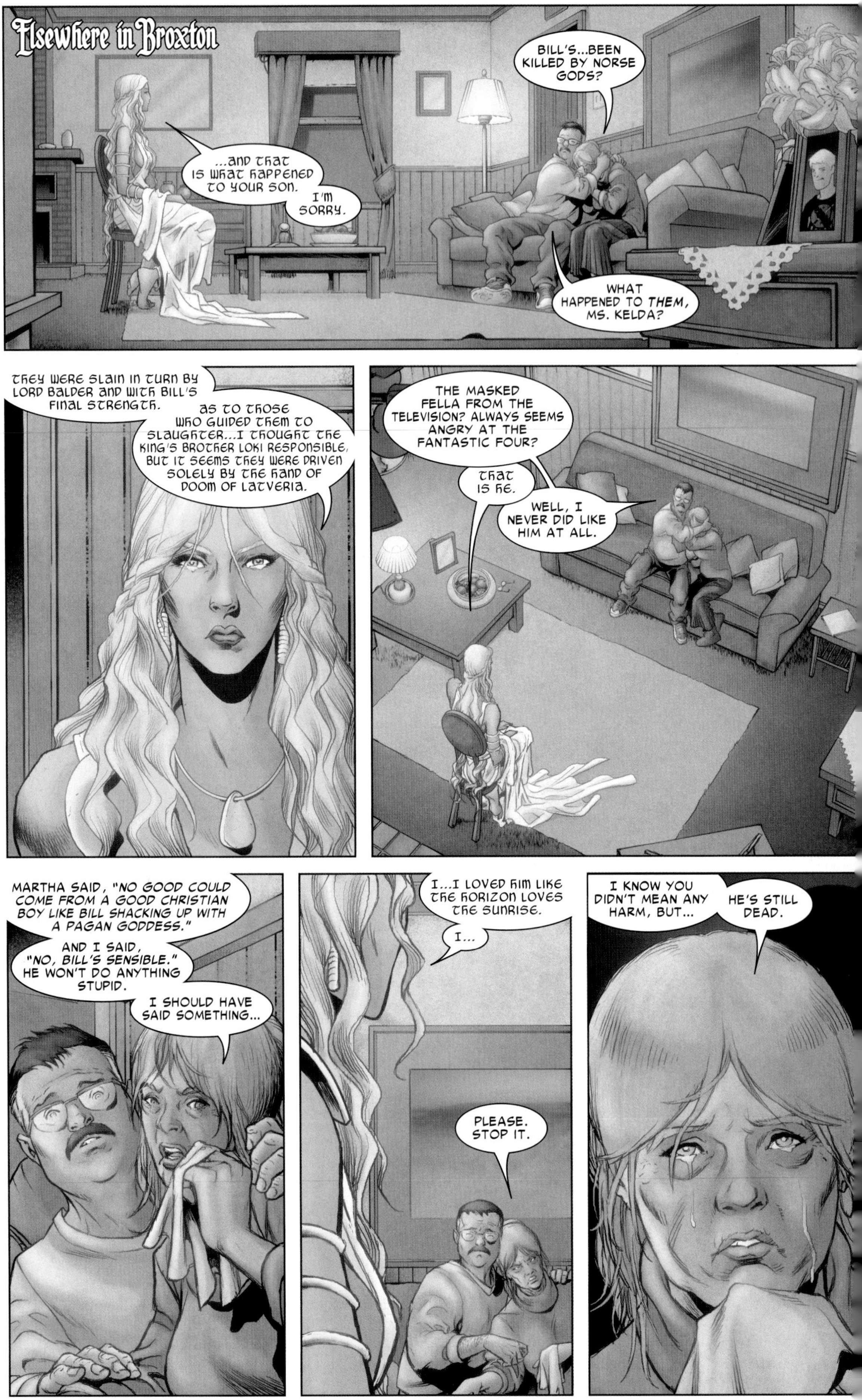
Elsewhere in Broxton
...AND THAT IS WHAT HAPPENED TO YOUR SON.
I'M SORRY.
BILL'S...BEEN KILLED BY NORSE GODS?
WHAT HAPPENED TO THEM, MS. KELDA?
THEY WERE SLAIN IN TURN BY LORD BALDER AND WITH BILL'S FINAL STRENGTH.
AS TO THOSE WHO GUIDED THEM TO SLAUGHTER...I THOUGHT THE KING'S BROTHER LOKI RESPONSIBLE, BUT IT SEEMS THEY WERE DRIVEN SOLELY BY THE HAND OF DOOM OF LATVERIA.
THE MASKED FELLA FROM THE TELEVISION? ALWAYS SEEMS ANGRY AT THE FANTASTIC FOUR?
THAT IS HE.
WELL, I NEVER DID LIKE HIM AT ALL.
MARTHA SAID, "NO GOOD COULD COME FROM A GOOD CHRISTIAN BOY LIKE BILL SHACKING UP WITH A PAGAN GODDESS."
AND I SAID, "NO, BILL'S SENSIBLE." HE WON'T DO ANYTHING STUPID.
I SHOULD HAVE SAID SOMETHING...
I...I LOVED HIM LIKE THE HORIZON LOVES THE SUNRISE.
I...
PLEASE. STOP IT.
I KNOW YOU DIDN'T MEAN ANY HARM, BUT...
HE'S STILL DEAD.

I THINK MAYBE YOU BETTER GO.

I SHALL. BUT I SHARE THE WOE THAT...

PLEASE GO. FANCY LINGO JUST MAKES IT WORSE.

ATTENTION!

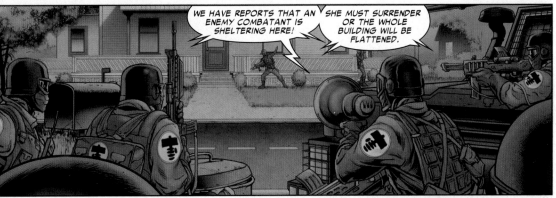

WE HAVE REPORTS THAT AN ENEMY COMBATANT IS SHELTERING HERE!

SHE MUST SURRENDER OR THE WHOLE BUILDING WILL BE FLATTENED.

YOU HAVE SIXTY SECONDS TO COMPLY.

WH-WHAT ARE YOU GOING TO DO?

IT WILL BE AS YOU WISHED...

I WILL LEAVE.

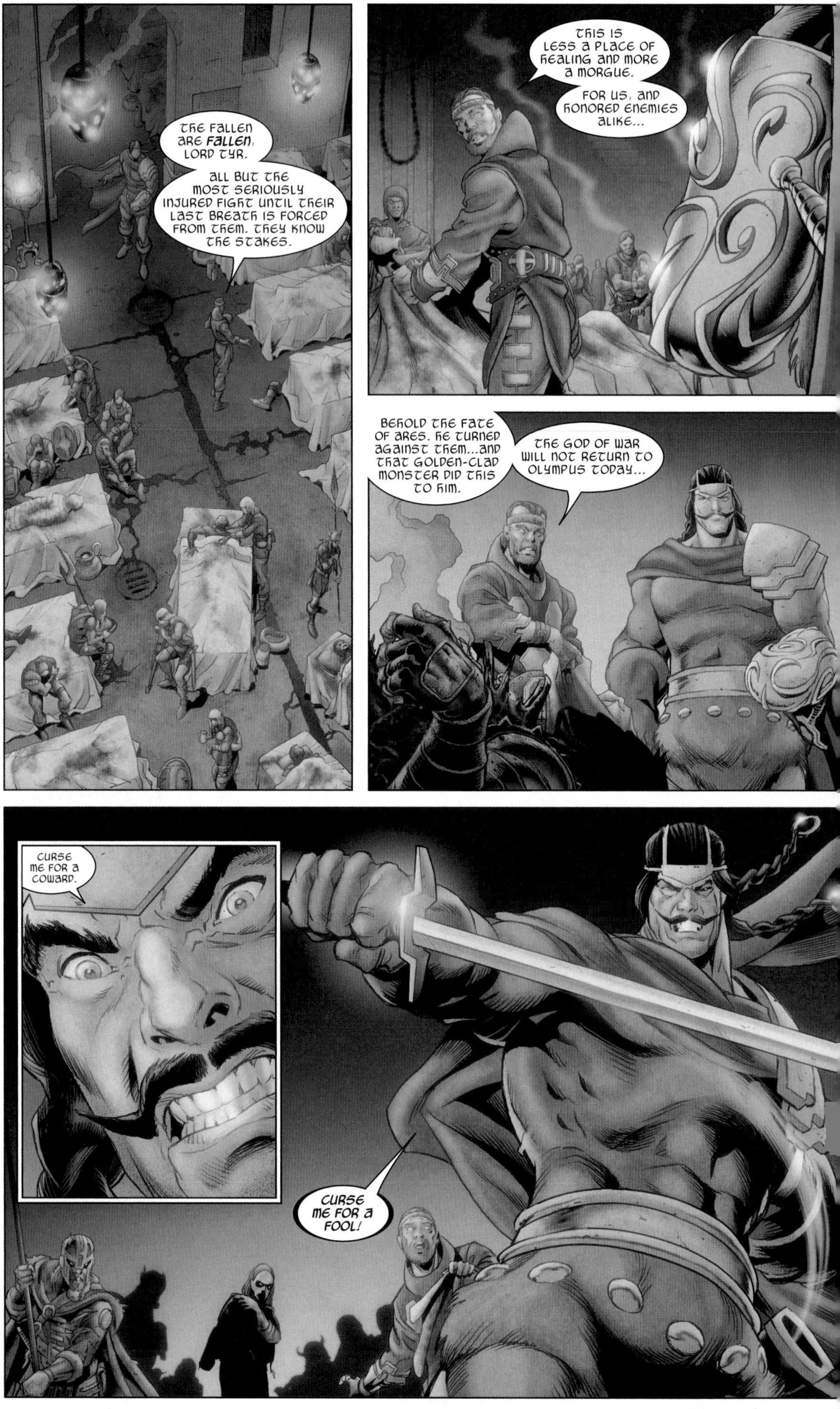
THE FALLEN ARE FALLEN, LORD TYR.
ALL BUT THE MOST SERIOUSLY INJURED FIGHT UNTIL THEIR LAST BREATH IS FORCED FROM THEM. THEY KNOW THE STAKES.
THIS IS LESS A PLACE OF HEALING AND MORE A MORGUE.
FOR US, AND HONORED ENEMIES ALIKE...
BEHOLD THE FATE OF ARES. HE TURNED AGAINST THEM...AND THAT GOLDEN-CLAD MONSTER DID THIS TO HIM.
THE GOD OF WAR WILL NOT RETURN TO OLYMPUS TODAY...
CURSE ME FOR A COWARD.
CURSE ME FOR A FOOL!

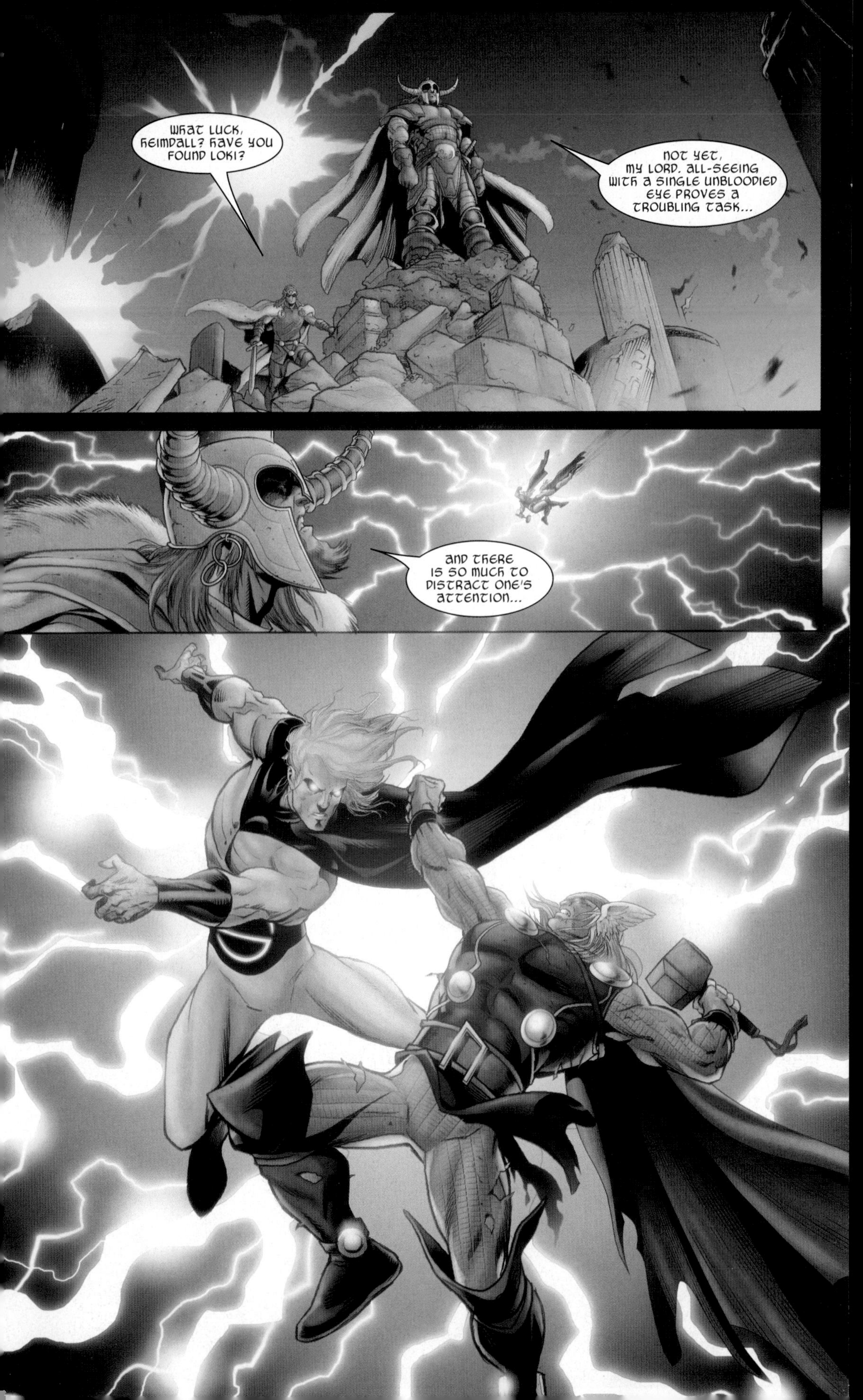
WHAT LUCK, HEIMDALL? HAVE YOU FOUND LOKI?
NOT YET, MY LORD. ALL-SEEING WITH A SINGLE UNBLOODIED EYE PROVES A TROUBLING TASK...
AND THERE IS SO MUCH TO DISTRACT ONE'S ATTENTION...

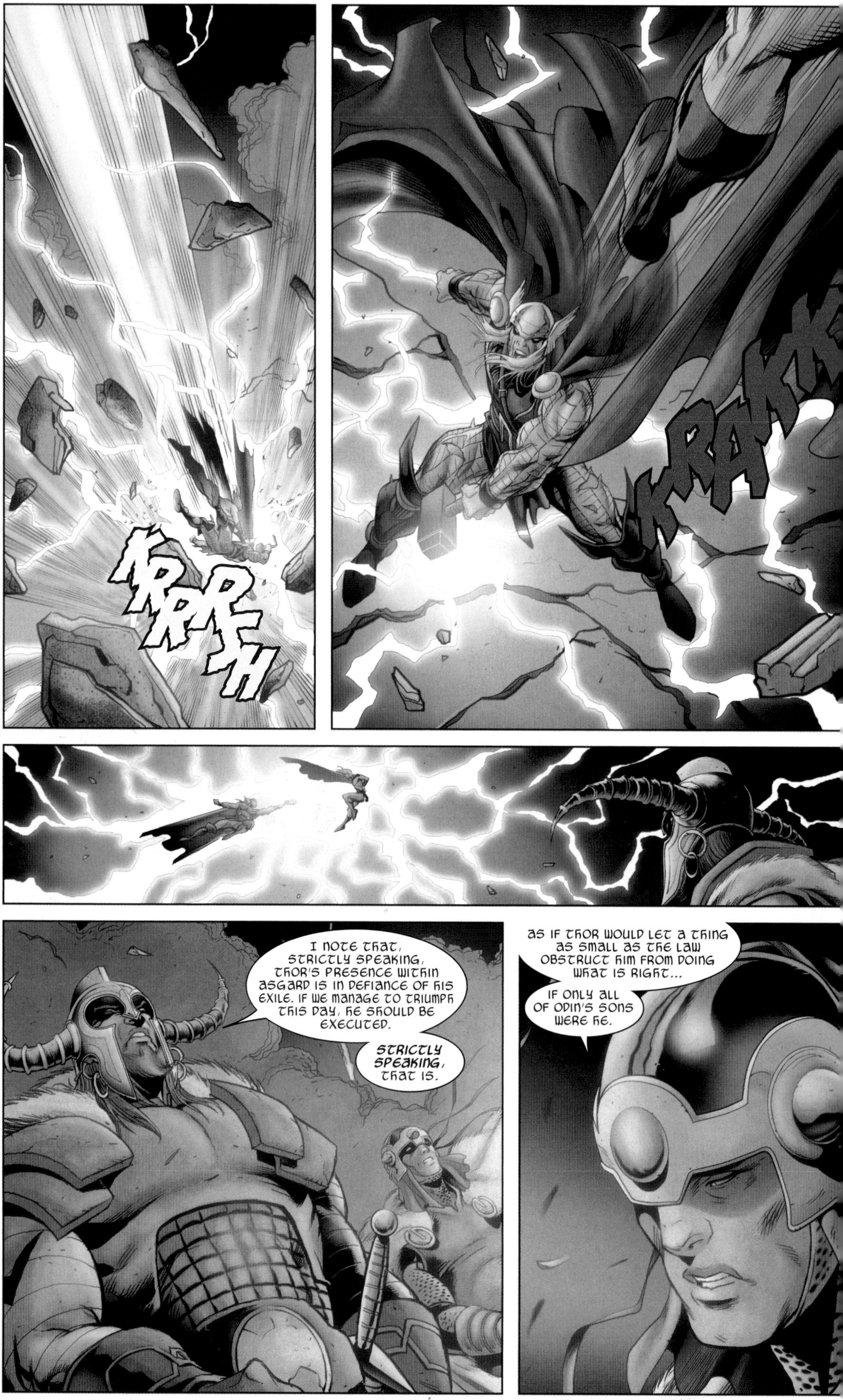
KRRRSH
KRAKK
I NOTE THAT, STRICTLY SPEAKING, THOR'S PRESENCE WITHIN ASGARD IS IN DEFIANCE OF HIS EXILE. IF WE MANAGE TO TRIUMPH THIS DAY, HE SHOULD BE EXECUTED.
STRICTLY SPEAKING, THAT IS.
AS IF THOR WOULD LET A THING AS SMALL AS THE LAW OBSTRUCT HIM FROM DOING WHAT IS RIGHT...
IF ONLY ALL OF ODIN'S SONS WERE HE.

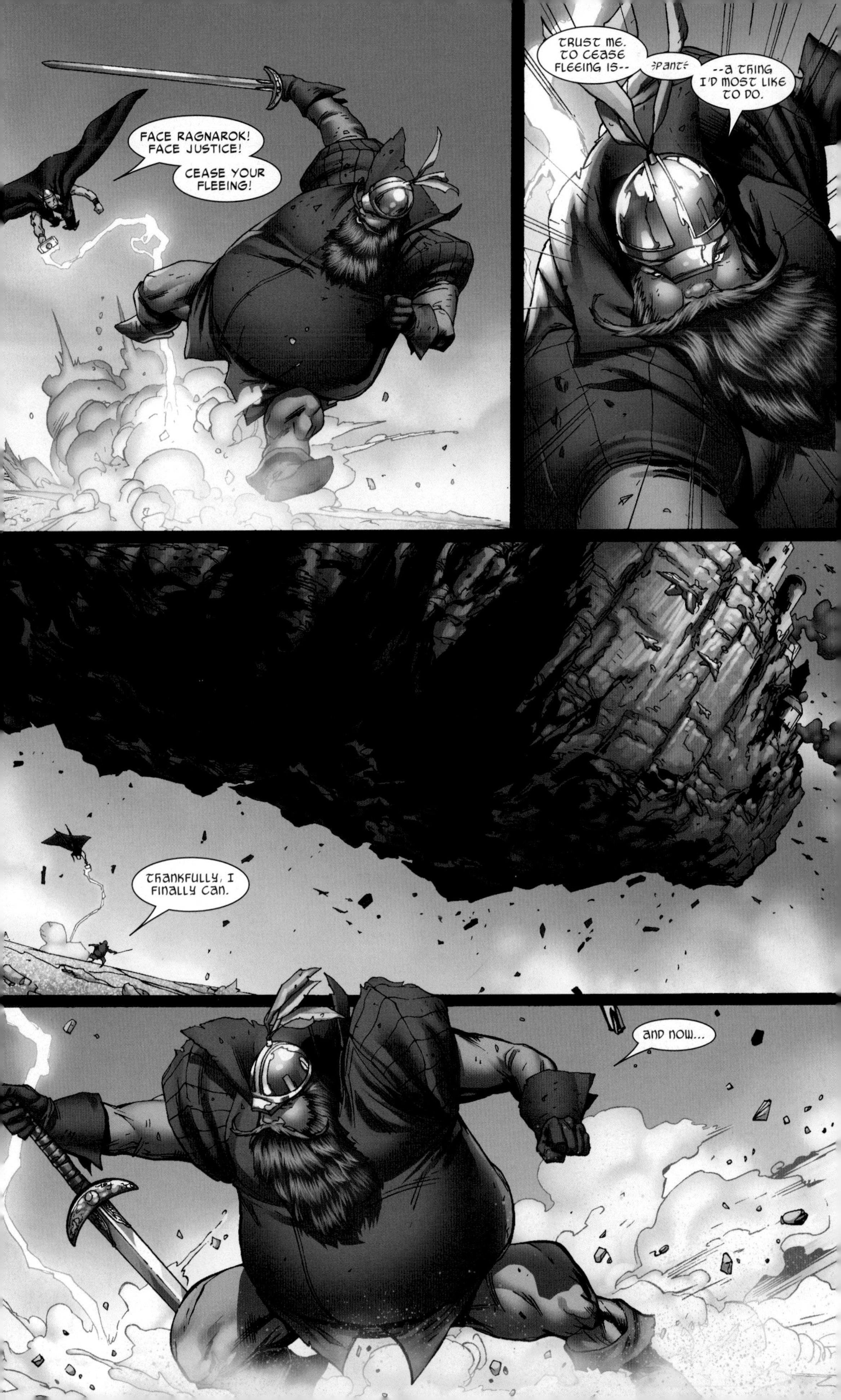
FACE RAGNAROK! FACE JUSTICE!
CEASE YOUR FLEEING!
TRUST ME. TO CEASE FLEEING IS--
PANT
--A THING I'D MOST LIKE TO DO.
THANKFULLY, I FINALLY CAN.
AND NOW...

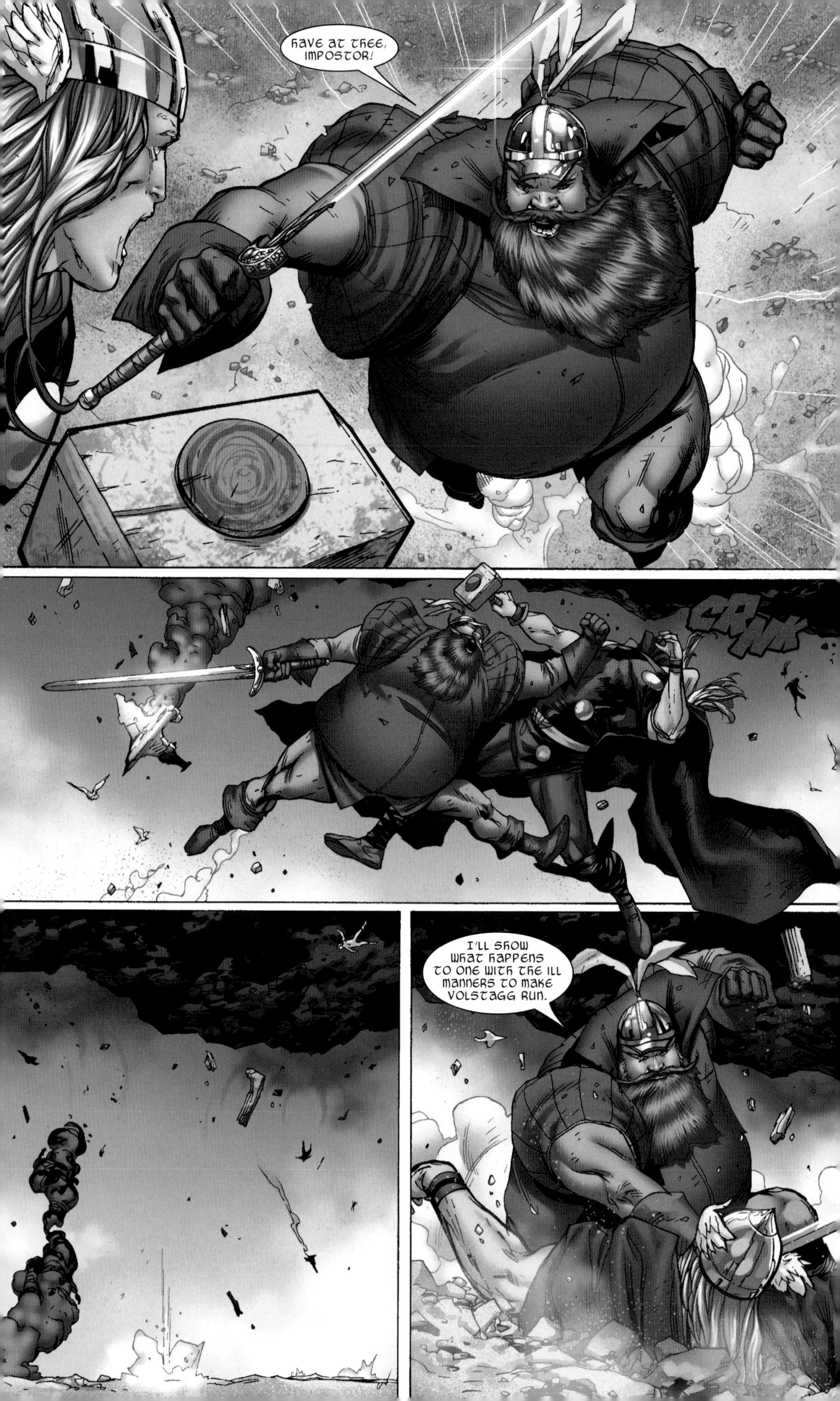
HAVE AT THEE, IMPOSTOR!
CRNK
I'LL SHOW WHAT HAPPENS TO ONE WITH THE ILL MANNERS TO MAKE VOLSTAGG RUN.

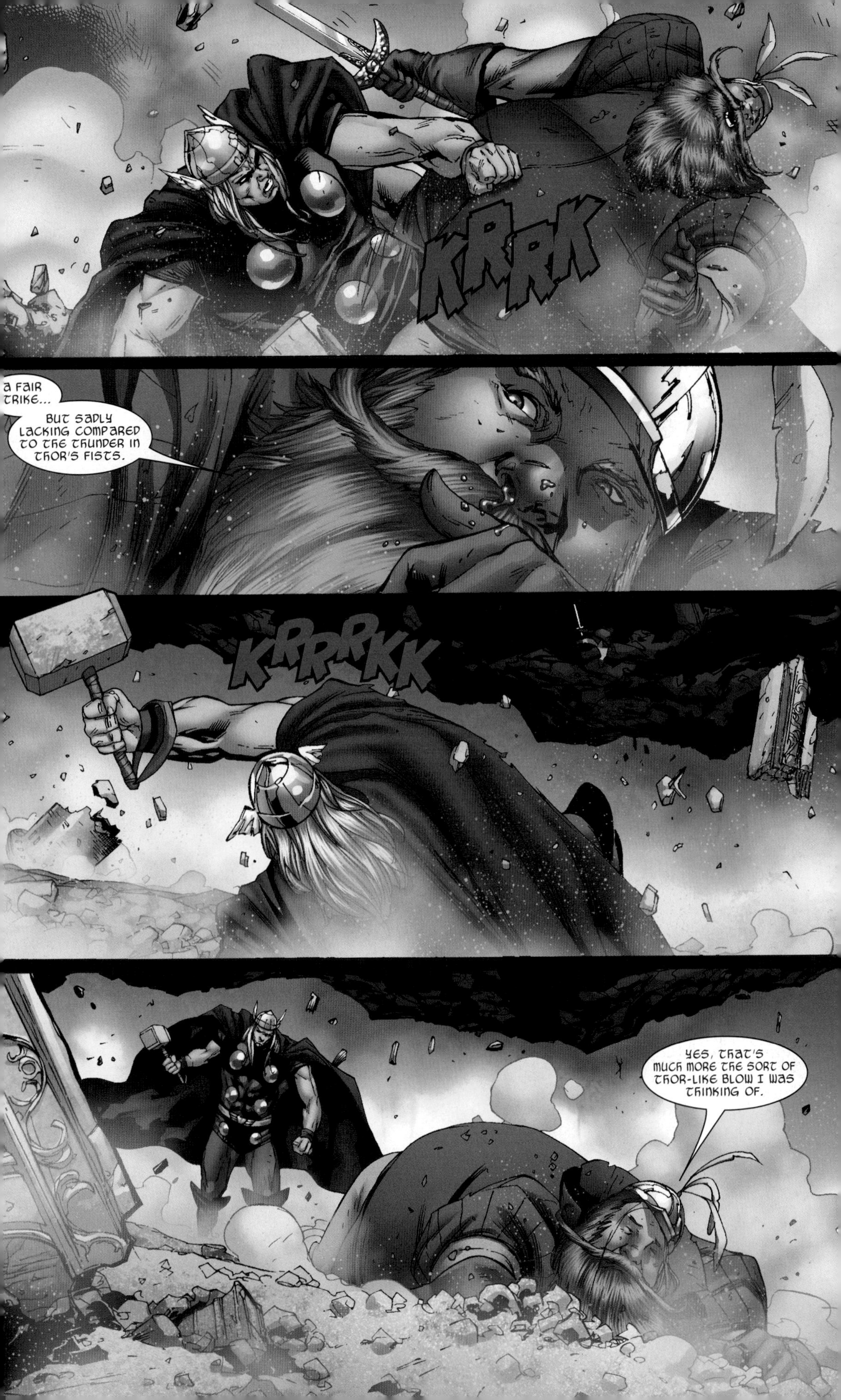
KRRK
A FAIR TRIKE...
BUT SADLY LACKING COMPARED TO THE THUNDER IN THOR'S FISTS.
KRRRKK
YES, THAT'S MUCH MORE THE SORT OF THOR-LIKE BLOW I WAS THINKING OF.

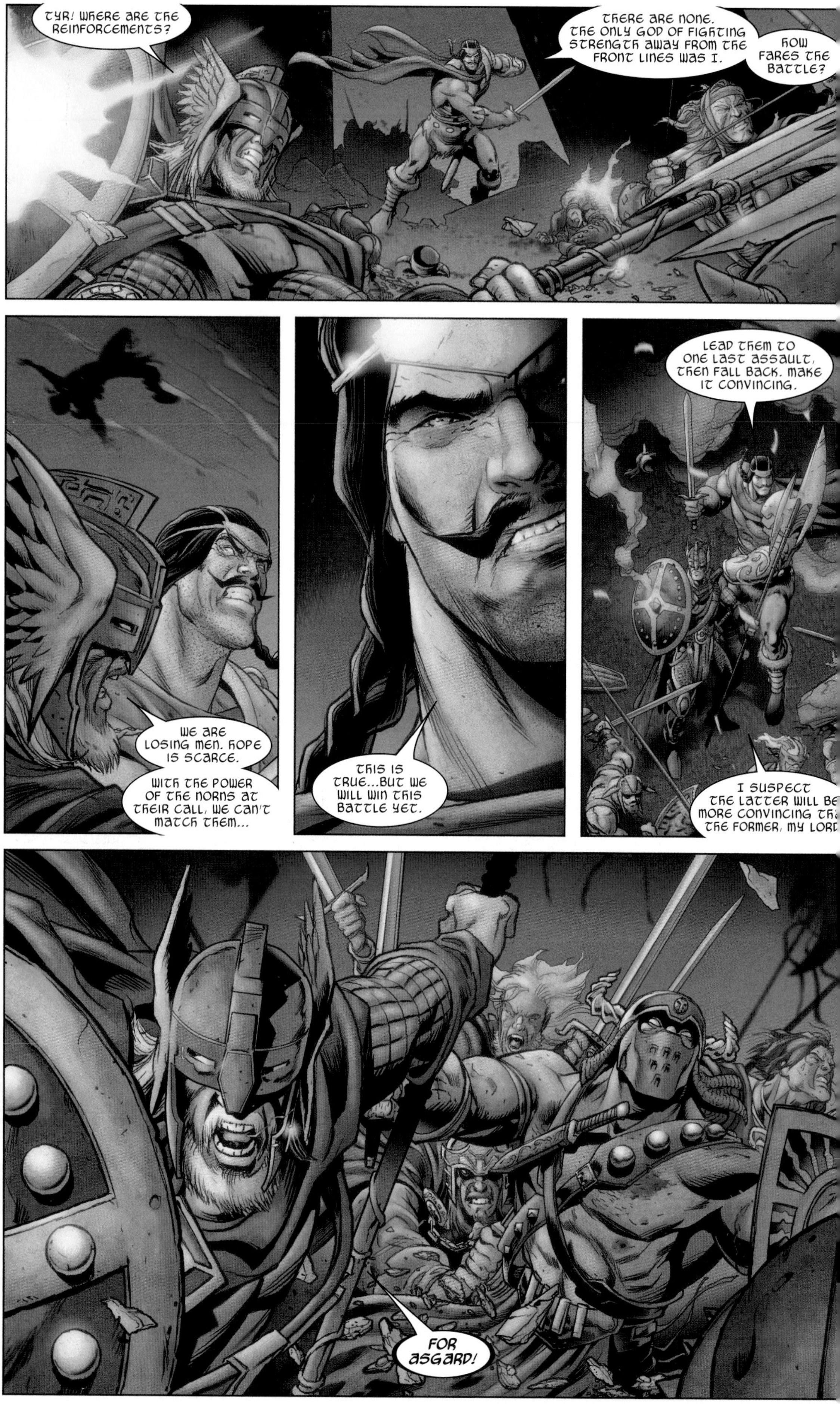
TYR! WHERE ARE THE REINFORCEMENTS?
THERE ARE NONE. THE ONLY GOD OF FIGHTING STRENGTH AWAY FROM THE FRONT LINES WAS I.
HOW FARES THE BATTLE?
WE ARE LOSING MEN. HOPE IS SCARCE.
WITH THE POWER OF THE NORNS AT THEIR CALL, WE CAN'T MATCH THEM...
THIS IS TRUE...BUT WE WILL WIN THIS BATTLE YET.
LEAD THEM TO ONE LAST ASSAULT, THEN FALL BACK. MAKE IT CONVINCING.
I SUSPECT THE LATTER WILL BE MORE CONVINCING THA THE FORMER, MY LORD
FOR ASGARD!

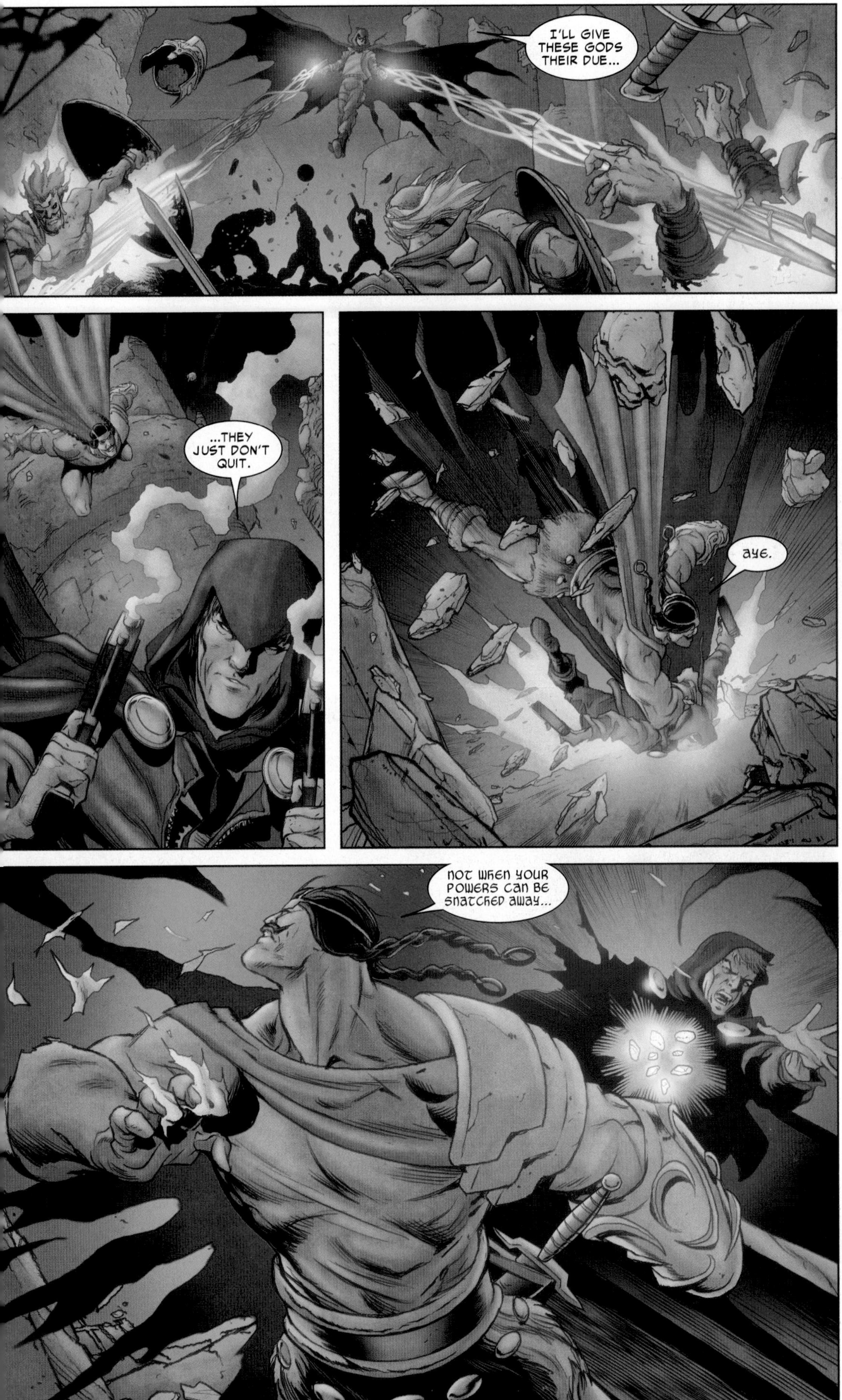
I'LL GIVE THESE GODS THEIR DUE...
...THEY JUST DON'T QUIT.
AYE.
NOT WHEN YOUR POWERS CAN BE SNATCHED AWAY...

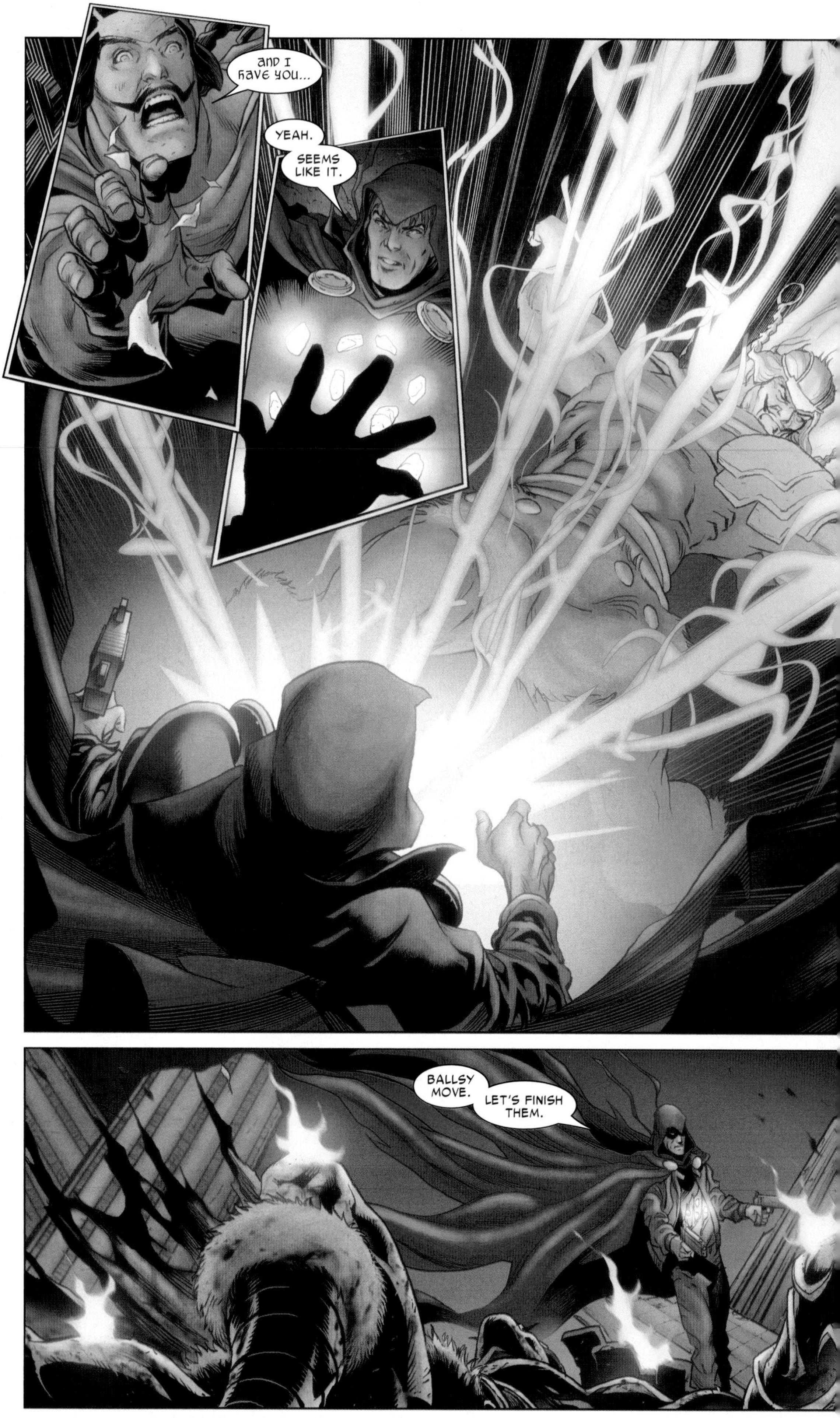
AND I HAVE YOU...
YEAH.
SEEMS LIKE IT.
BALLSY MOVE.
LET'S FINISH THEM.

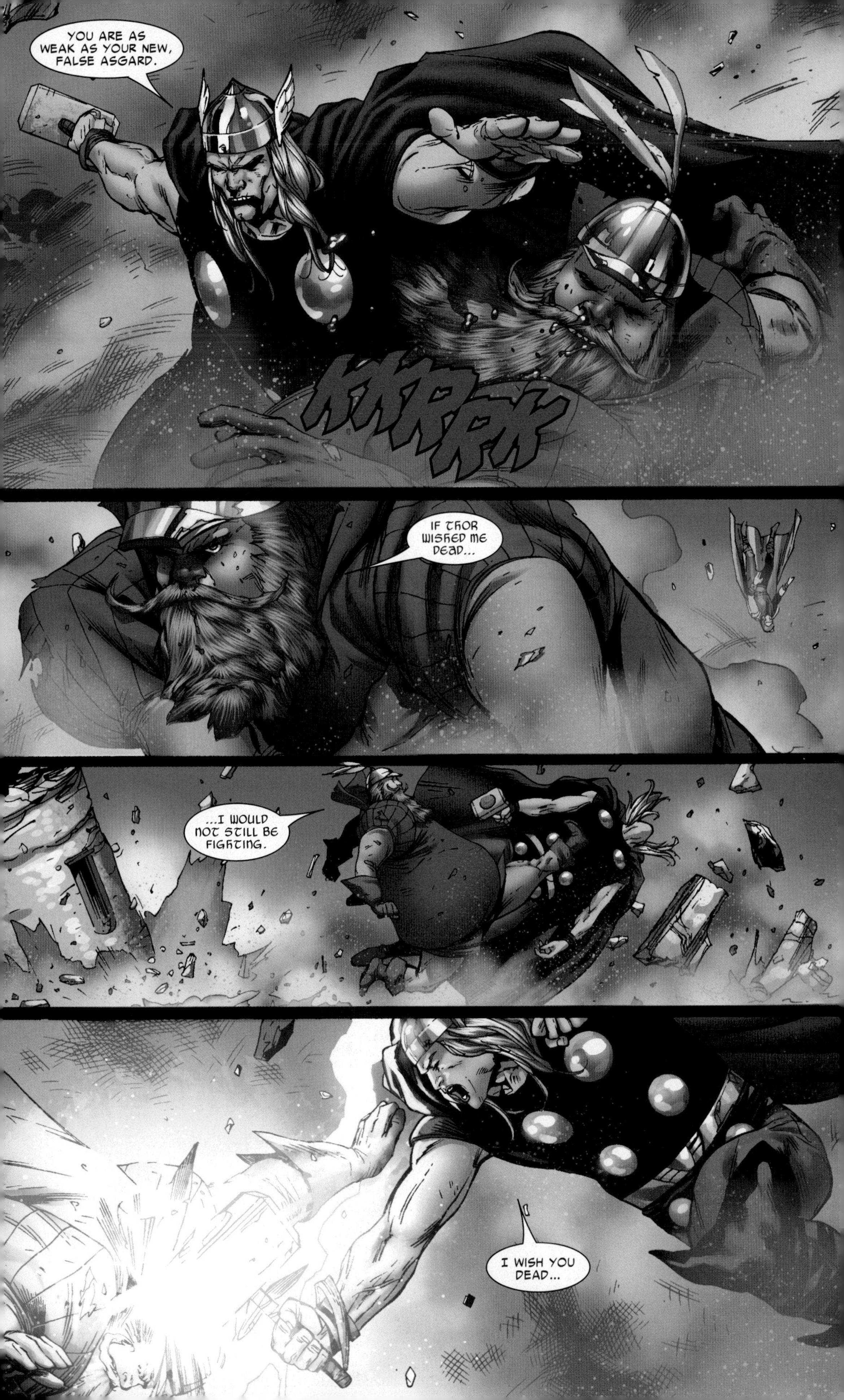
YOU ARE AS WEAK AS YOUR NEW, FALSE ASGARD.
KKRRK
IF THOR WISHED ME DEAD...
...I WOULD NOT STILL BE FIGHTING.
I WISH YOU DEAD...

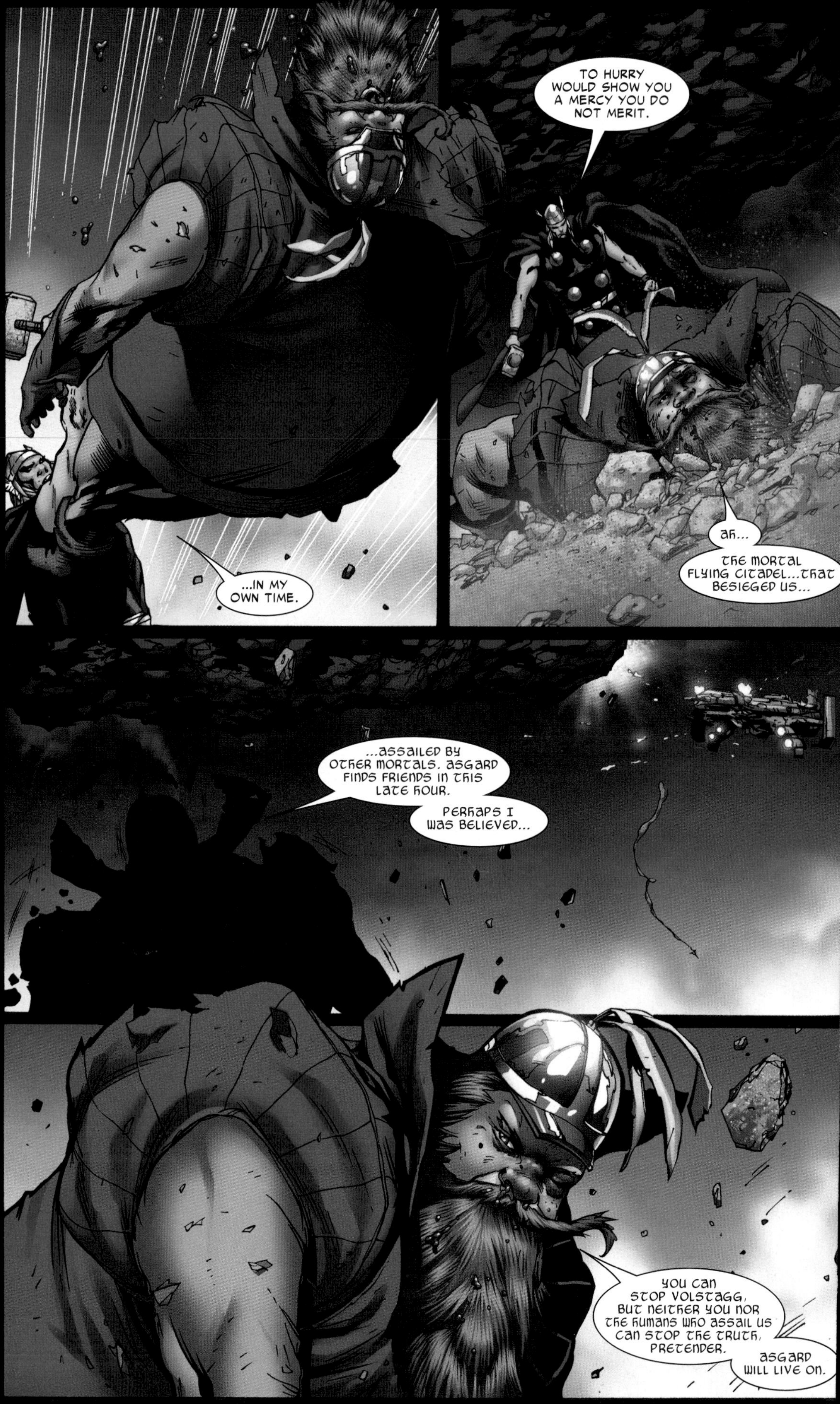
...IN MY OWN TIME.
TO HURRY WOULD SHOW YOU A MERCY YOU DO NOT MERIT.
AH...
THE MORTAL FLYING CITADEL...THAT BESIEGED US...
...ASSAILED BY OTHER MORTALS. ASGARD FINDS FRIENDS IN THIS LATE HOUR.
PERHAPS I WAS BELIEVED...
YOU CAN STOP VOLSTAGG, BUT NEITHER YOU NOR THE HUMANS WHO ASSAIL US CAN STOP THE TRUTH, PRETENDER.
ASGARD WILL LIVE ON.

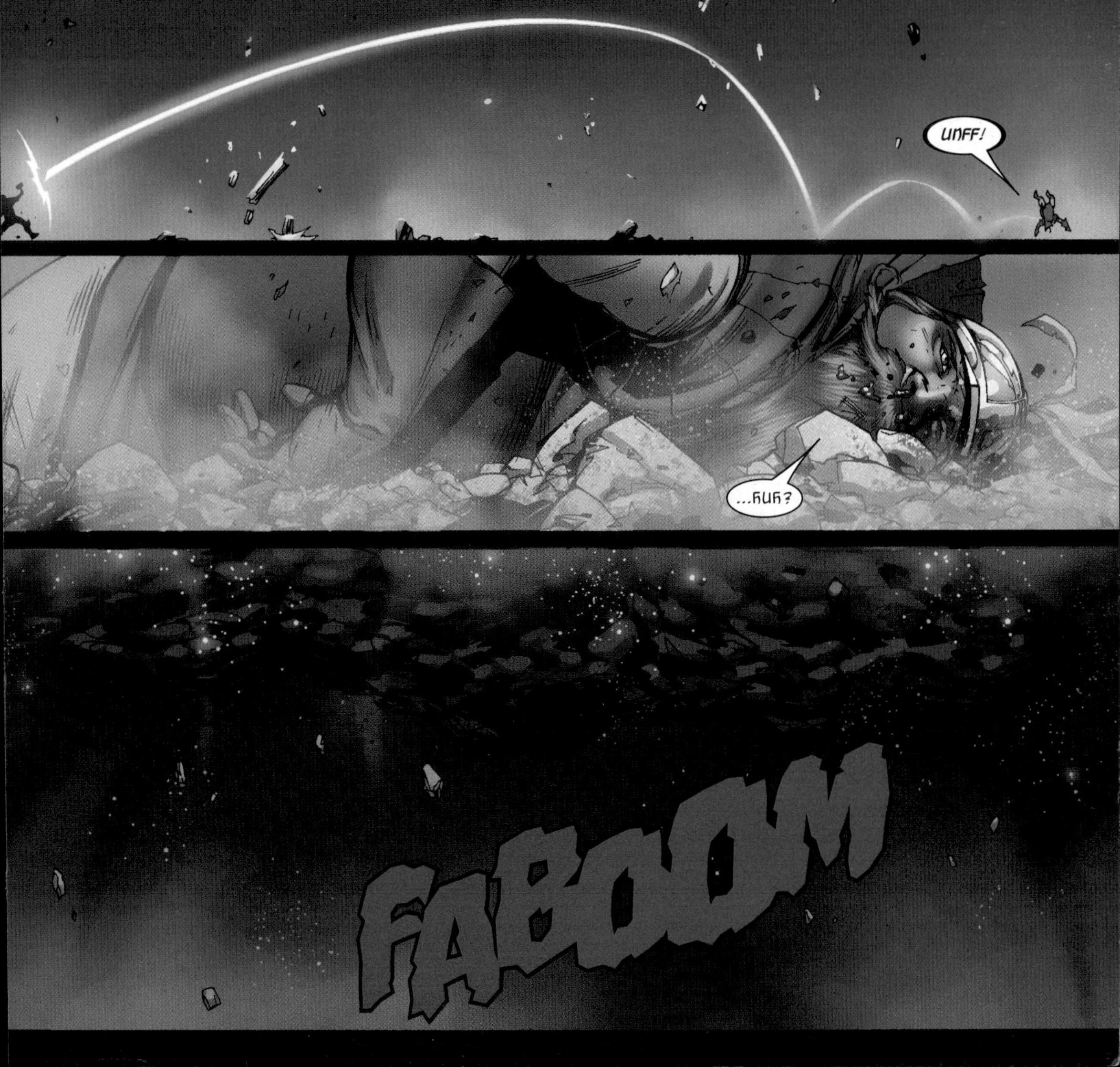
UNFF!
...HUH?
FABOOM

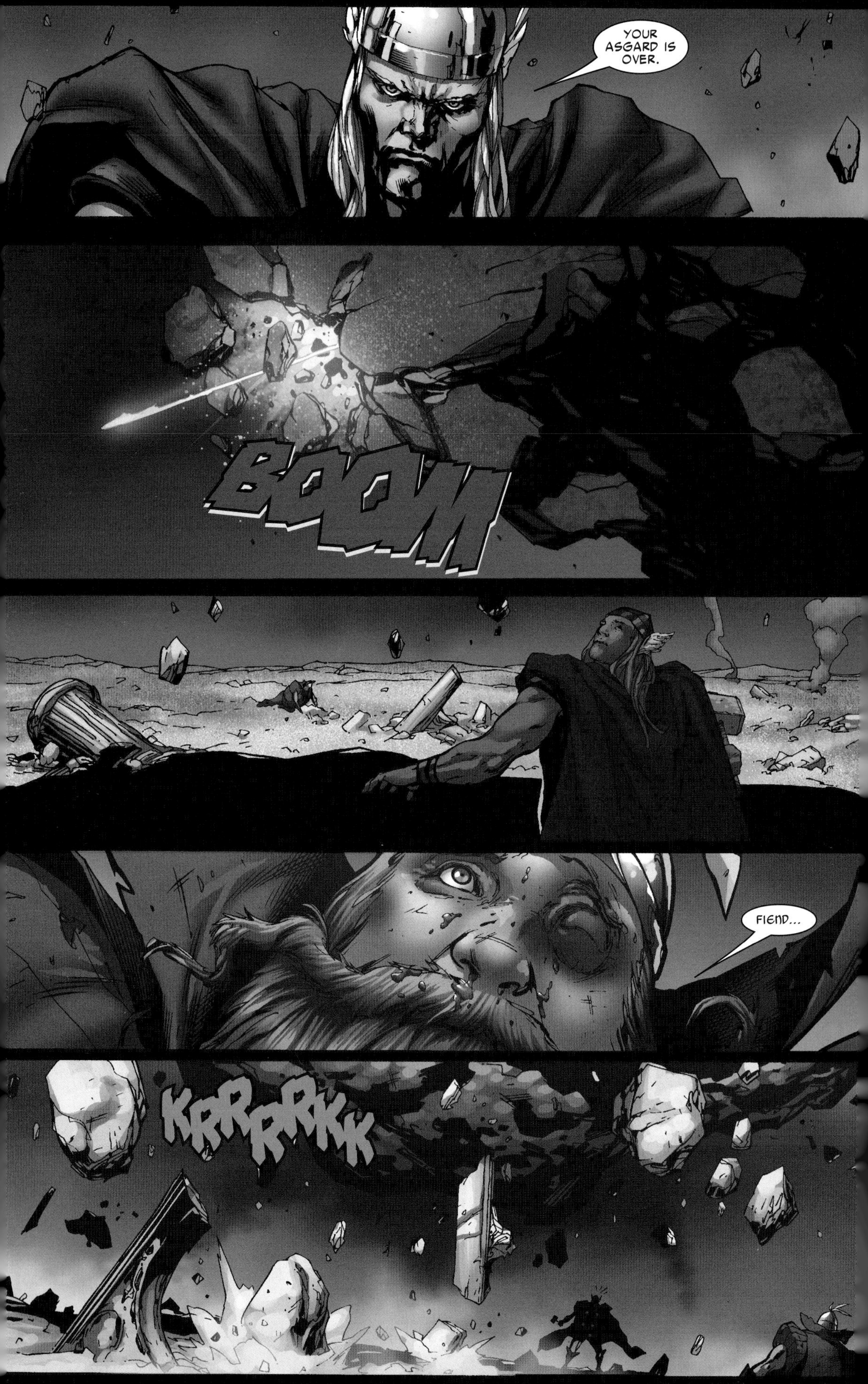
YOUR ASGARD IS OVER.
BOOM
FIEND...
KRRRRKKK

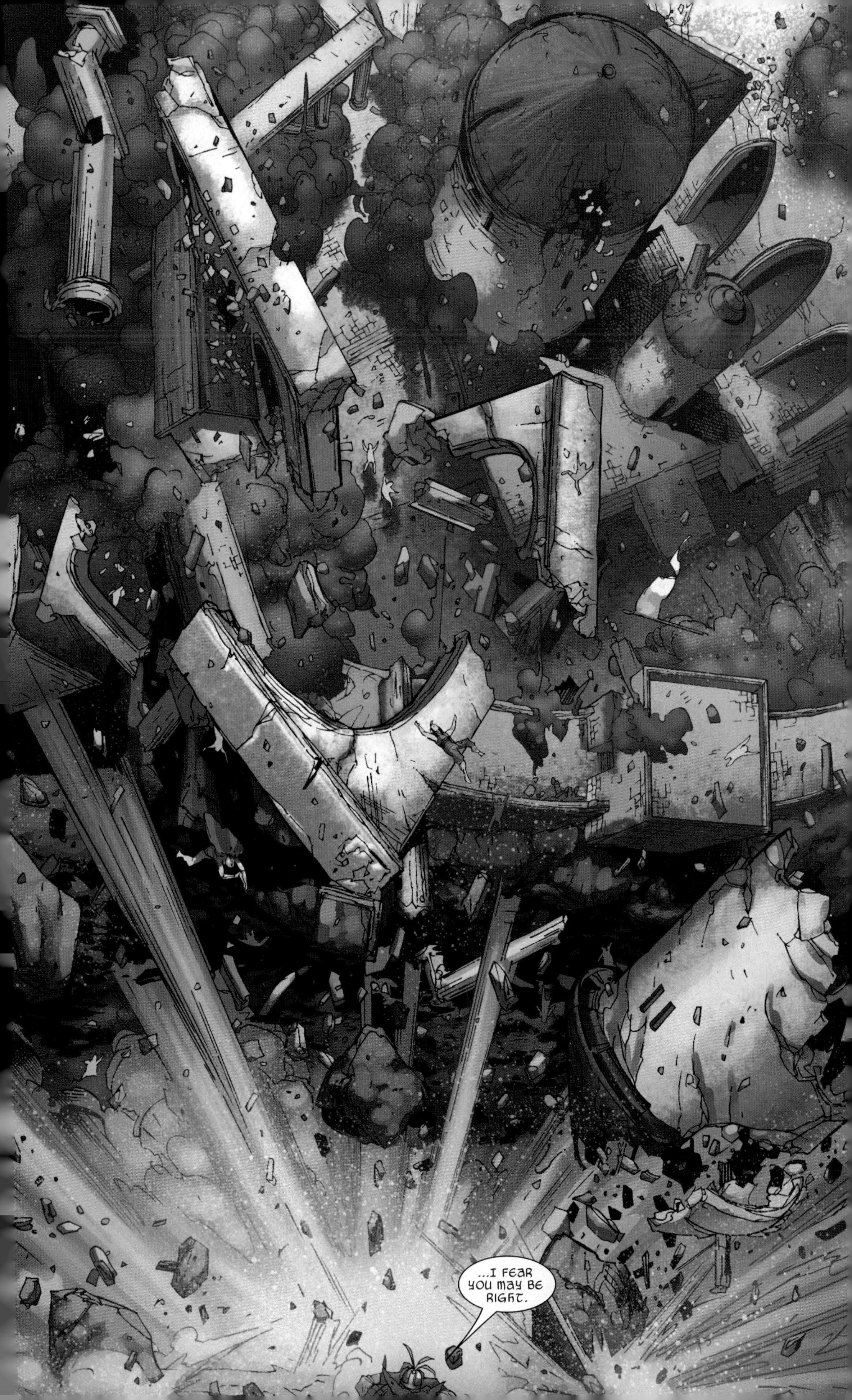
...I FEAR YOU MAY BE RIGHT.

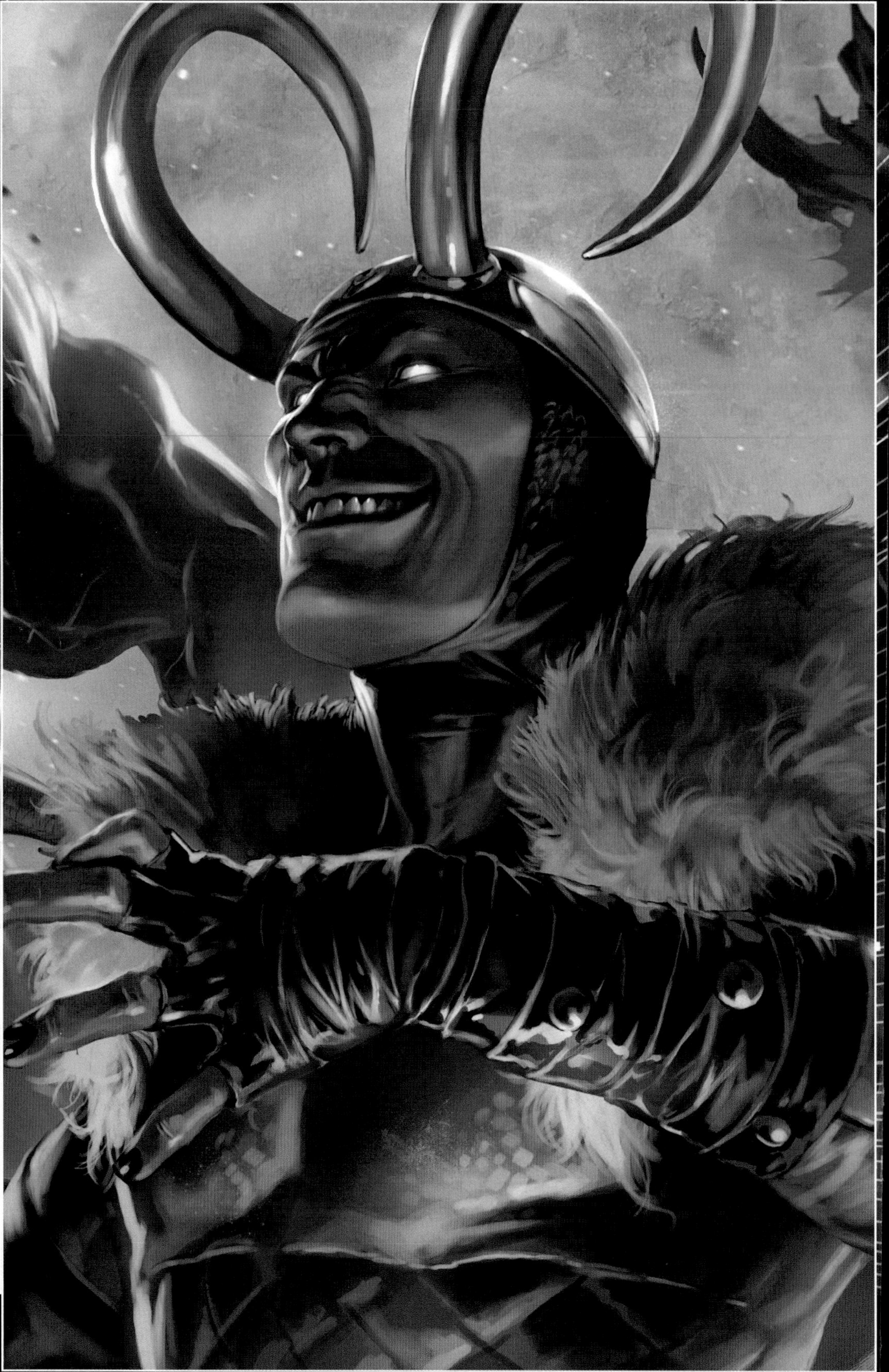

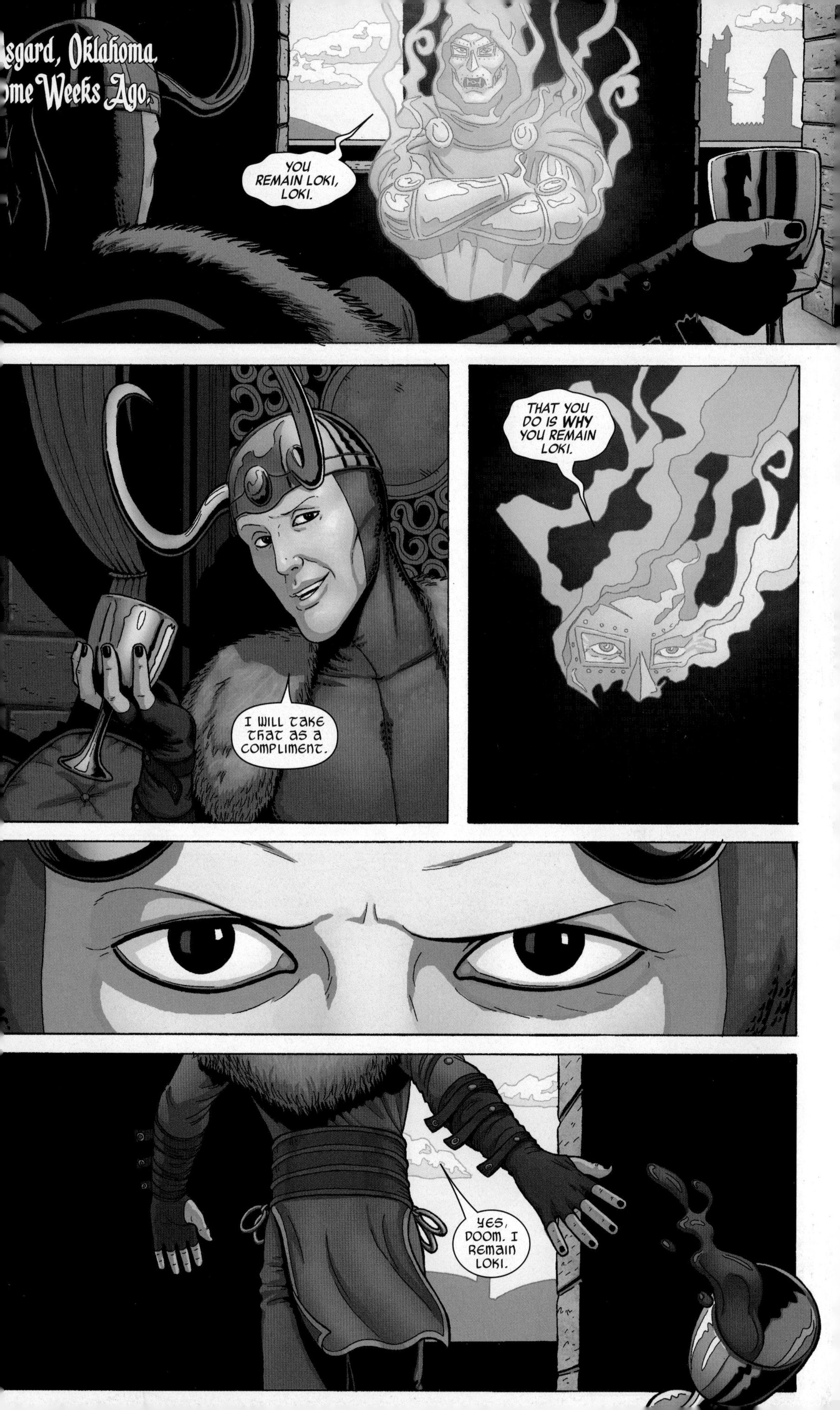
Asgard, Oklahoma.
Some Weeks Ago.
YOU REMAIN LOKI, LOKI.
I WILL TAKE THAT AS A COMPLIMENT.
THAT YOU DO IS WHY YOU REMAIN LOKI.
YES, DOOM. I REMAIN LOKI.

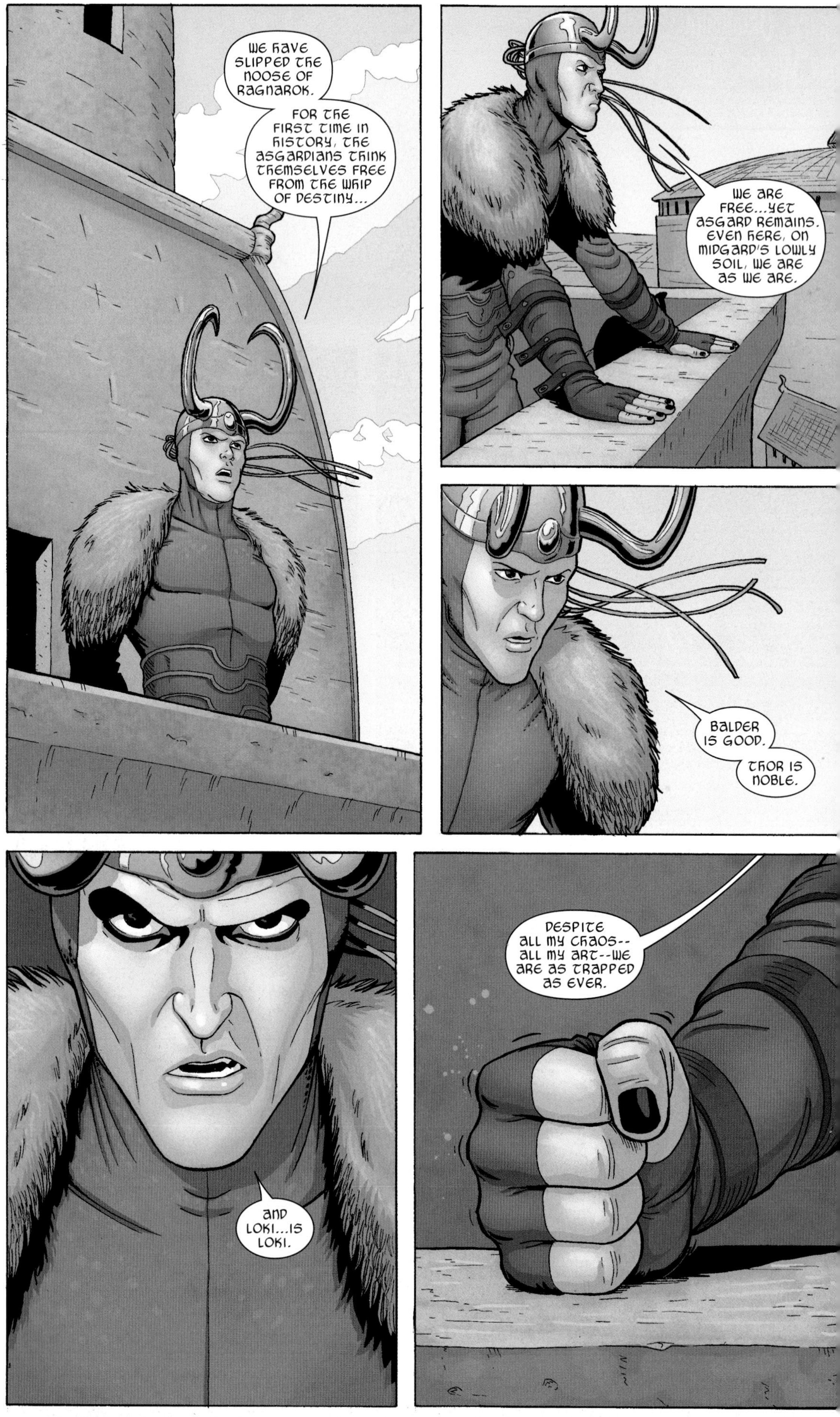
WE HAVE SLIPPED THE NOOSE OF RAGNAROK.
FOR THE FIRST TIME IN HISTORY, THE ASGARDIANS THINK THEMSELVES FREE FROM THE WHIP OF DESTINY...
WE ARE FREE...YET ASGARD REMAINS. EVEN HERE, ON MIDGARD'S LOWLY SOIL, WE ARE AS WE ARE.
BALDER IS GOOD.
THOR IS NOBLE.
AND LOKI...IS LOKI.
DESPITE ALL MY CHAOS--ALL MY ART--WE ARE AS TRAPPED AS EVER.

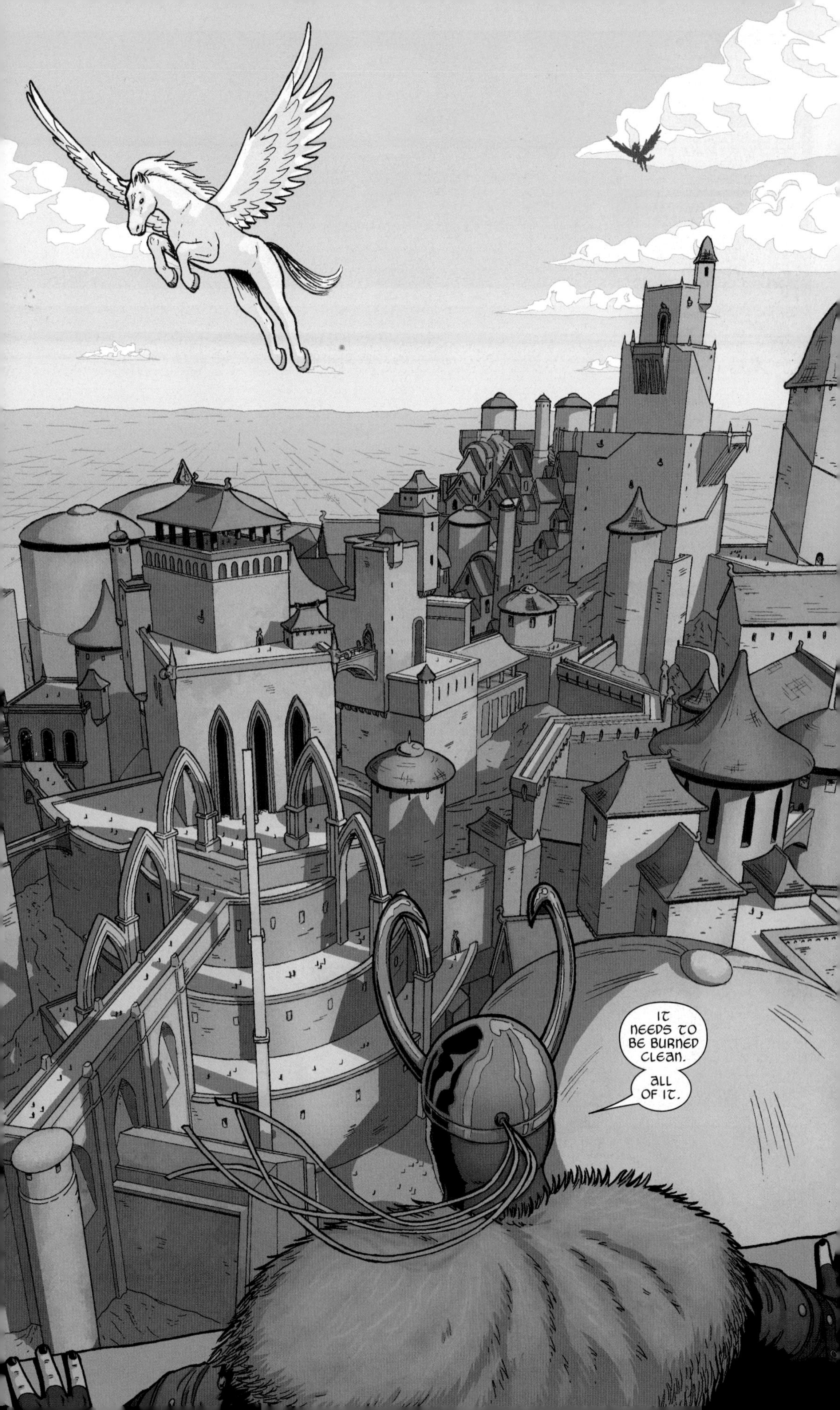
IT NEEDS TO BE BURNED CLEAN.
ALL OF IT.

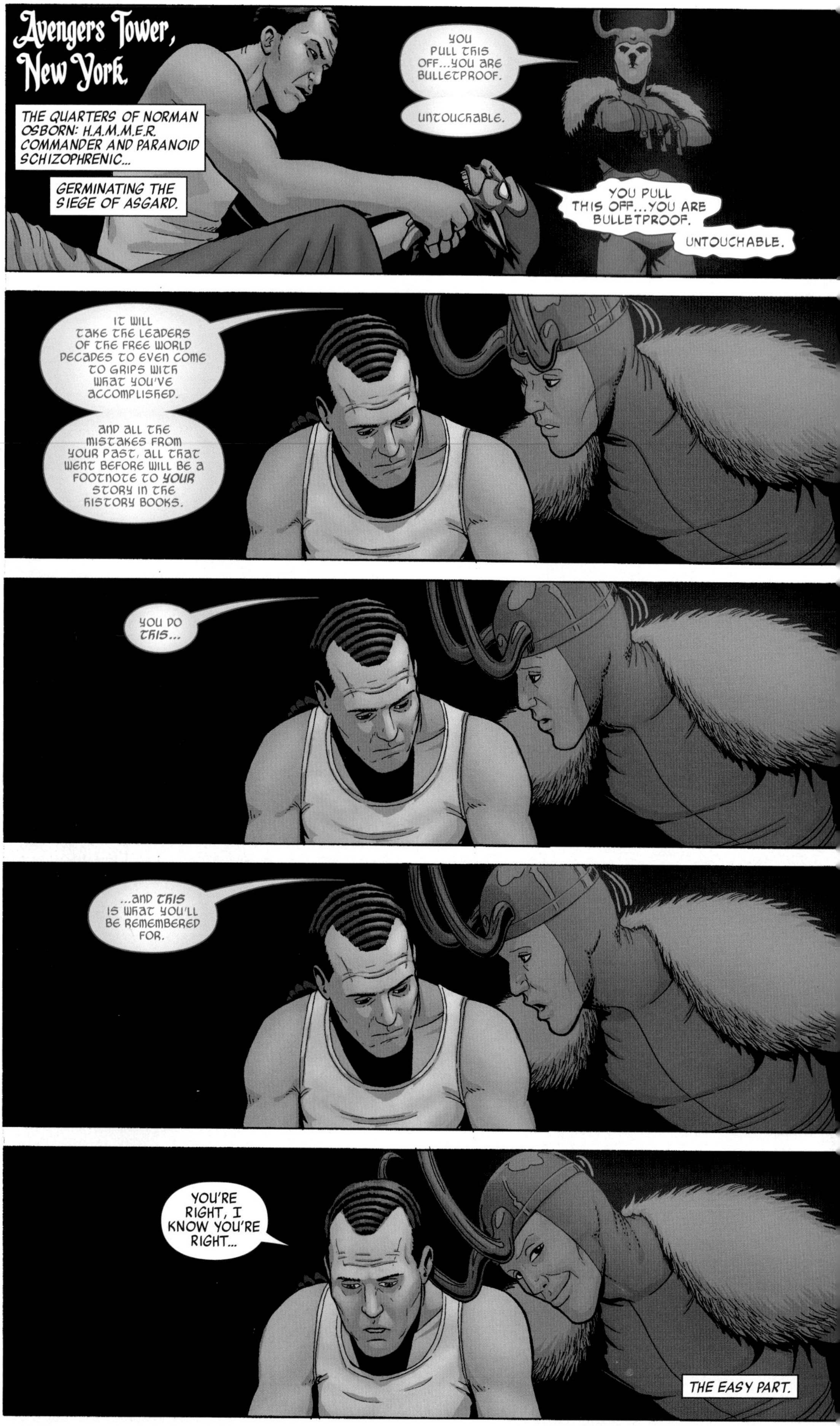
Avengers Tower, New York.
THE QUARTERS OF NORMAN OSBORN: H.A.M.M.E.R. COMMANDER AND PARANOID SCHIZOPHRENIC...
GERMINATING THE SIEGE OF ASGARD.
YOU PULL THIS OFF...YOU ARE BULLETPROOF.
UNTOUCHABLE.
YOU PULL THIS OFF...YOU ARE BULLETPROOF.
UNTOUCHABLE.
IT WILL TAKE THE LEADERS OF THE FREE WORLD DECADES TO EVEN COME TO GRIPS WITH WHAT YOU'VE ACCOMPLISHED.
AND ALL THE MISTAKES FROM YOUR PAST, ALL THAT WENT BEFORE WILL BE A FOOTNOTE TO YOUR STORY IN THE HISTORY BOOKS.
YOU DO THIS...
...AND THIS IS WHAT YOU'LL BE REMEMBERED FOR.
YOU'RE RIGHT, I KNOW YOU'RE RIGHT...
THE EASY PART.

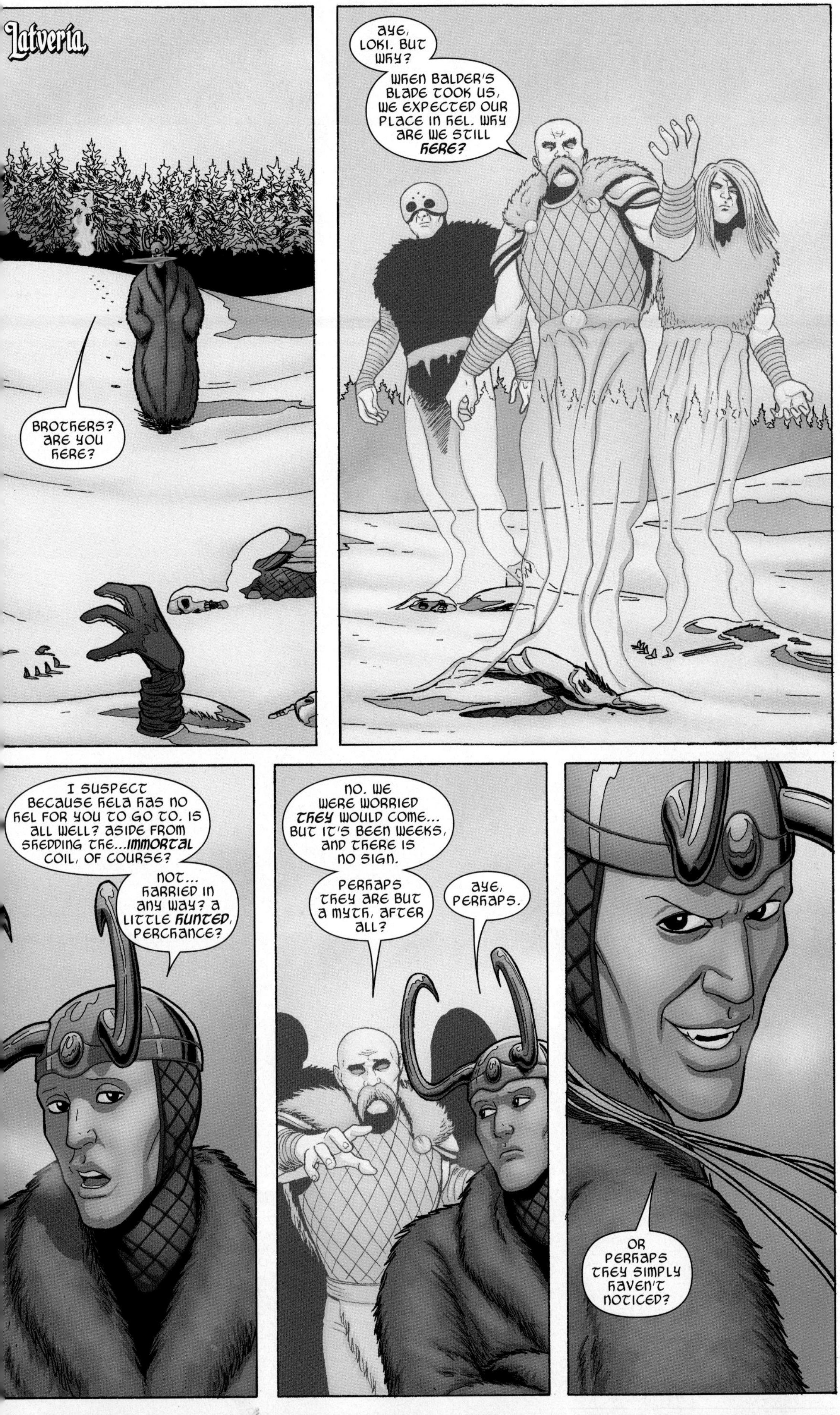
Latveria.
BROTHERS? ARE YOU HERE?
AYE, LOKI. BUT WHY?
WHEN BALDER'S BLADE TOOK US, WE EXPECTED OUR PLACE IN HEL. WHY ARE WE STILL HERE?
I SUSPECT BECAUSE HELA HAS NO HEL FOR YOU TO GO TO. IS ALL WELL? ASIDE FROM SHEDDING THE...IMMORTAL COIL, OF COURSE?
NOT... HARRIED IN ANY WAY? A LITTLE HUNTED, PERCHANCE?
NO. WE WERE WORRIED THEY WOULD COME... BUT IT'S BEEN WEEKS, AND THERE IS NO SIGN.
PERHAPS THEY ARE BUT A MYTH, AFTER ALL?
AYE, PERHAPS.
OR PERHAPS THEY SIMPLY HAVEN'T NOTICED?

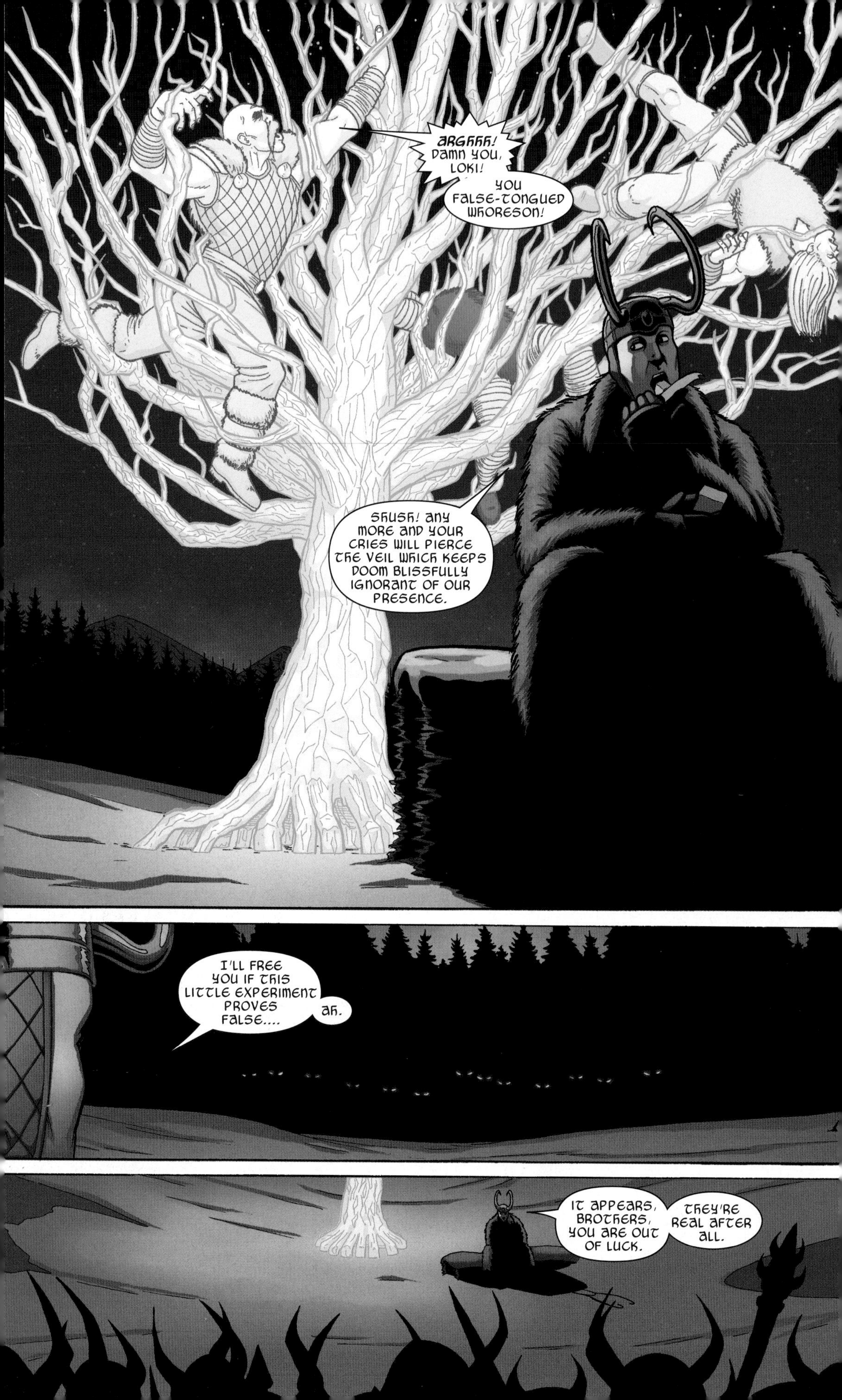
ARGHHH! DAMN YOU, LOKI!
YOU FALSE-TONGUED WHORESON!
SHUSH! ANY MORE AND YOUR CRIES WILL PIERCE THE VEIL WHICH KEEPS DOOM BLISSFULLY IGNORANT OF OUR PRESENCE.
I'LL FREE YOU IF THIS LITTLE EXPERIMENT PROVES FALSE....
AH.
IT APPEARS, BROTHERS, YOU ARE OUT OF LUCK.
THEY'RE REAL AFTER ALL.

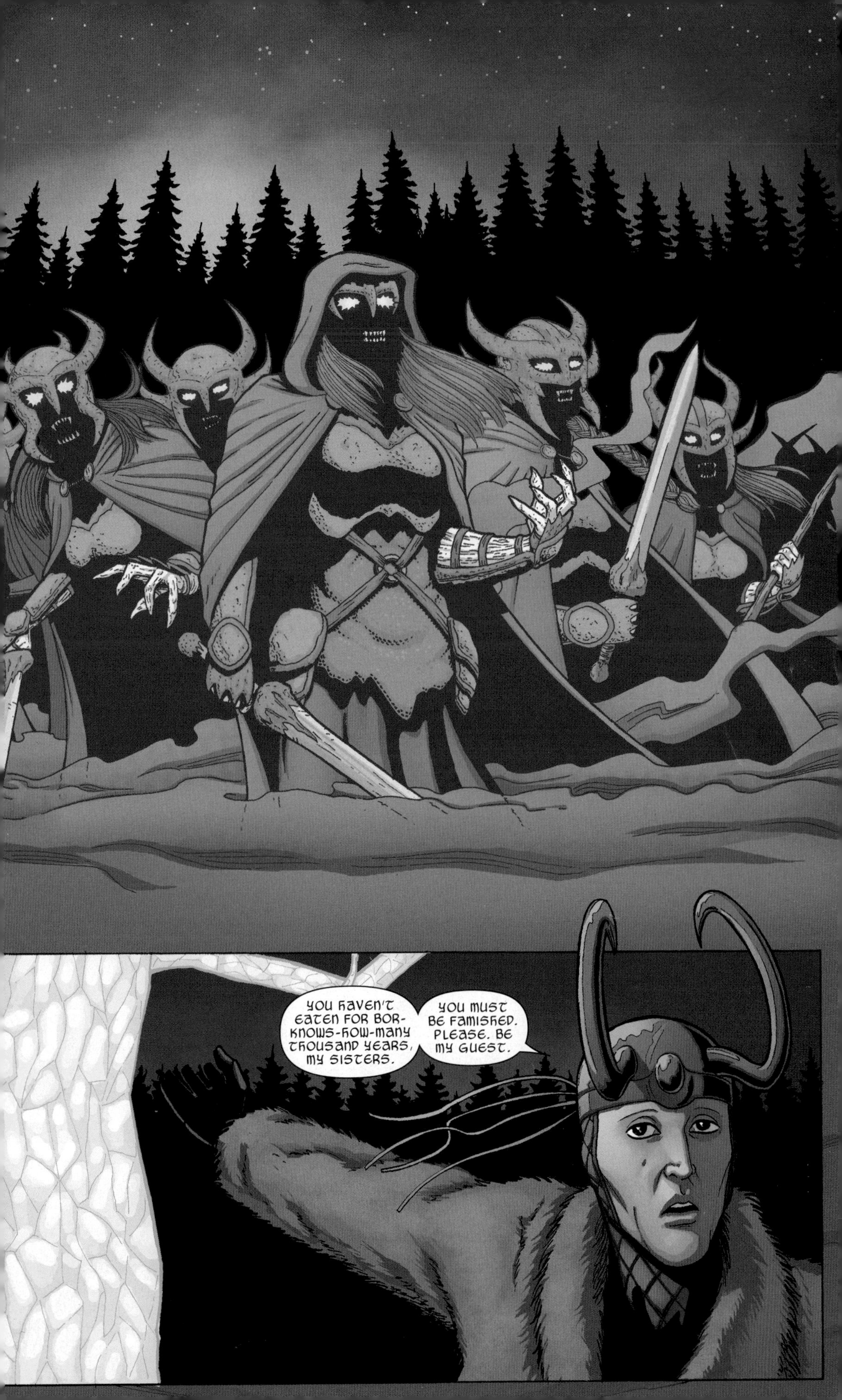
YOU HAVEN'T EATEN FOR BOR-KNOWS-HOW-MANY THOUSAND YEARS, MY SISTERS.
YOU MUST BE FAMISHED. PLEASE. BE MY GUEST.

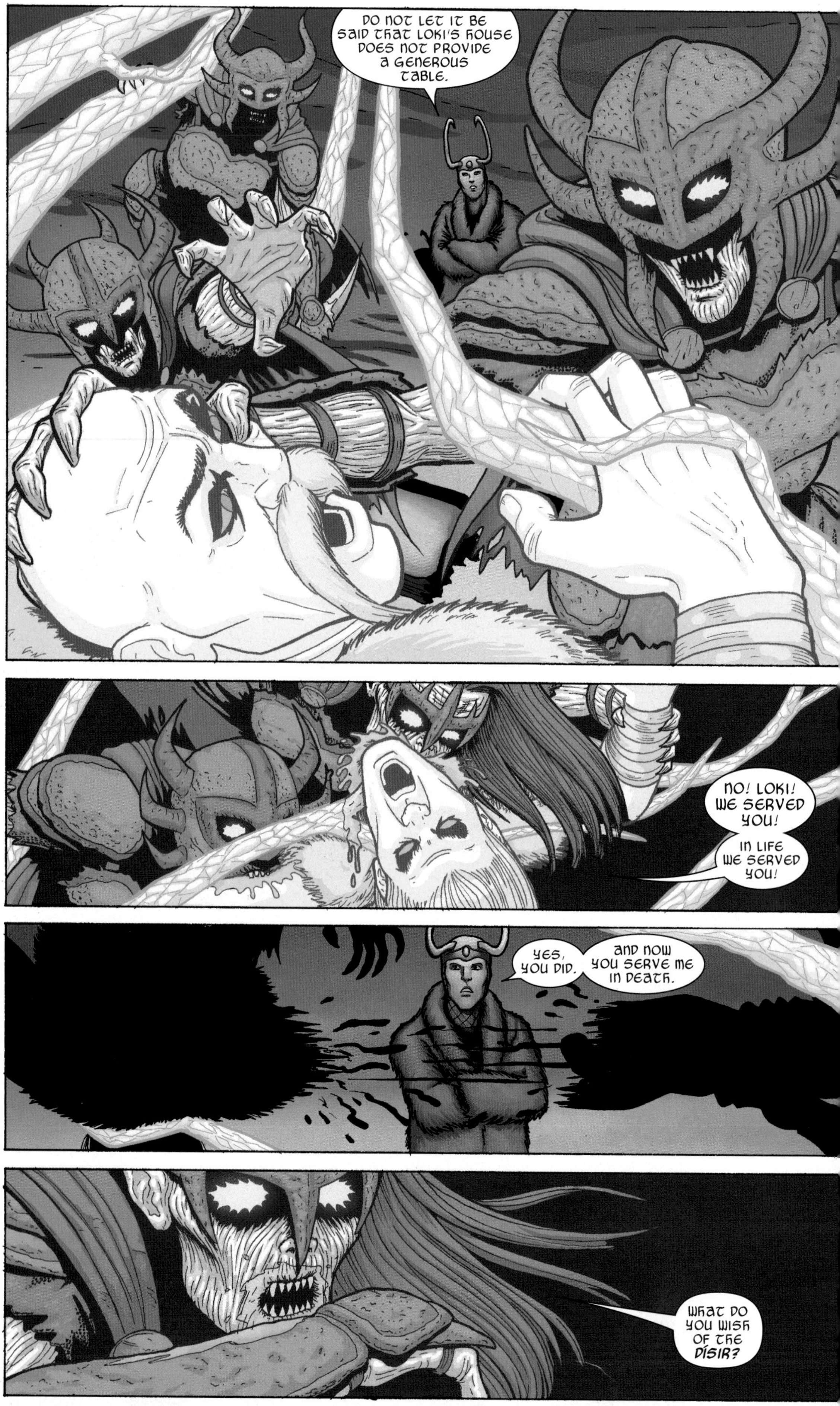
DO NOT LET IT BE SAID THAT LOKI'S HOUSE DOES NOT PROVIDE A GENEROUS TABLE.
NO! LOKI! WE SERVED YOU!
IN LIFE WE SERVED YOU!
YES, YOU DID.
AND NOW YOU SERVE ME IN DEATH.
WHAT DO YOU WISH OF THE DÍSIR?

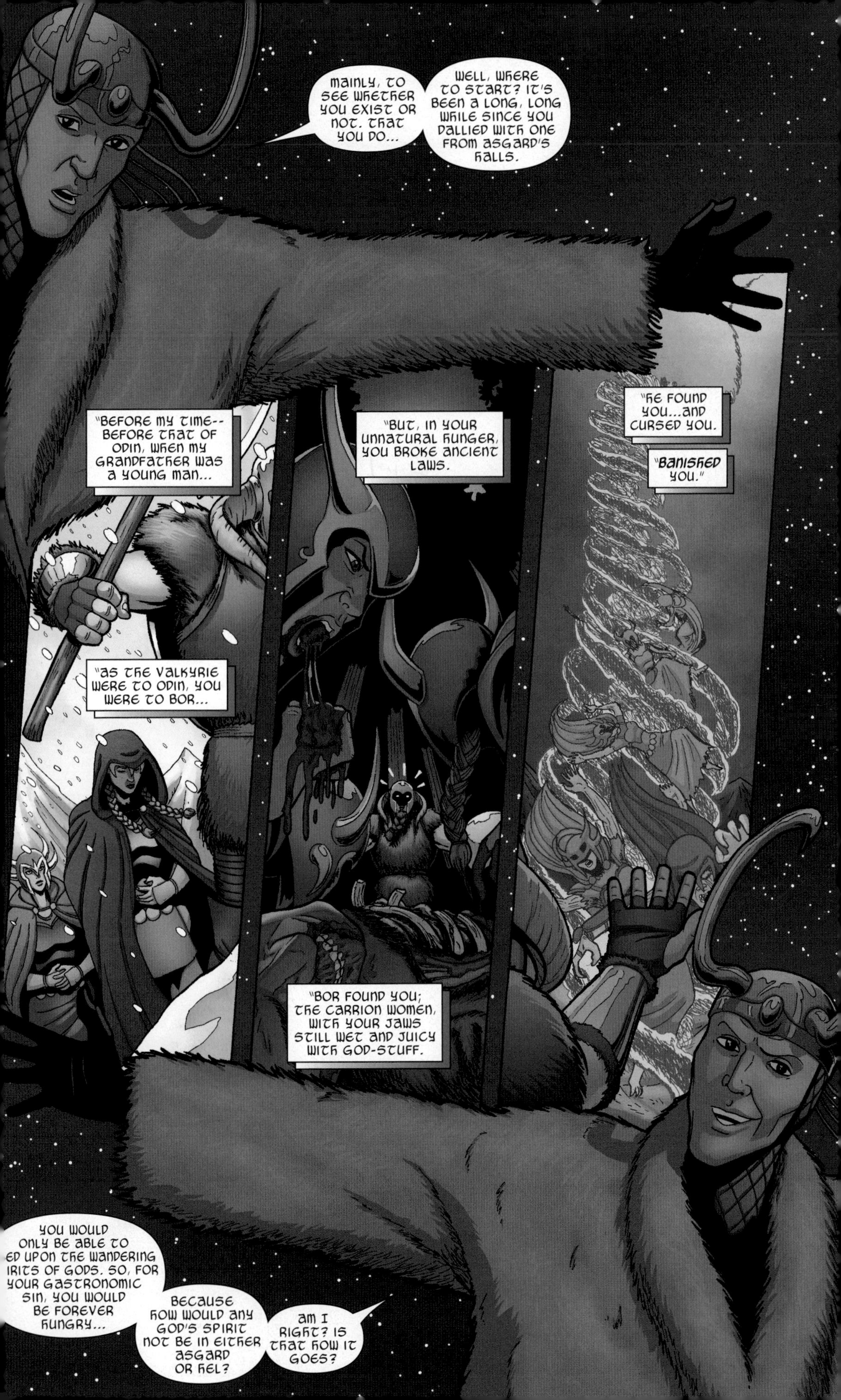

MAINLY, TO SEE WHETHER YOU EXIST OR NOT. THAT YOU DO...
WELL, WHERE TO START? IT'S BEEN A LONG, LONG WHILE SINCE YOU DALLIED WITH ONE FROM ASGARD'S HALLS.
"BEFORE MY TIME-- BEFORE THAT OF ODIN, WHEN MY GRANDFATHER WAS A YOUNG MAN...
"AS THE VALKYRIE WERE TO ODIN, YOU WERE TO BOR...
"BUT, IN YOUR UNNATURAL HUNGER, YOU BROKE ANCIENT LAWS.
"BOR FOUND YOU; THE CARRION WOMEN, WITH YOUR JAWS STILL WET AND JUICY WITH GOD-STUFF.
"HE FOUND YOU...AND CURSED YOU.
"BANISHED YOU."
YOU WOULD ONLY BE ABLE TO ED UPON THE WANDERING IRITS OF GODS. SO, FOR YOUR GASTRONOMIC SIN, YOU WOULD BE FOREVER HUNGRY...
BECAUSE HOW WOULD ANY GOD'S SPIRIT NOT BE IN EITHER ASGARD OR HEL?
AM I RIGHT? IS THAT HOW IT GOES?

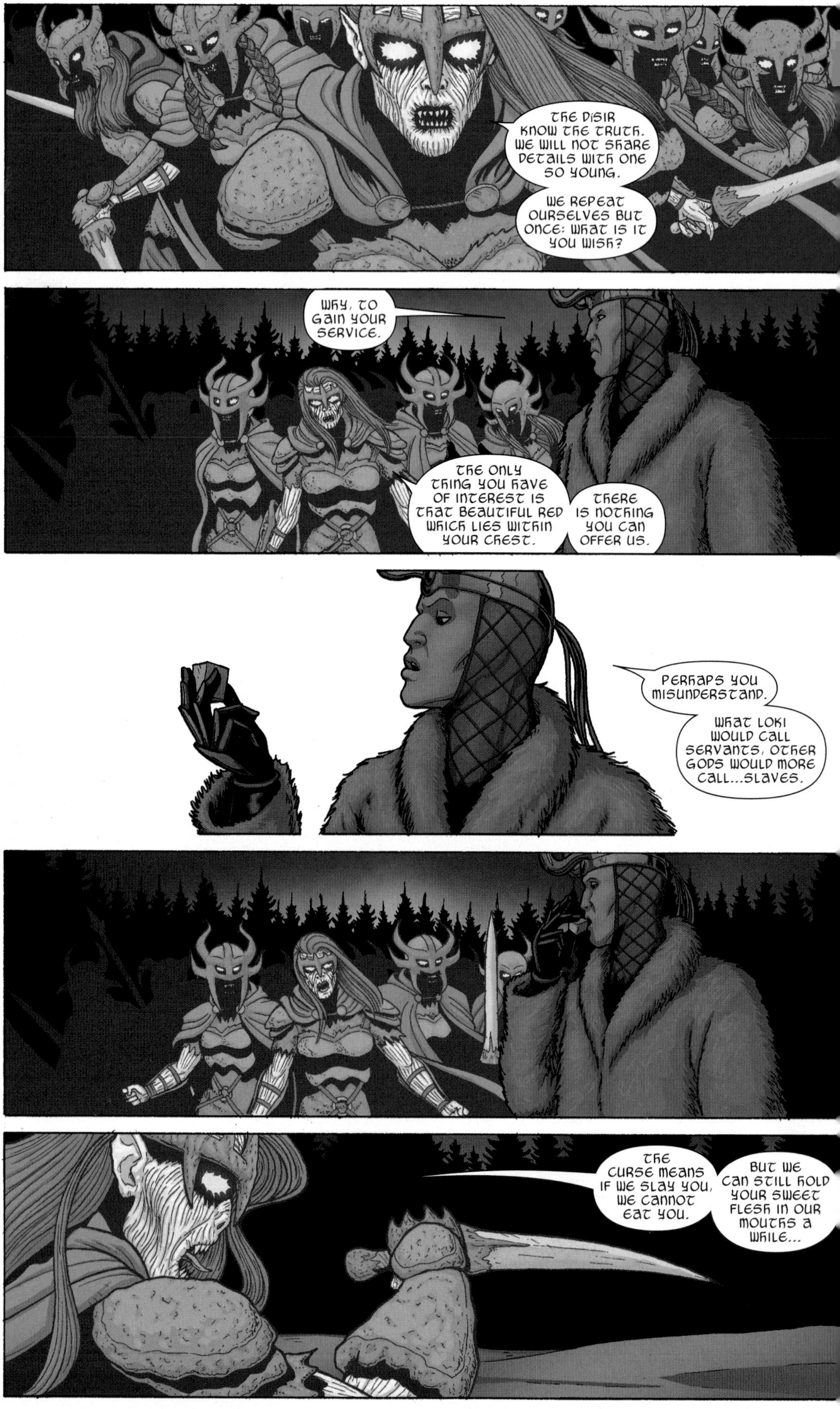

THE DISIR KNOW THE TRUTH. WE WILL NOT SHARE DETAILS WITH ONE SO YOUNG.
WE REPEAT OURSELVES BUT ONCE: WHAT IS IT YOU WISH?
WHY, TO GAIN YOUR SERVICE.
THE ONLY THING YOU HAVE OF INTEREST IS THAT BEAUTIFUL RED WHICH LIES WITHIN YOUR CHEST.
THERE IS NOTHING YOU CAN OFFER US.
PERHAPS YOU MISUNDERSTAND.
WHAT LOKI WOULD CALL SERVANTS, OTHER GODS WOULD MORE CALL...SLAVES.
THE CURSE MEANS IF WE SLAY YOU, WE CANNOT EAT YOU.
BUT WE CAN STILL HOLD YOUR SWEET FLESH IN OUR MOUTHS A WHILE...

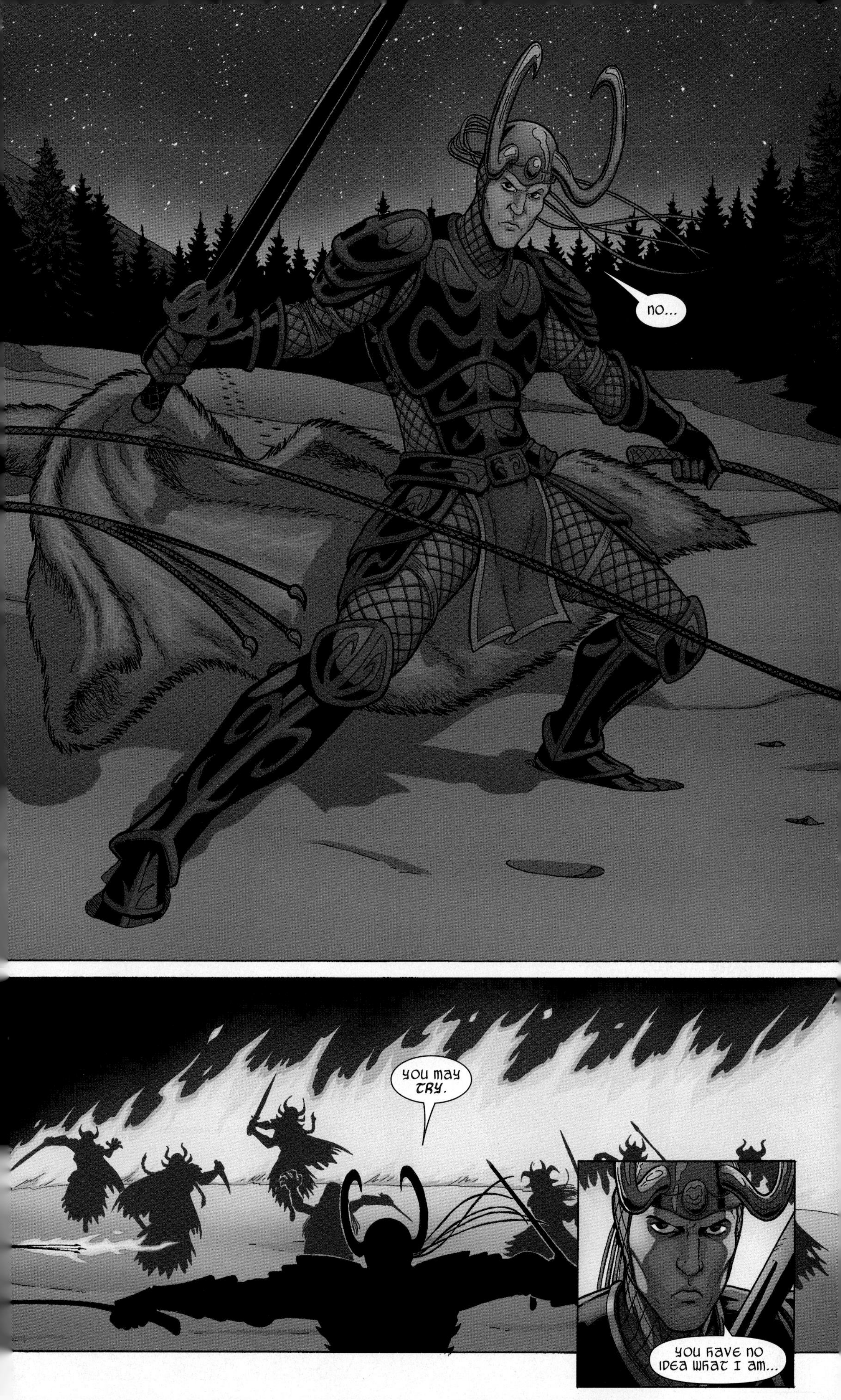
NO...
YOU MAY TRY.
YOU HAVE NO IDEA WHAT I AM...

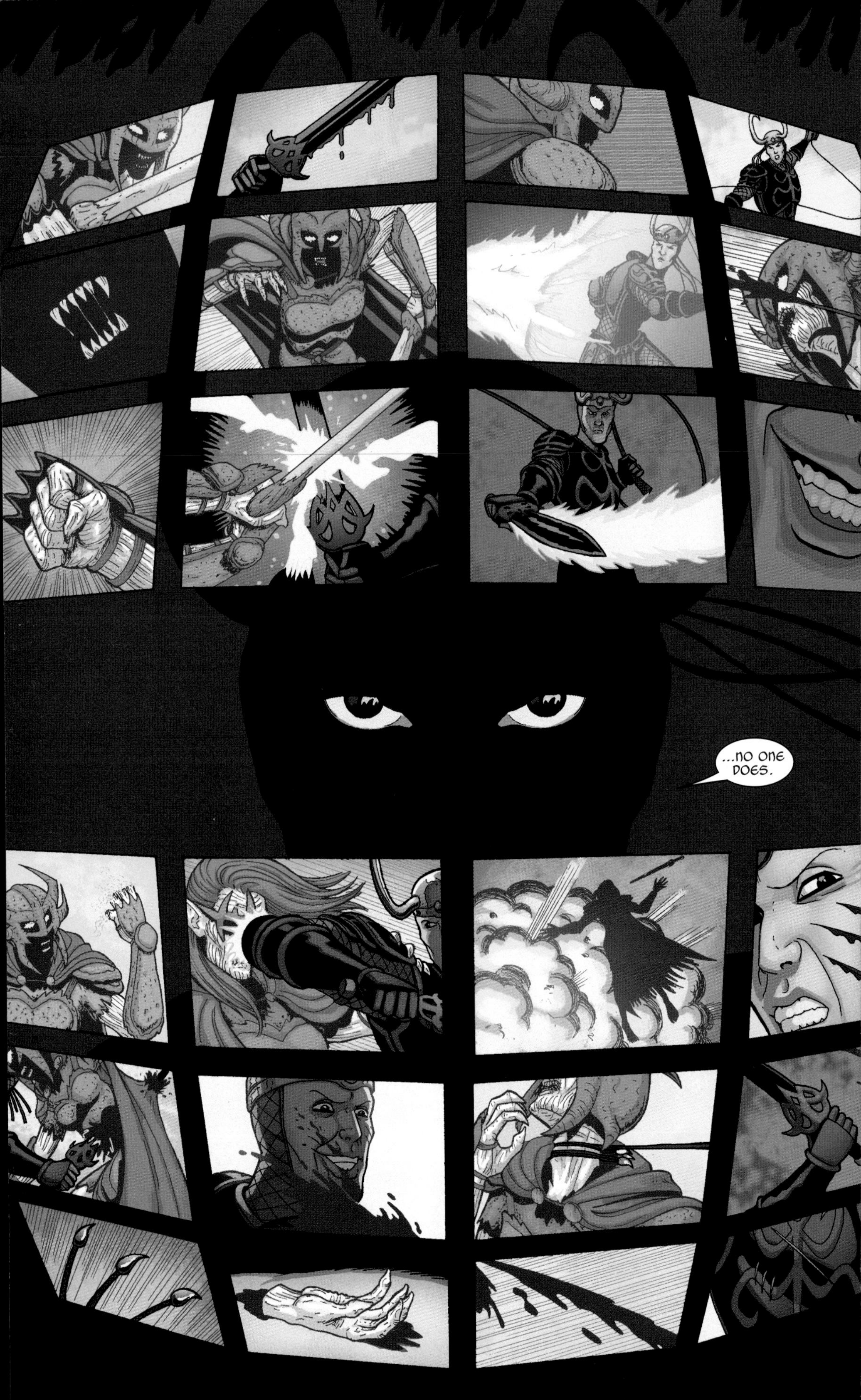
...NO ONE DOES.

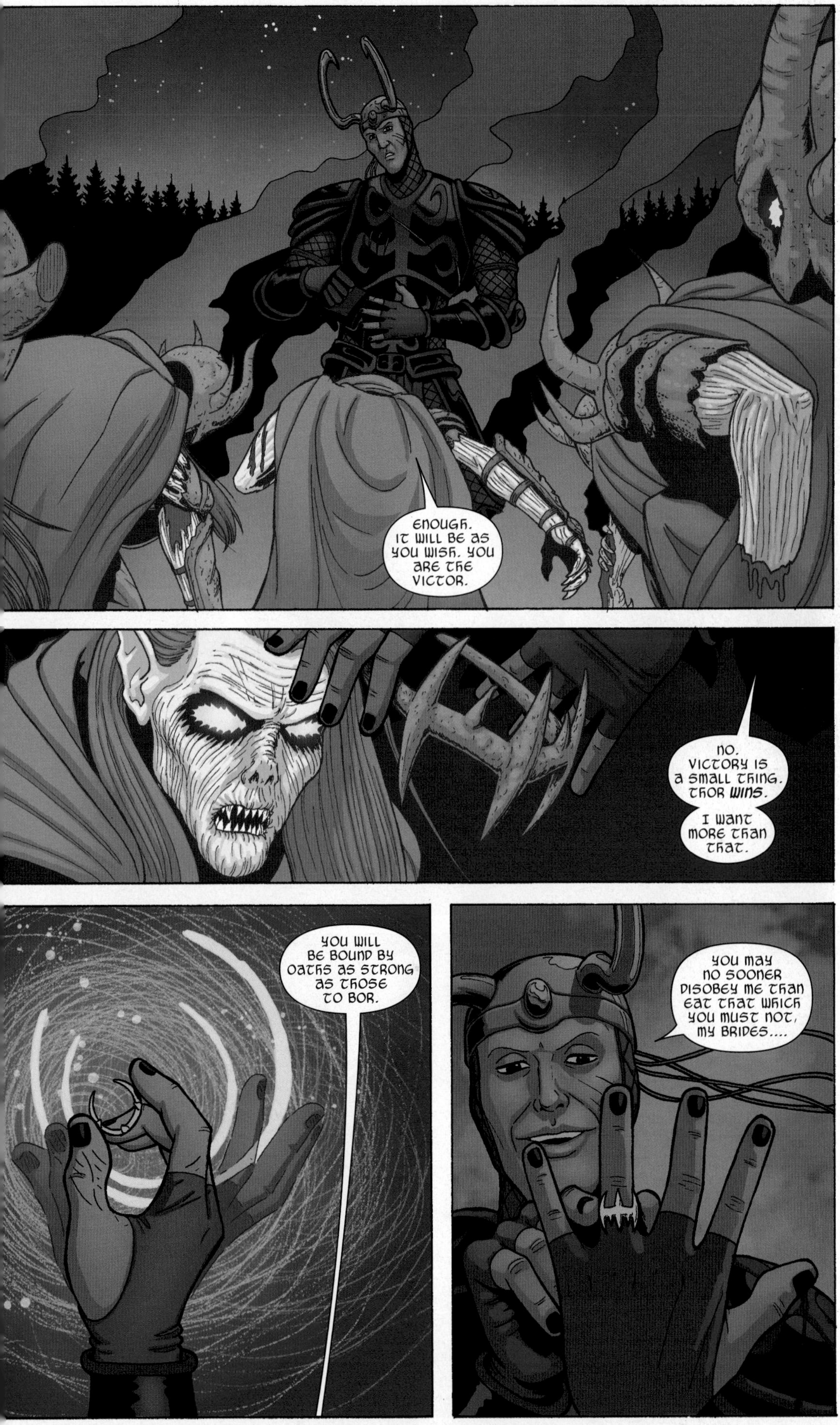
ENOUGH. IT WILL BE AS YOU WISH. YOU ARE THE VICTOR.
NO. VICTORY IS A SMALL THING. THOR WINS.
I WANT MORE THAN THAT.
YOU WILL BE BOUND BY OATHS AS STRONG AS THOSE TO BOR.
YOU MAY NO SOONER DISOBEY ME THAN EAT THAT WHICH YOU MUST NOT, MY BRIDES....

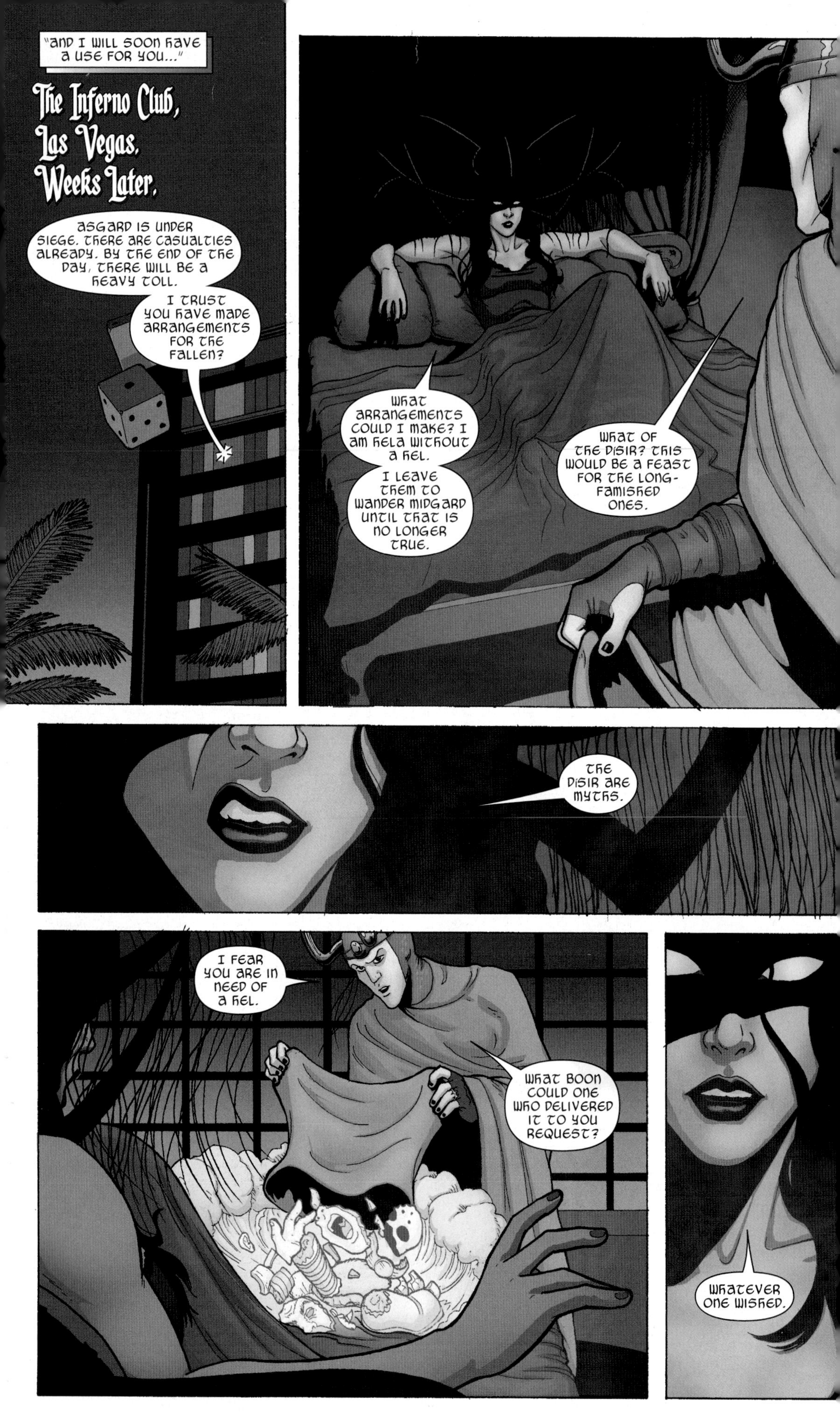
"AND I WILL SOON HAVE A USE FOR YOU..."
The Inferno Club, Las Vegas. Weeks Later.
ASGARD IS UNDER SIEGE. THERE ARE CASUALTIES ALREADY. BY THE END OF THE DAY, THERE WILL BE A HEAVY TOLL.
I TRUST YOU HAVE MADE ARRANGEMENTS FOR THE FALLEN?
WHAT ARRANGEMENTS COULD I MAKE? I AM HELA WITHOUT A HEL.
I LEAVE THEM TO WANDER MIDGARD UNTIL THAT IS NO LONGER TRUE.
WHAT OF THE DISIR? THIS WOULD BE A FEAST FOR THE LONG-FAMISHED ONES.
THE DISIR ARE MYTHS.
I FEAR YOU ARE IN NEED OF A HEL.
WHAT BOON COULD ONE WHO DELIVERED IT TO YOU REQUEST?
WHATEVER ONE WISHED.

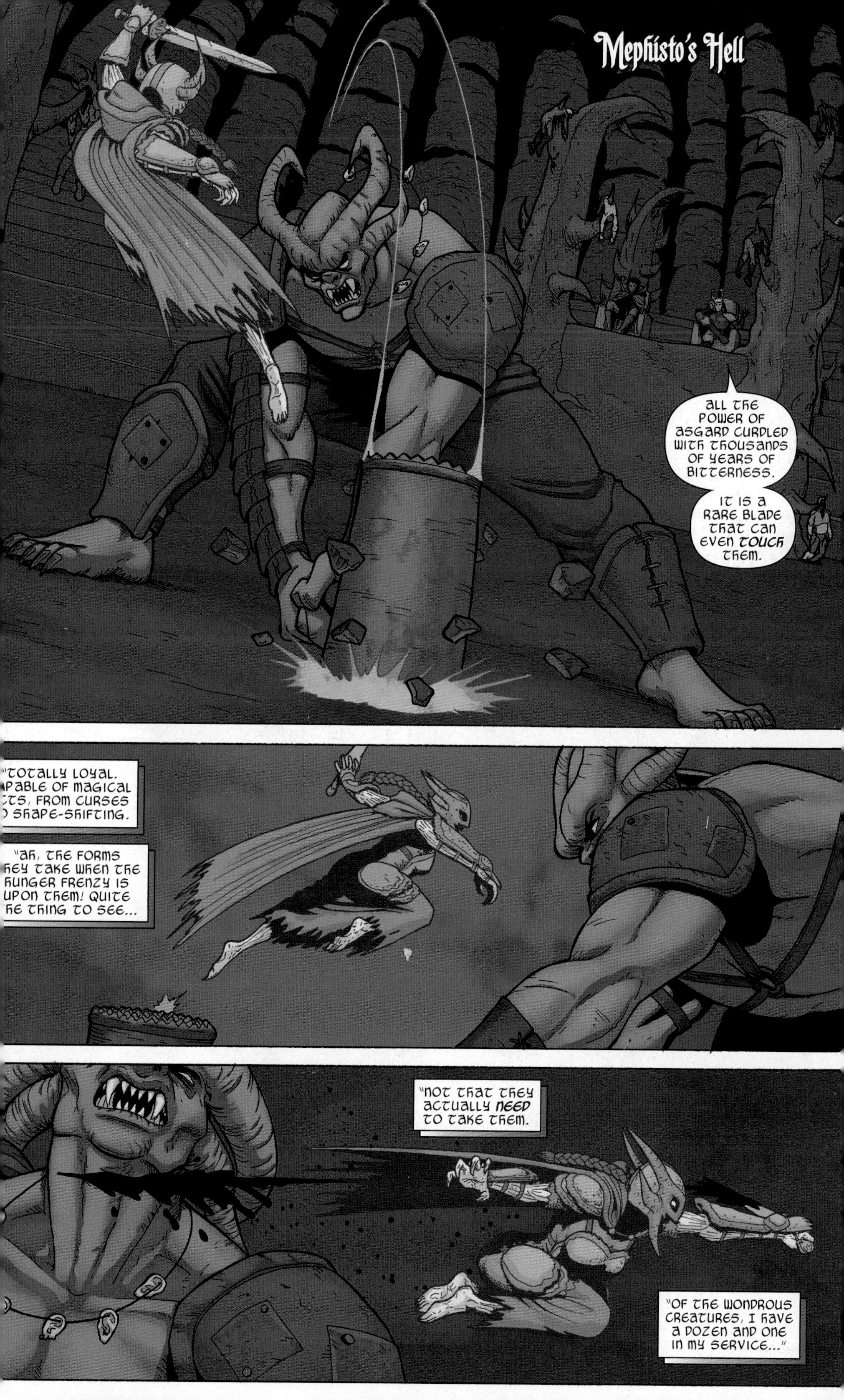
Mephisto's Hell
ALL THE POWER OF ASGARD CURDLED WITH THOUSANDS OF YEARS OF BITTERNESS.
IT IS A RARE BLADE THAT CAN EVEN TOUCH THEM.
"TOTALLY LOYAL. PABLE OF MAGICAL CTS, FROM CURSES D SHAPE-SHIFTING.
"AH, THE FORMS HEY TAKE WHEN THE HUNGER FRENZY IS UPON THEM! QUITE HE THING TO SEE...
"NOT THAT THEY ACTUALLY NEED TO TAKE THEM.
"OF THE WONDROUS CREATURES, I HAVE A DOZEN AND ONE IN MY SERVICE..."

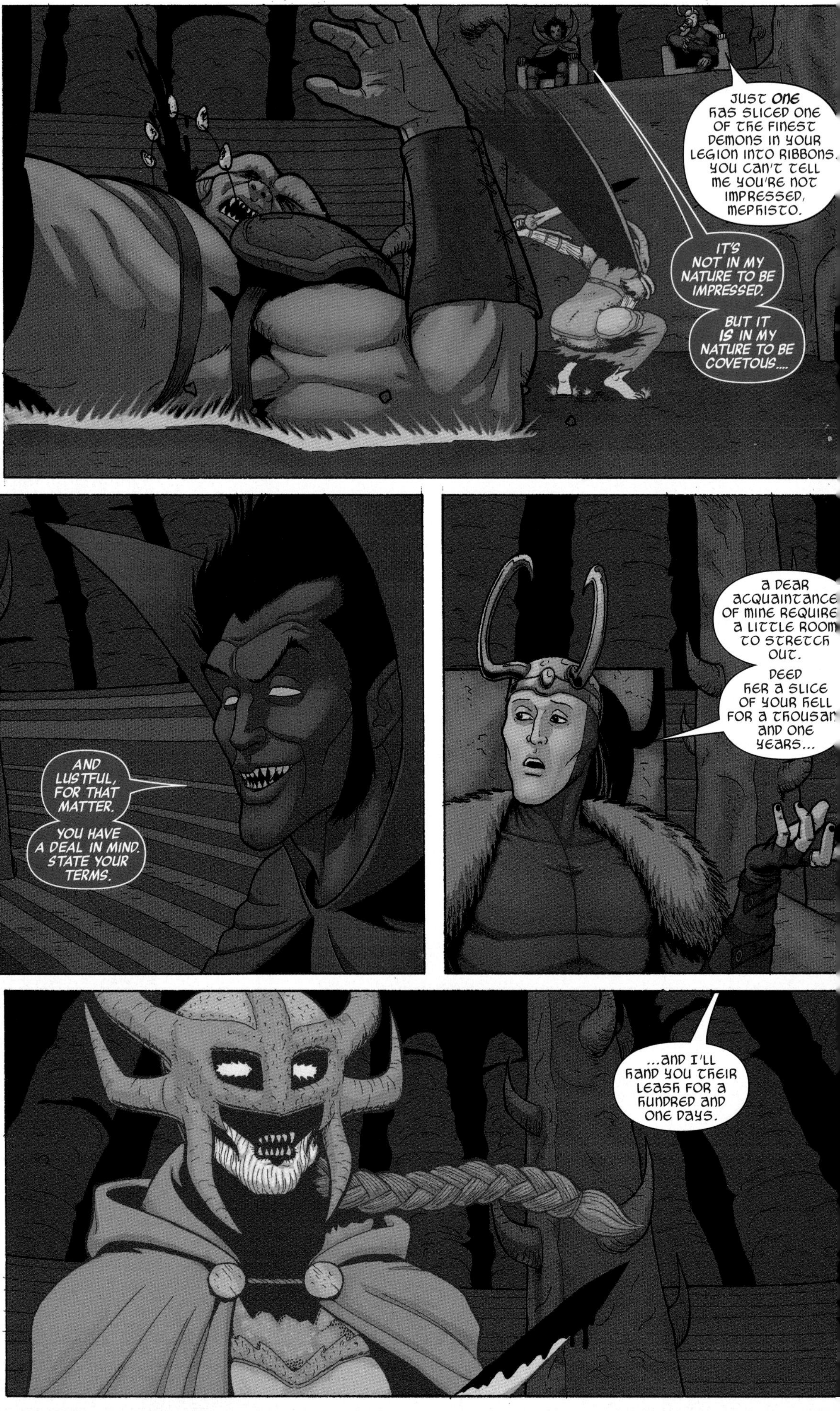
JUST ONE HAS SLICED ONE OF THE FINEST DEMONS IN YOUR LEGION INTO RIBBONS. YOU CAN'T TELL ME YOU'RE NOT IMPRESSED, MEPHISTO.
IT'S NOT IN MY NATURE TO BE IMPRESSED.
BUT IT IS IN MY NATURE TO BE COVETOUS....
AND LUSTFUL, FOR THAT MATTER.
YOU HAVE A DEAL IN MIND. STATE YOUR TERMS.
A DEAR ACQUAINTANCE OF MINE REQUIRE A LITTLE ROOM TO STRETCH OUT.
DEED HER A SLICE OF YOUR HELL FOR A THOUSAN AND ONE YEARS...
...AND I'LL HAND YOU THEIR LEASH FOR A HUNDRED AND ONE DAYS.

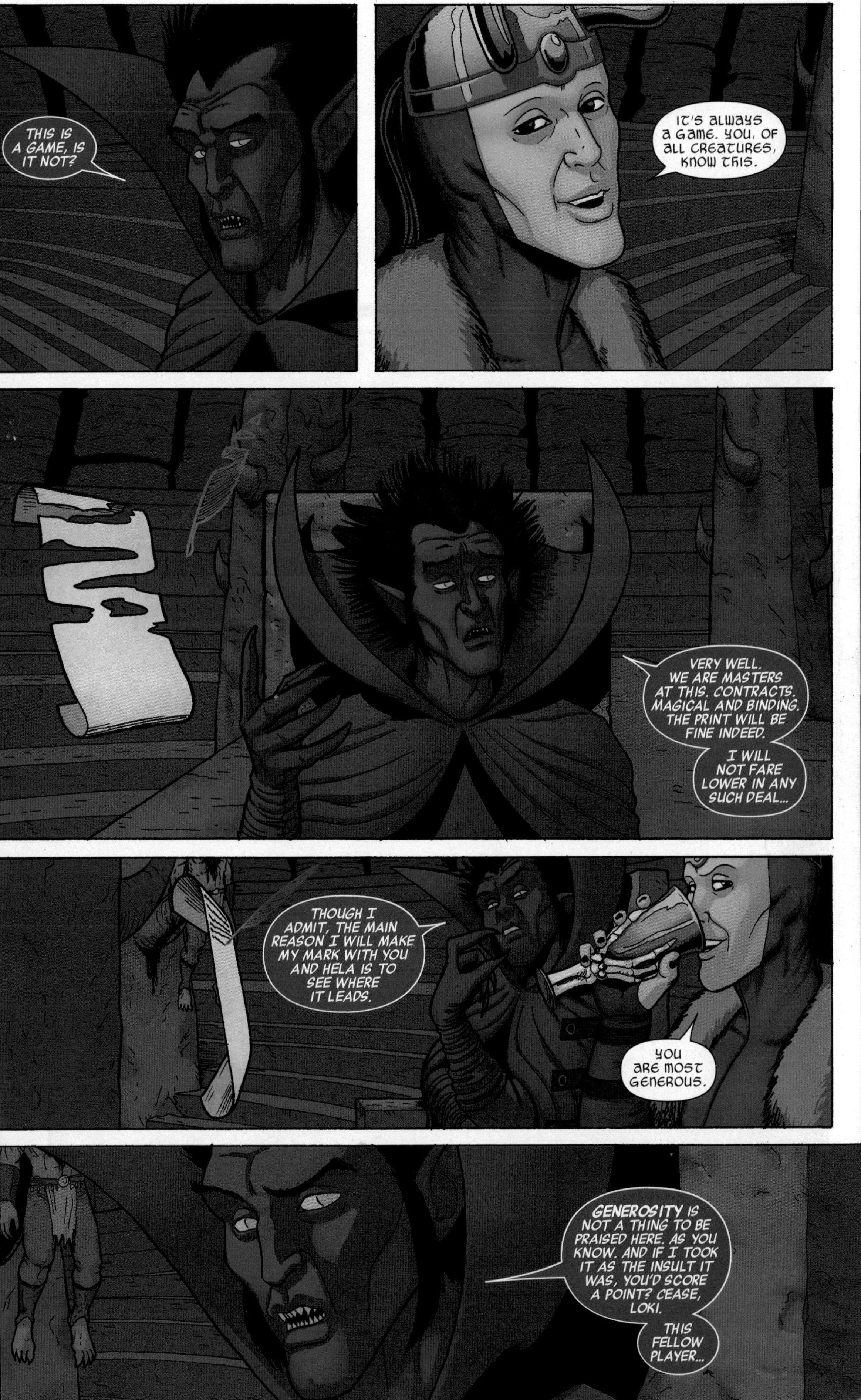
THIS IS A GAME, IS IT NOT?
IT'S ALWAYS A GAME. YOU, OF ALL CREATURES, KNOW THIS.
VERY WELL. WE ARE MASTERS AT THIS. CONTRACTS. MAGICAL AND BINDING. THE PRINT WILL BE FINE INDEED.
I WILL NOT FARE LOWER IN ANY SUCH DEAL...
THOUGH I ADMIT, THE MAIN REASON I WILL MAKE MY MARK WITH YOU AND HELA IS TO SEE WHERE IT LEADS.
YOU ARE MOST GENEROUS.
GENEROSITY IS NOT A THING TO BE PRAISED HERE, AS YOU KNOW. AND IF I TOOK IT AS THE INSULT IT WAS, YOU'D SCORE A POINT? CEASE, LOKI.
THIS FELLOW PLAYER...

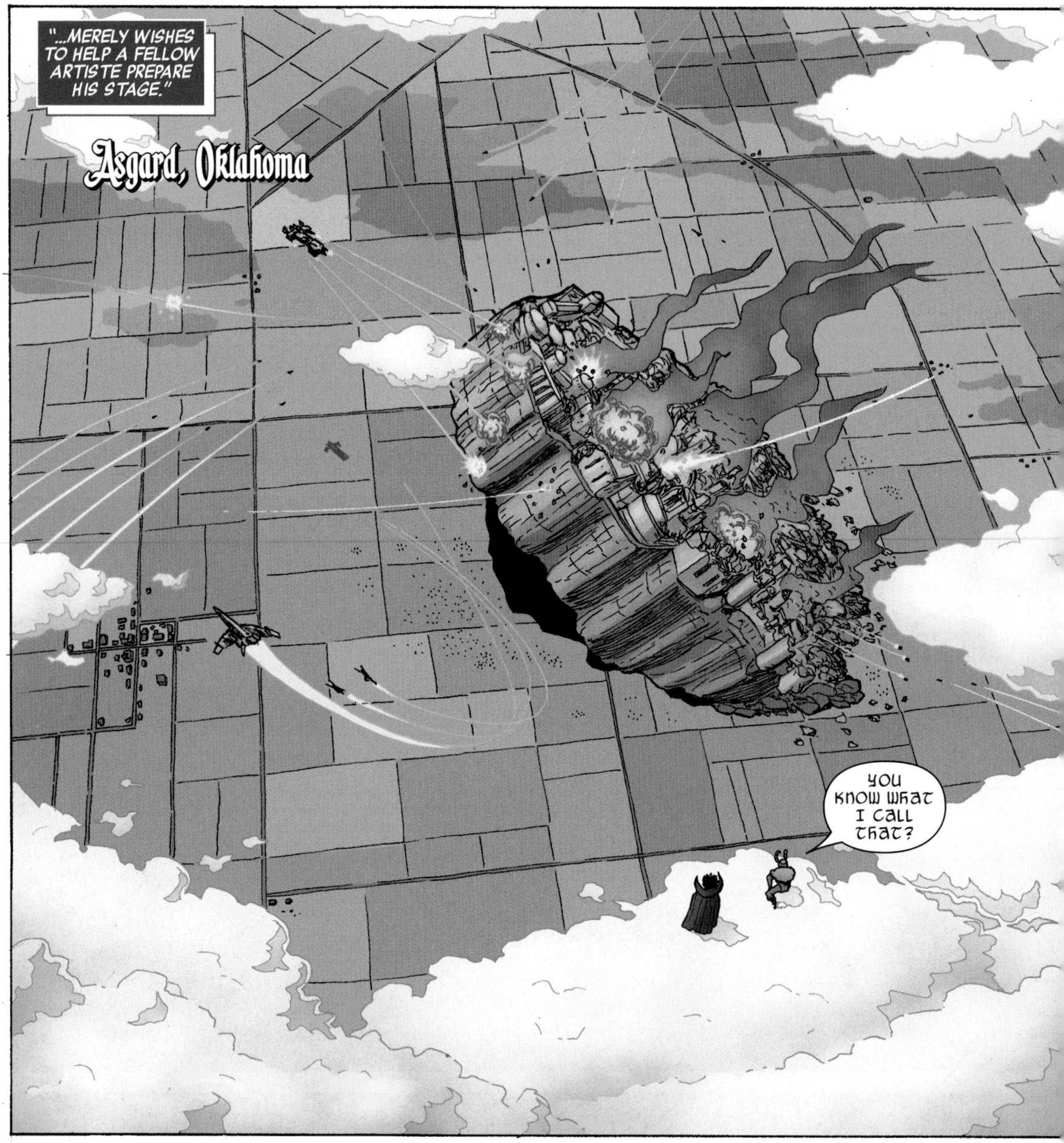
"...MERELY WISHES TO HELP A FELLOW ARTISTE PREPARE HIS STAGE."
Asgard, Oklahoma
YOU KNOW WHAT I CALL THAT?
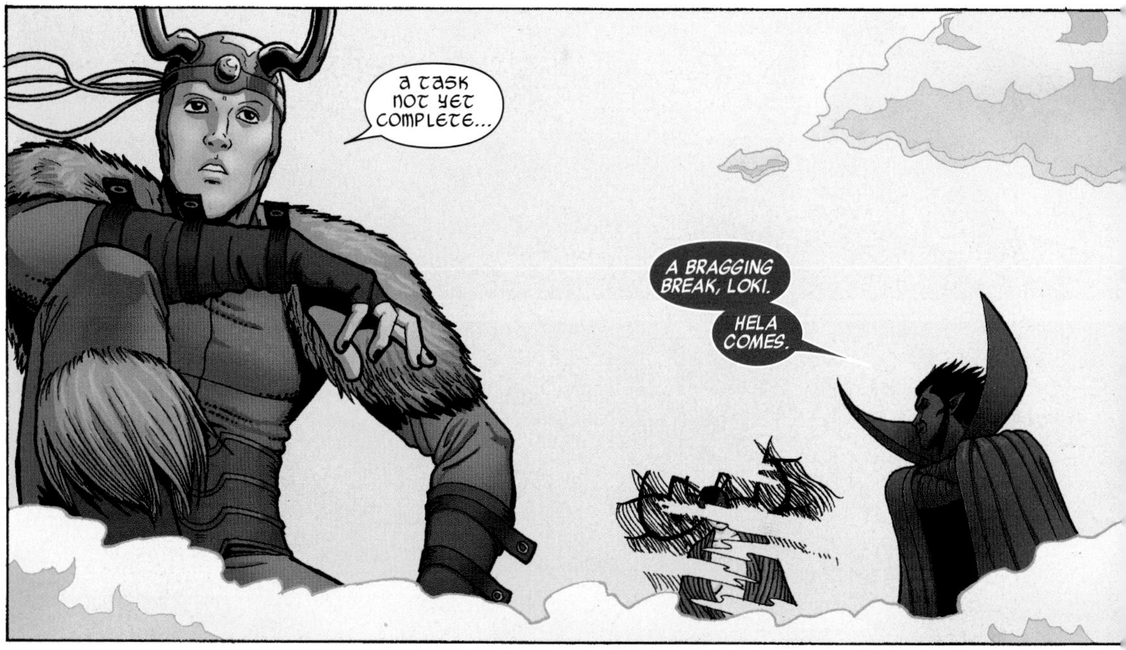
A TASK NOT YET COMPLETE...
A BRAGGING BREAK, LOKI.
HELA COMES.

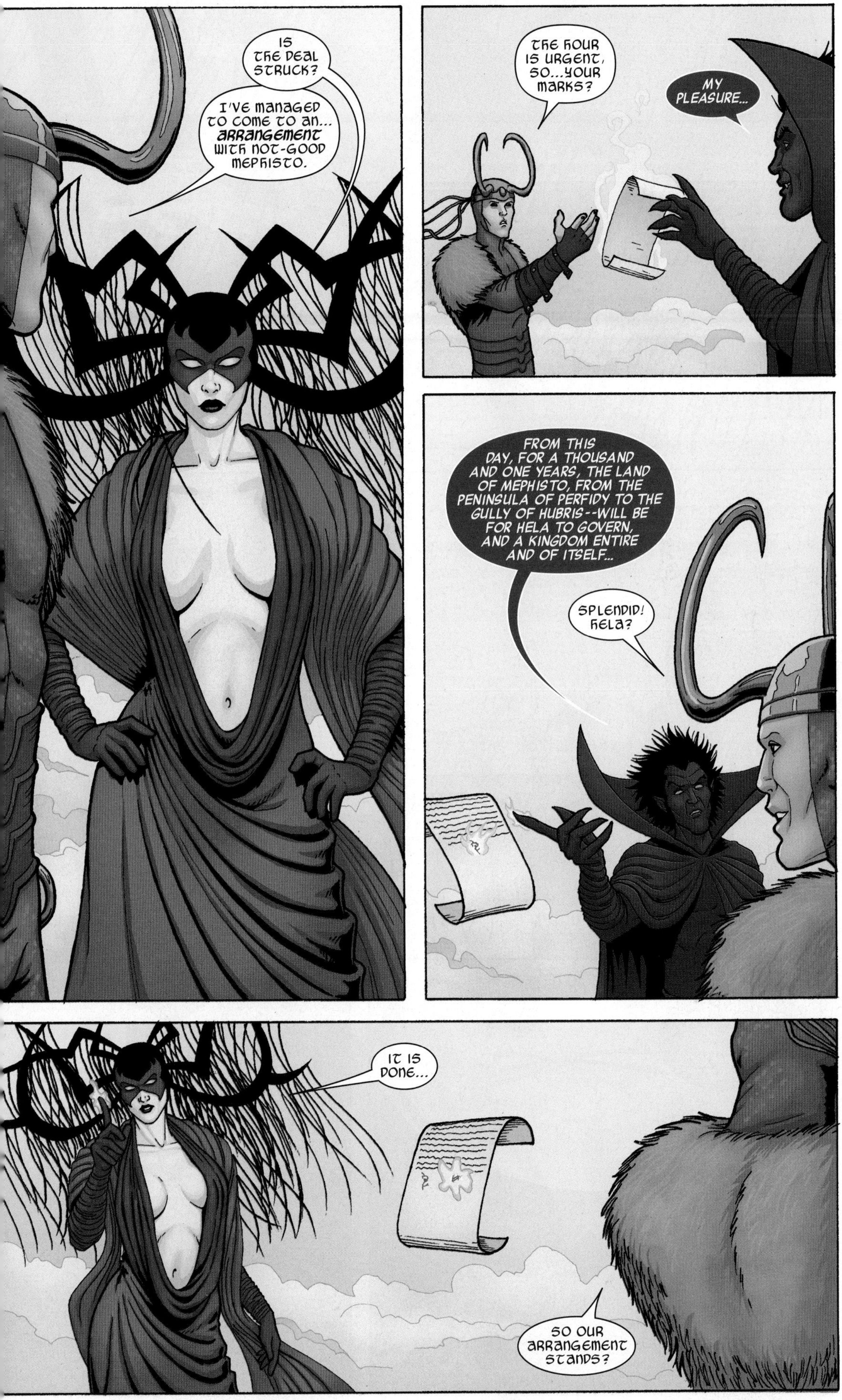

IS THE DEAL STRUCK?
I'VE MANAGED TO COME TO AN... ARRANGEMENT WITH NOT-GOOD MEPHISTO.
THE HOUR IS URGENT, SO...YOUR MARKS?
MY PLEASURE...
FROM THIS DAY, FOR A THOUSAND AND ONE YEARS, THE LAND OF MEPHISTO, FROM THE PENINSULA OF PERFIDY TO THE GULLY OF HUBRIS--WILL BE FOR HELA TO GOVERN, AND A KINGDOM ENTIRE AND OF ITSELF...
SPLENDID! HELA?
IT IS DONE...
SO OUR ARRANGEMENT STANDS?

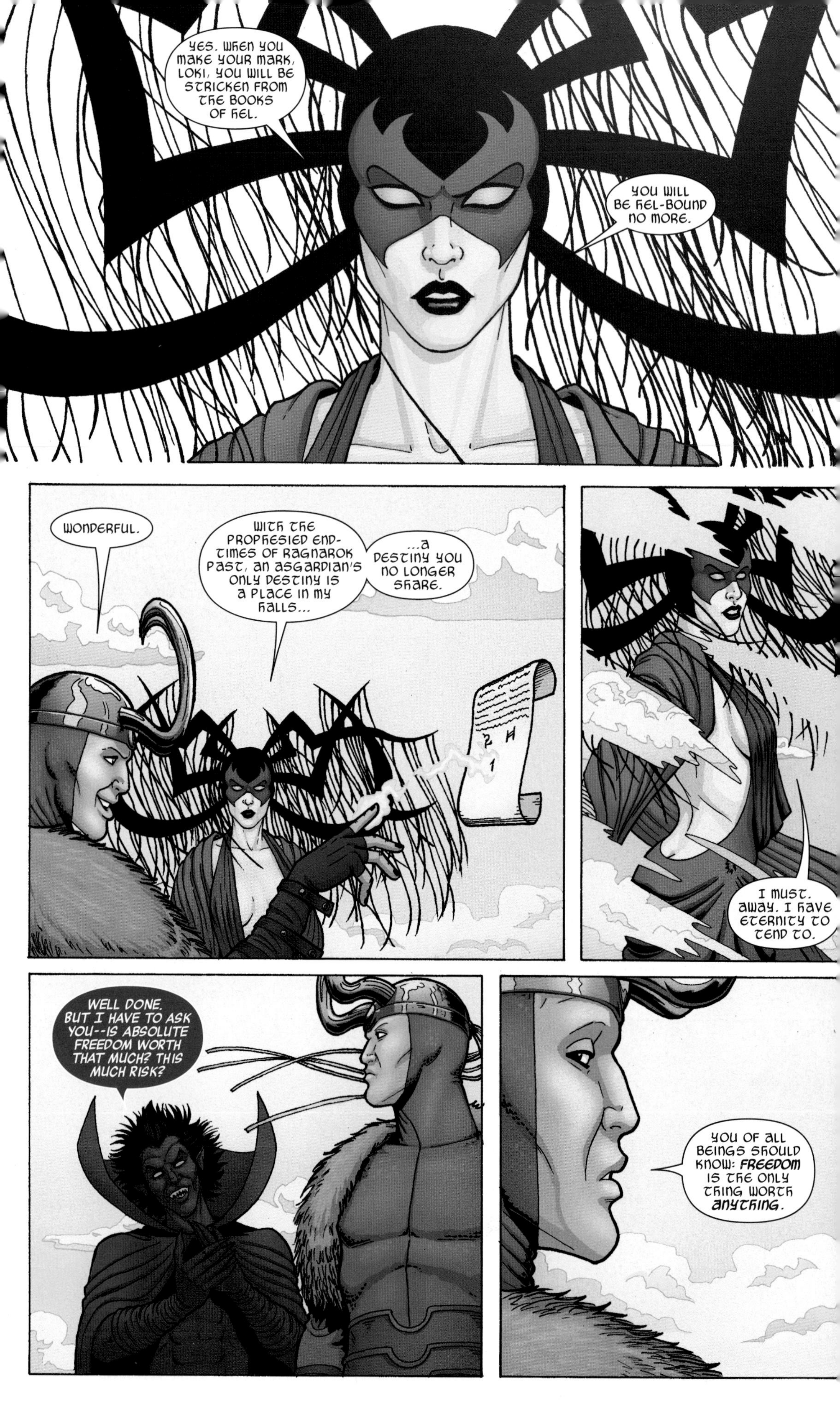
YES. WHEN YOU MAKE YOUR MARK, LOKI, YOU WILL BE STRICKEN FROM THE BOOKS OF HEL.
YOU WILL BE HEL-BOUND NO MORE.
WONDERFUL.
WITH THE PROPHESIED END-TIMES OF RAGNAROK PAST, AN ASGARDIAN'S ONLY DESTINY IS A PLACE IN MY HALLS...
...A DESTINY YOU NO LONGER SHARE.
I MUST. AWAY. I HAVE ETERNITY TO TEND TO.
WELL DONE. BUT I HAVE TO ASK YOU--IS ABSOLUTE FREEDOM WORTH THAT MUCH? THIS MUCH RISK?
YOU OF ALL BEINGS SHOULD KNOW: FREEDOM IS THE ONLY THING WORTH ANYTHING.

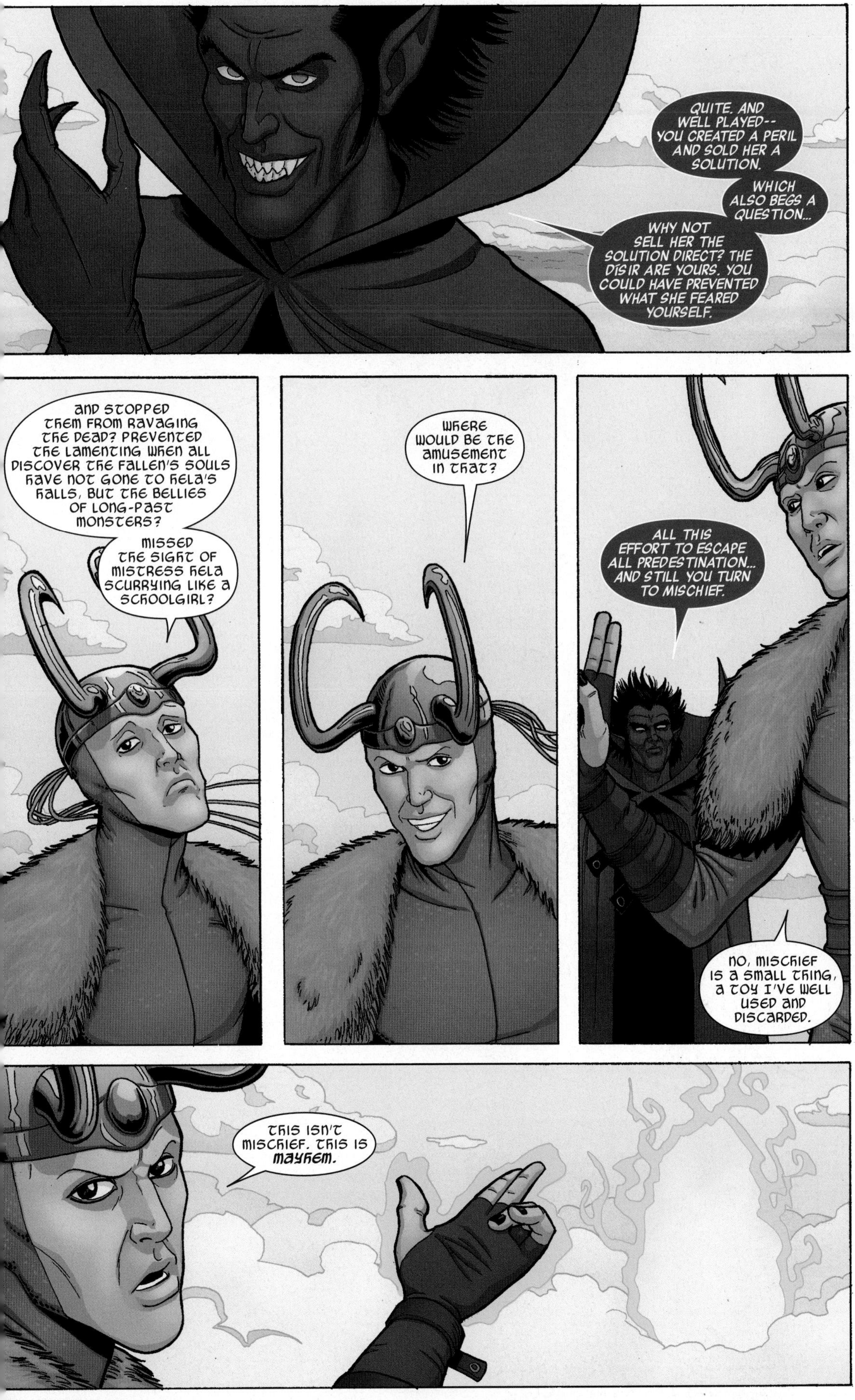
QUITE. AND WELL PLAYED-- YOU CREATED A PERIL AND SOLD HER A SOLUTION.
WHICH ALSO BEGS A QUESTION...
WHY NOT SELL HER THE SOLUTION DIRECT? THE DÍSIR ARE YOURS. YOU COULD HAVE PREVENTED WHAT SHE FEARED YOURSELF.
AND STOPPED THEM FROM RAVAGING THE DEAD? PREVENTED THE LAMENTING WHEN ALL DISCOVER THE FALLEN'S SOULS HAVE NOT GONE TO HELA'S HALLS, BUT THE BELLIES OF LONG-PAST MONSTERS?
MISSED THE SIGHT OF MISTRESS HELA SCURRYING LIKE A SCHOOLGIRL?
WHERE WOULD BE THE AMUSEMENT IN THAT?
ALL THIS EFFORT TO ESCAPE ALL PREDESTINATION... AND STILL YOU TURN TO MISCHIEF.
NO, MISCHIEF IS A SMALL THING, A TOY I'VE WELL USED AND DISCARDED.
THIS ISN'T MISCHIEF. THIS IS *MAYHEM.*

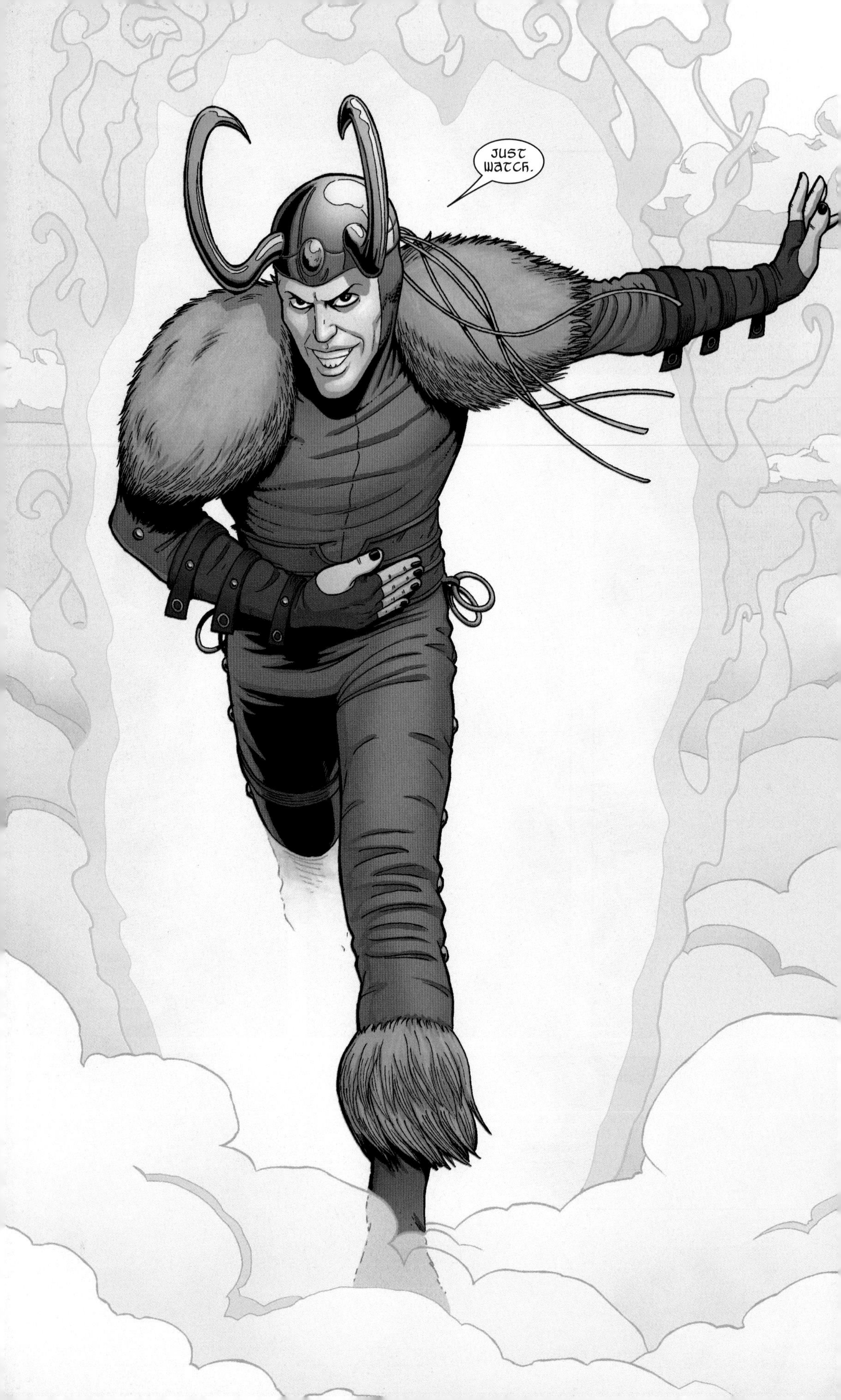
JUST WATCH.

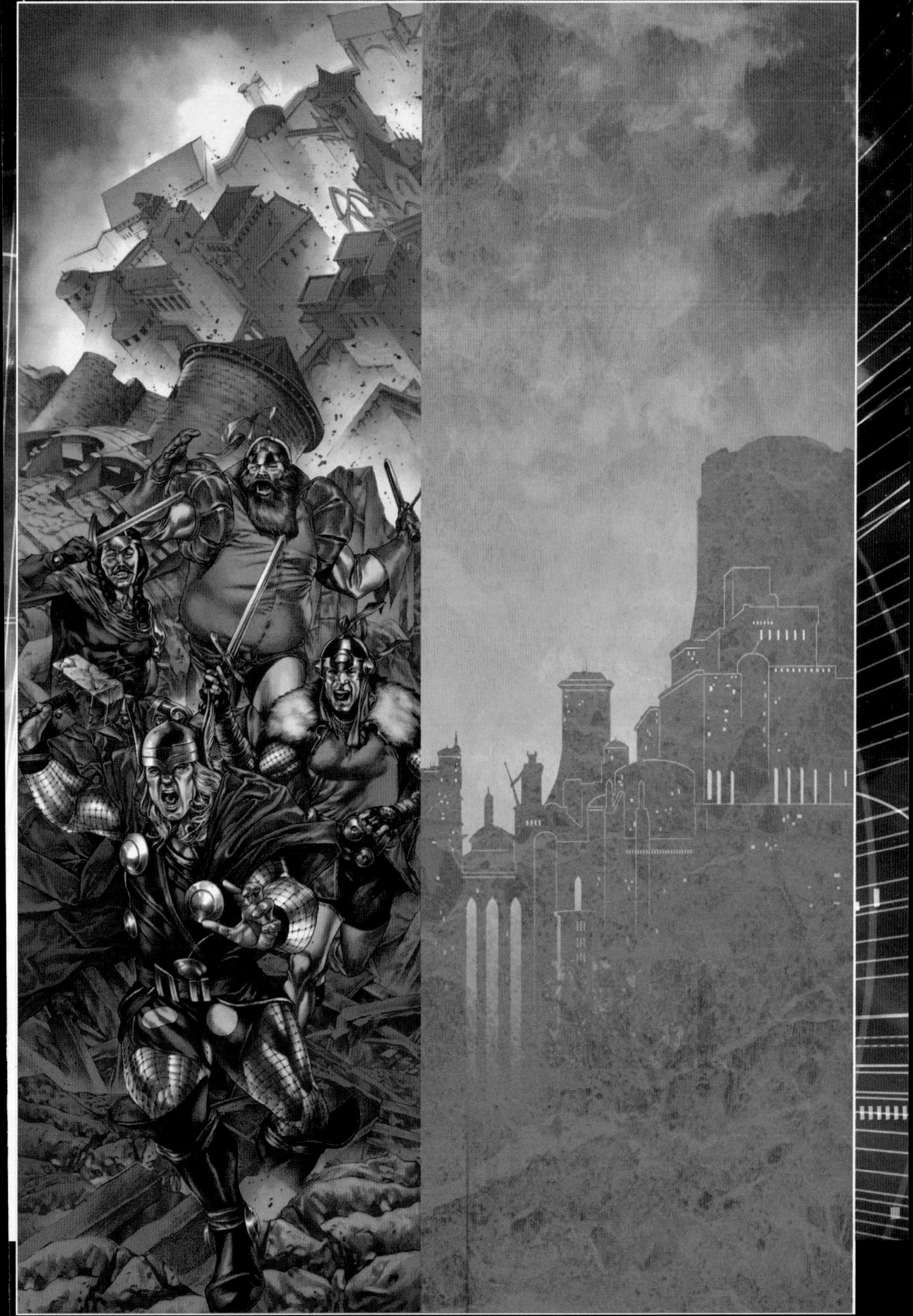

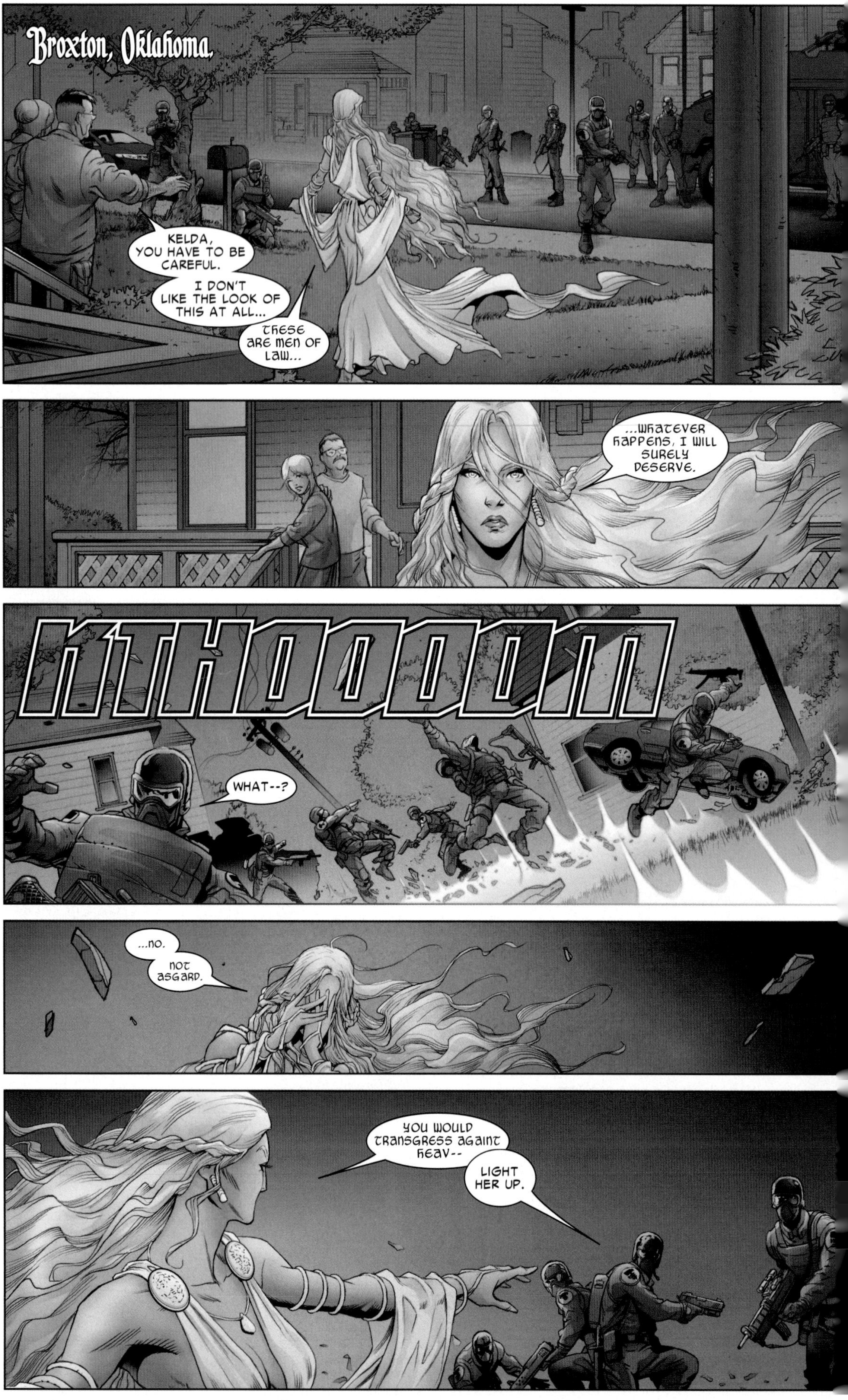
Broxton, Oklahoma.
KELDA, YOU HAVE TO BE CAREFUL.
I DON'T LIKE THE LOOK OF THIS AT ALL...
THESE ARE MEN OF LAW...
...WHATEVER HAPPENS, I WILL SURELY DESERVE.
KTHOOOOM
WHAT--?
...NO. NOT ASGARD.
YOU WOULD TRANSGRESS AGAINT HEAV--
LIGHT HER UP.

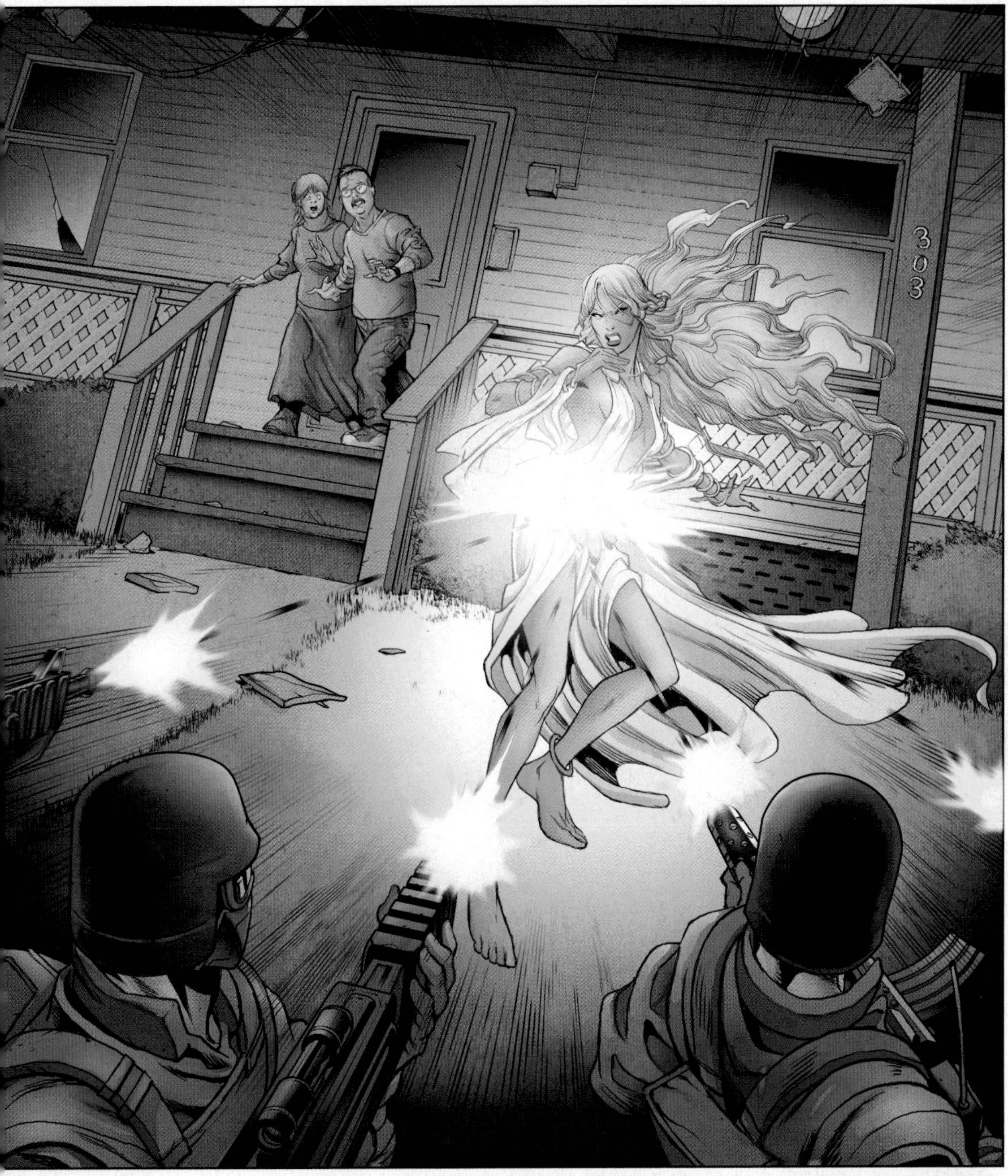
303

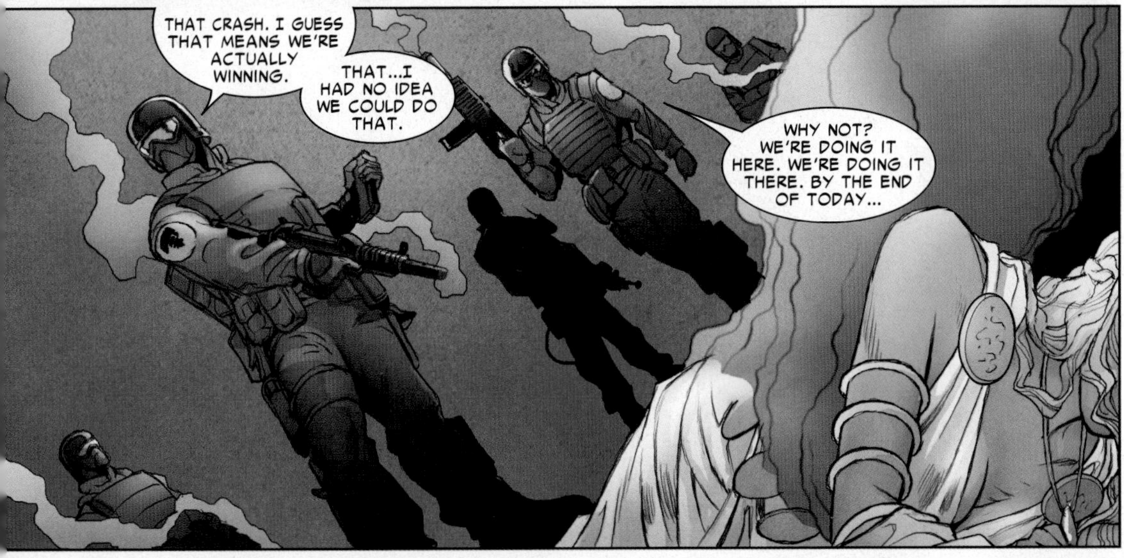
THAT CRASH. I GUESS THAT MEANS WE'RE ACTUALLY WINNING.
THAT...I HAD NO IDEA WE COULD DO THAT.
WHY NOT? WE'RE DOING IT HERE. WE'RE DOING IT THERE. BY THE END OF TODAY...

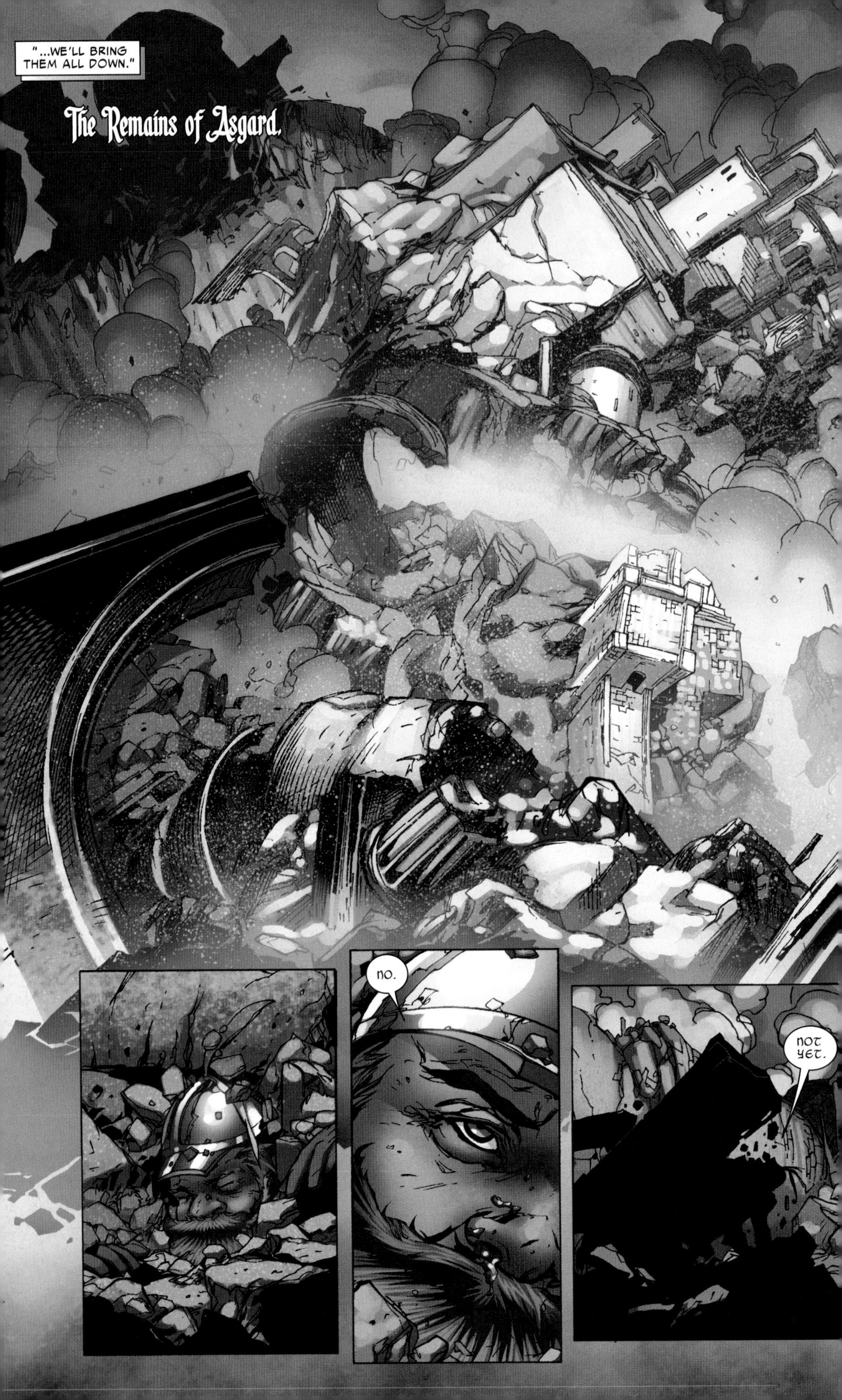
"...WE'LL BRING THEM ALL DOWN."
The Remains of Asgard.
NO.
NOT YET.

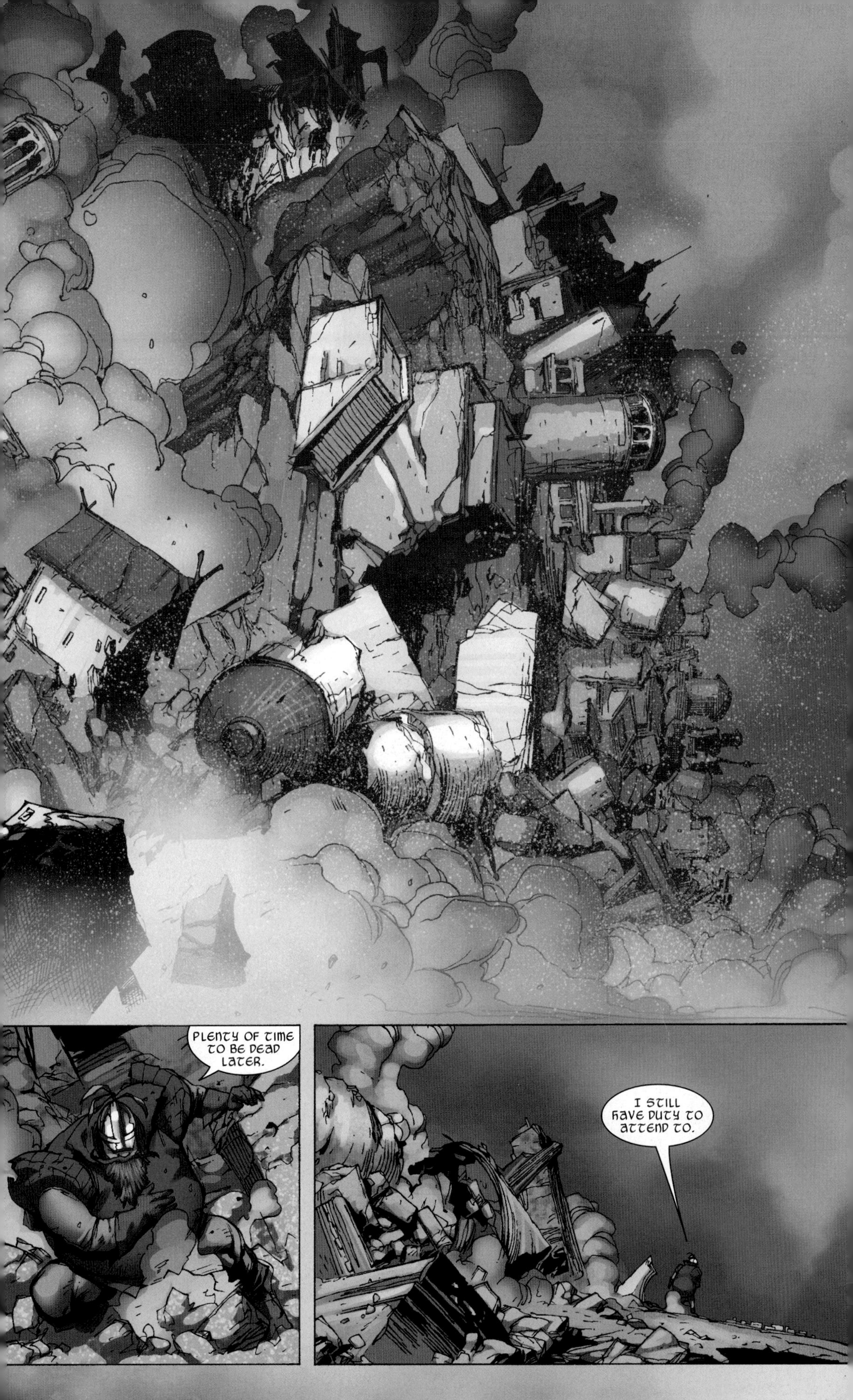
PLENTY OF TIME TO BE DEAD LATER.
I STILL HAVE DUTY TO ATTEND TO.

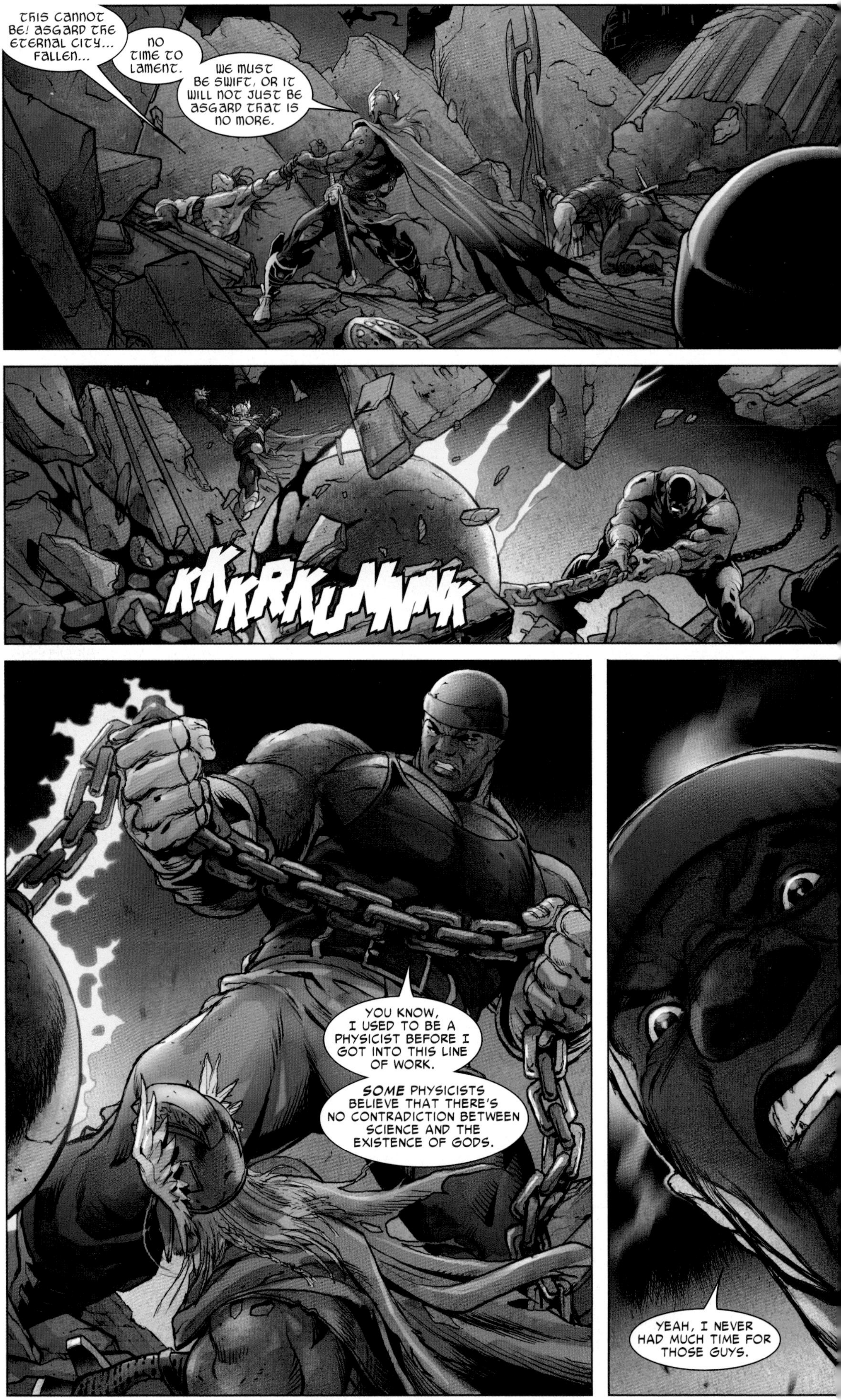
THIS CANNOT BE! ASGARD THE ETERNAL CITY... FALLEN...
NO TIME TO LAMENT.
WE MUST BE SWIFT, OR IT WILL NOT JUST BE ASGARD THAT IS NO MORE.
KKKRKUNNNK
YOU KNOW, I USED TO BE A PHYSICIST BEFORE I GOT INTO THIS LINE OF WORK.
SOME PHYSICISTS BELIEVE THAT THERE'S NO CONTRADICTION BETWEEN SCIENCE AND THE EXISTENCE OF GODS.
YEAH, I NEVER HAD MUCH TIME FOR THOSE GUYS.

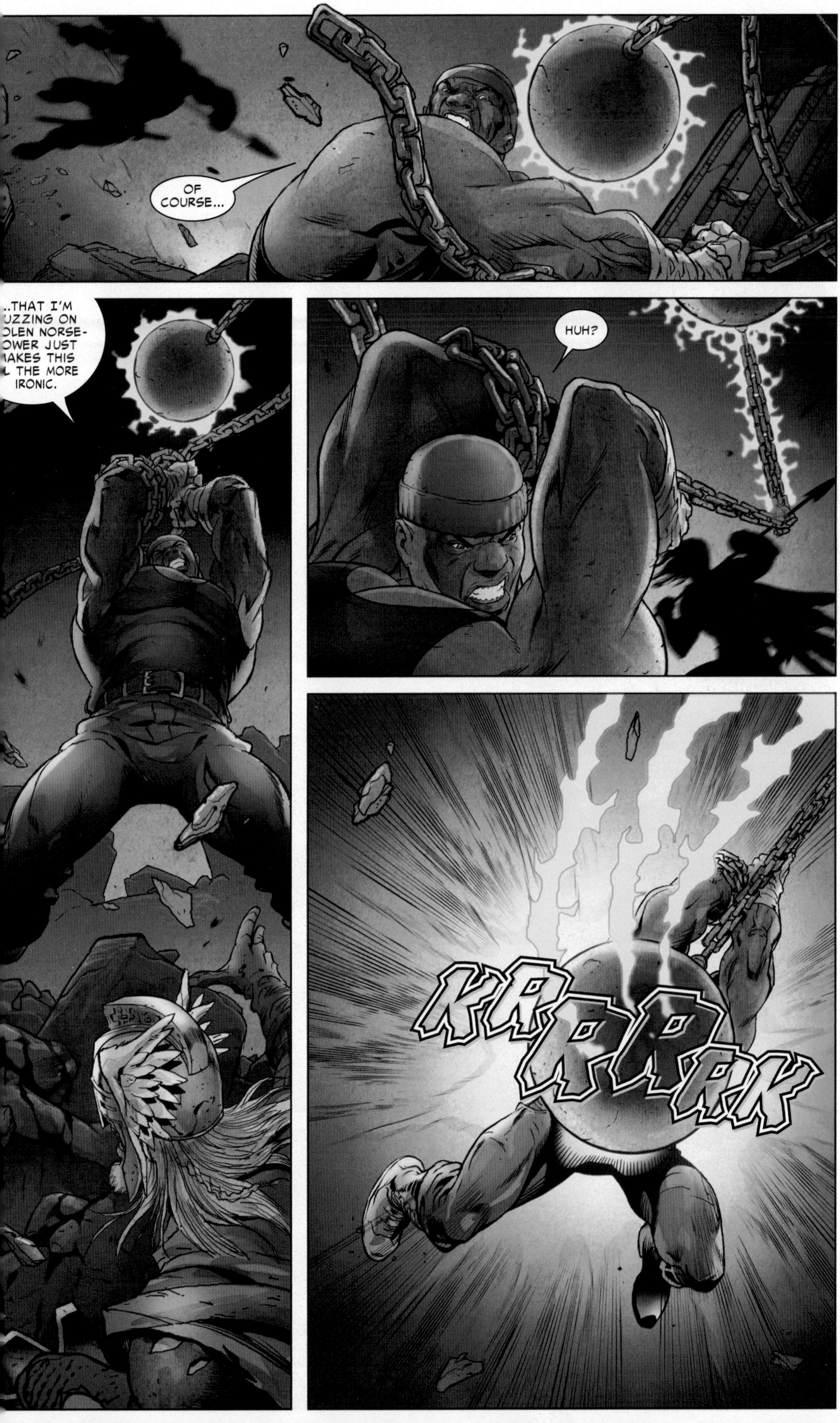
OF COURSE...
...THAT I'M
UZZING ON
OLEN NORSE-
OWER JUST
AKES THIS
L THE MORE
IRONIC.
HUH?
KRRRAK

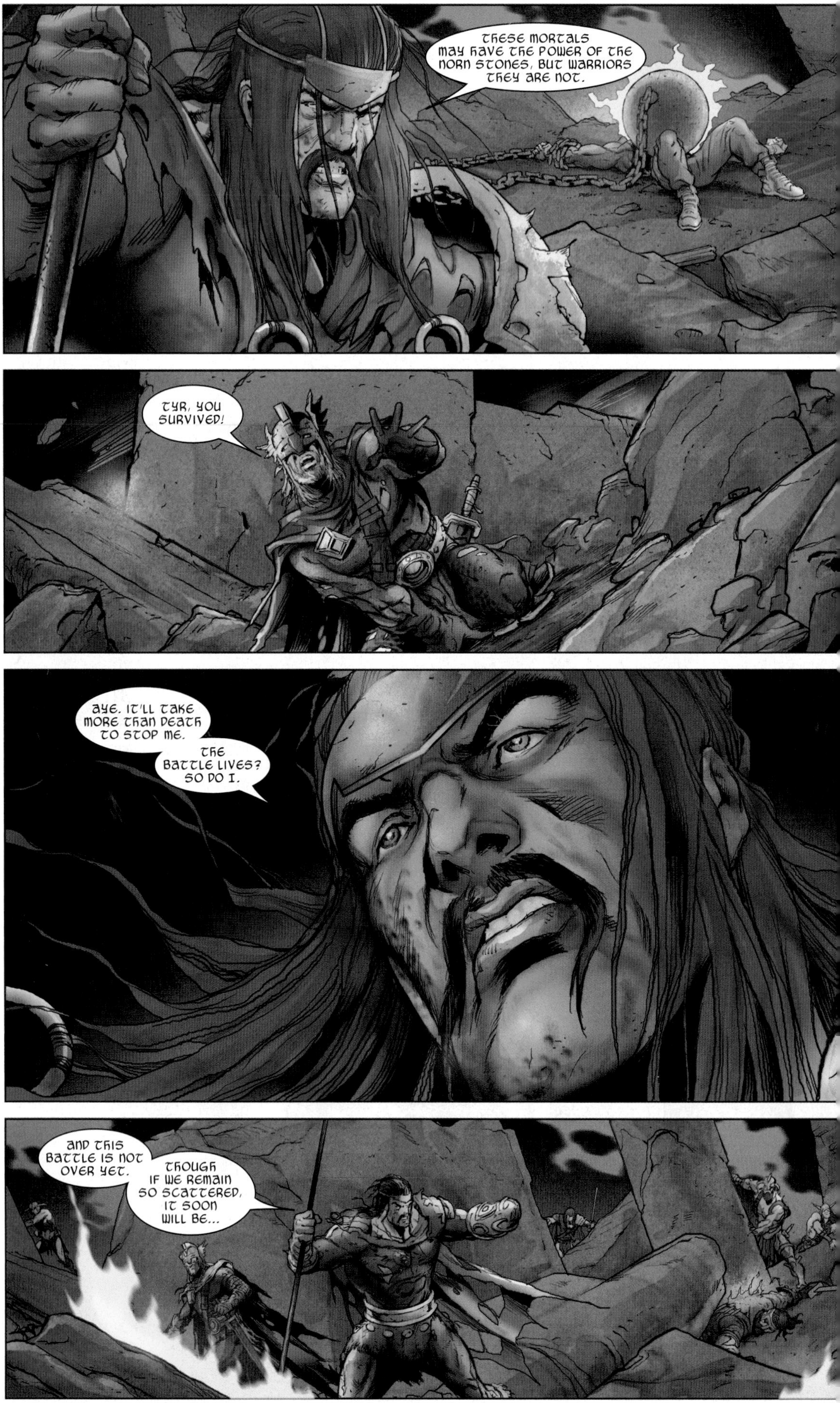
THESE MORTALS MAY HAVE THE POWER OF THE NORN STONES, BUT WARRIORS THEY ARE NOT.
TYR, YOU SURVIVED!
AYE. IT'LL TAKE MORE THAN DEATH TO STOP ME.
THE BATTLE LIVES? SO DO I.
AND THIS BATTLE IS NOT OVER YET.
THOUGH IF WE REMAIN SO SCATTERED, IT SOON WILL BE...

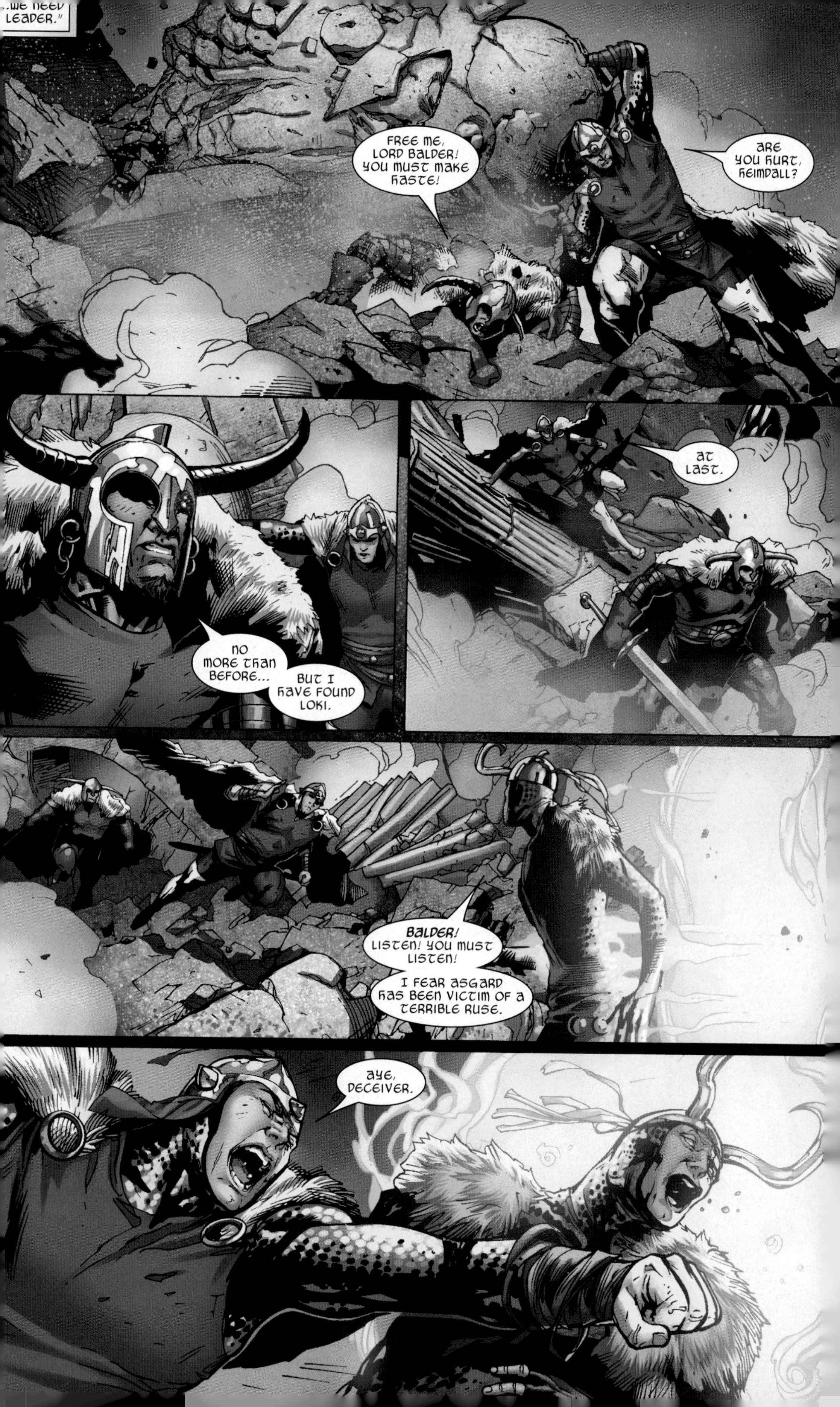
"...WE NEED LEADER."
FREE ME, LORD BALDER! YOU MUST MAKE HASTE!
ARE YOU HURT, HEIMDALL?
NO MORE THAN BEFORE...
BUT I HAVE FOUND LOKI.
AT LAST.
BALDER! LISTEN! YOU MUST LISTEN!
I FEAR ASGARD HAS BEEN VICTIM OF A TERRIBLE RUSE.
AYE, DECEIVER.

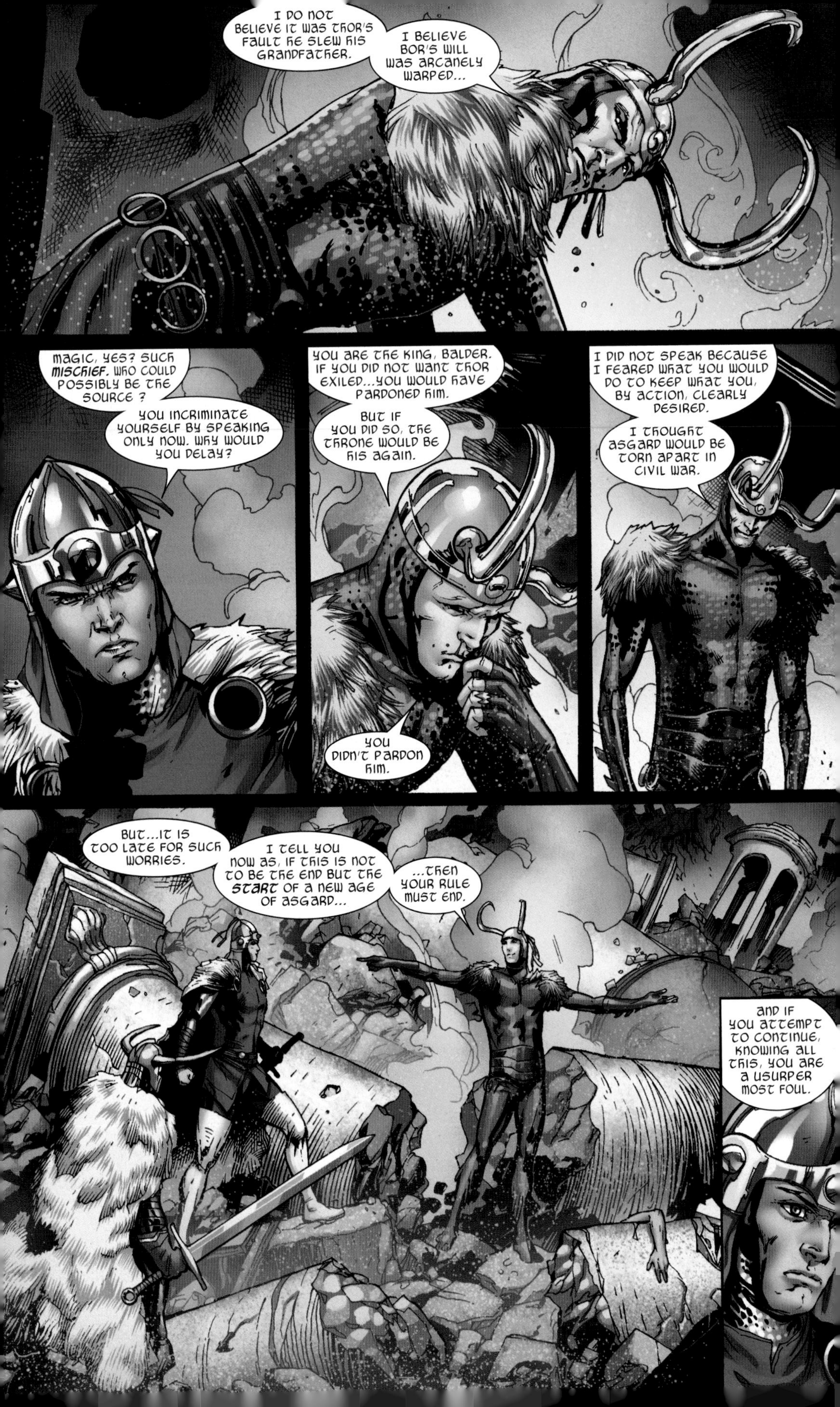

I DO NOT BELIEVE IT WAS THOR'S FAULT HE SLEW HIS GRANDFATHER.
I BELIEVE BOR'S WILL WAS ARCANELY WARPED...
MAGIC, YES? SUCH MISCHIEF. WHO COULD POSSIBLY BE THE SOURCE ?
YOU INCRIMINATE YOURSELF BY SPEAKING ONLY NOW. WHY WOULD YOU DELAY?
YOU ARE THE KING, BALDER. IF YOU DID NOT WANT THOR EXILED...YOU WOULD HAVE PARDONED HIM.
BUT IF YOU DID SO, THE THRONE WOULD BE HIS AGAIN.
YOU DIDN'T PARDON HIM.
I DID NOT SPEAK BECAUSE I FEARED WHAT YOU WOULD DO TO KEEP WHAT YOU, BY ACTION, CLEARLY DESIRED.
I THOUGHT ASGARD WOULD BE TORN APART IN CIVIL WAR.
BUT...IT IS TOO LATE FOR SUCH WORRIES.
I TELL YOU NOW AS, IF THIS IS NOT TO BE THE END BUT THE START OF A NEW AGE OF ASGARD...
...THEN YOUR RULE MUST END.
AND IF YOU ATTEMPT TO CONTINUE, KNOWING ALL THIS, YOU ARE A USURPER MOST FOUL.

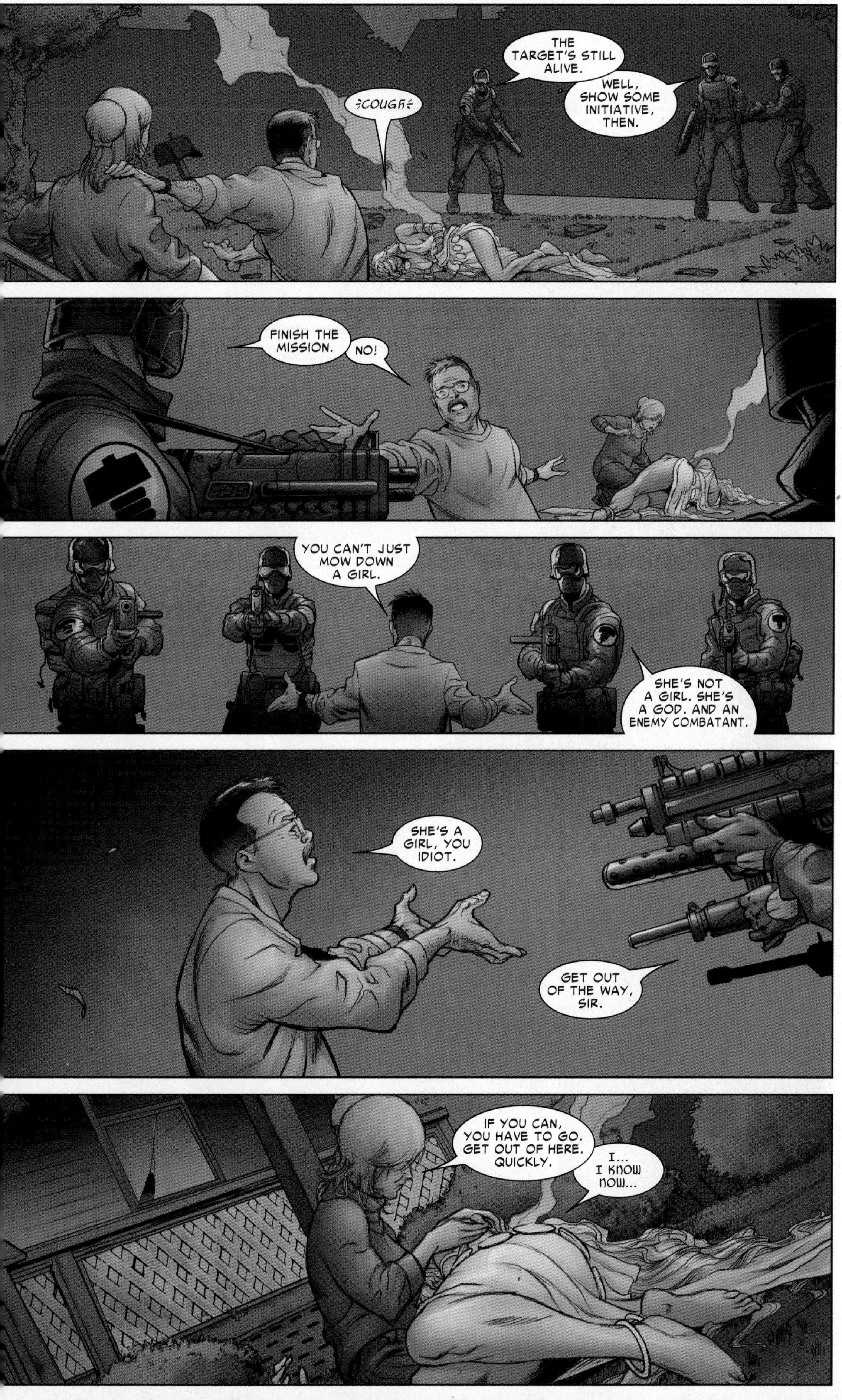

THE TARGET'S STILL ALIVE.
COUGH
WELL, SHOW SOME INITIATIVE, THEN.
FINISH THE MISSION.
NO!
YOU CAN'T JUST MOW DOWN A GIRL.
SHE'S NOT A GIRL. SHE'S A GOD. AND AN ENEMY COMBATANT.
SHE'S A GIRL, YOU IDIOT.
GET OUT OF THE WAY, SIR.
IF YOU CAN, YOU HAVE TO GO. GET OUT OF HERE. QUICKLY.
I... I KNOW NOW...

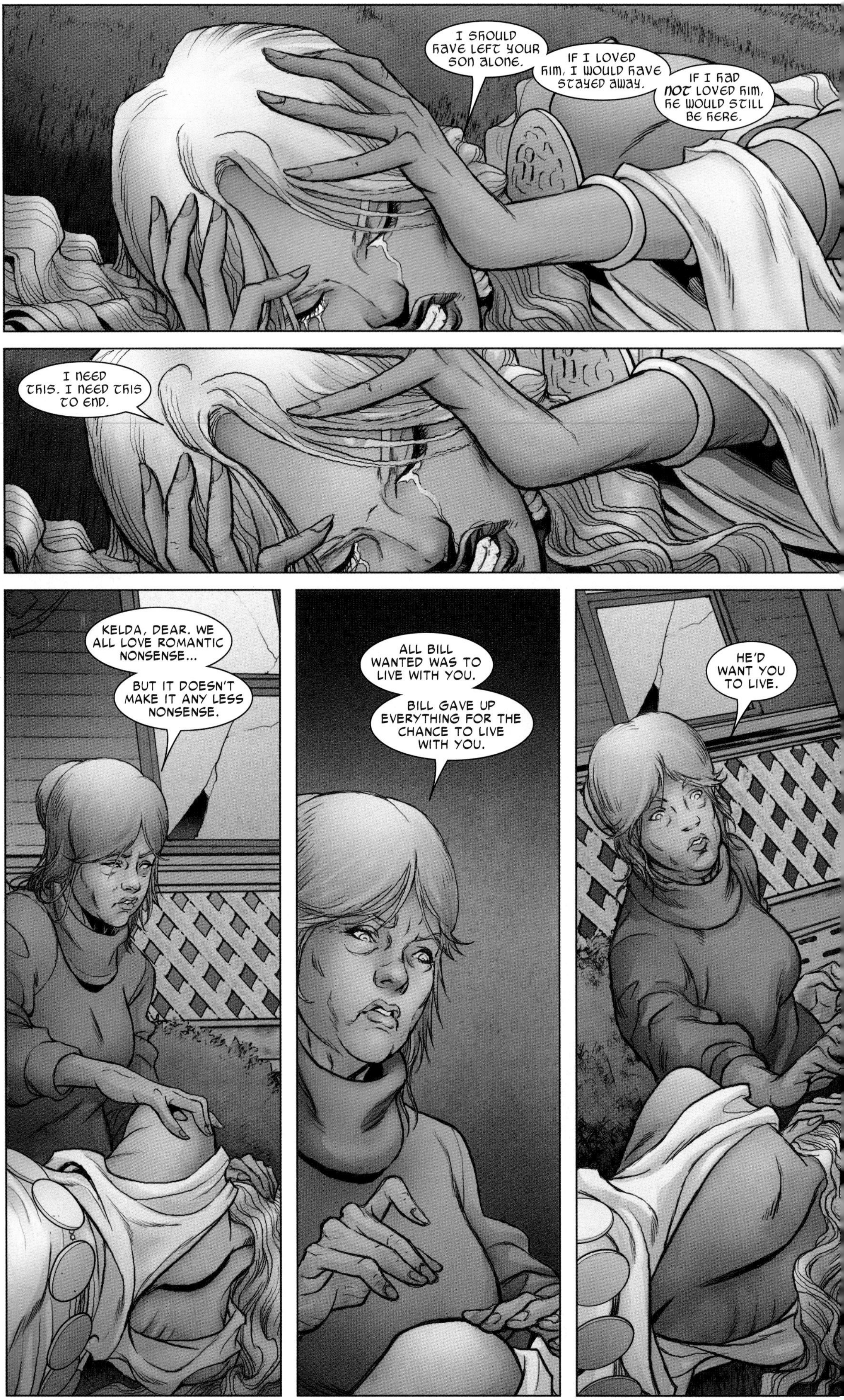
I SHOULD HAVE LEFT YOUR SON ALONE.
IF I LOVED HIM, I WOULD HAVE STAYED AWAY.
IF I HAD NOT LOVED HIM, HE WOULD STILL BE HERE.
I NEED THIS. I NEED THIS TO END.
KELDA, DEAR. WE ALL LOVE ROMANTIC NONSENSE...
BUT IT DOESN'T MAKE IT ANY LESS NONSENSE.
ALL BILL WANTED WAS TO LIVE WITH YOU.
BILL GAVE UP EVERYTHING FOR THE CHANCE TO LIVE WITH YOU.
HE'D WANT YOU TO LIVE.

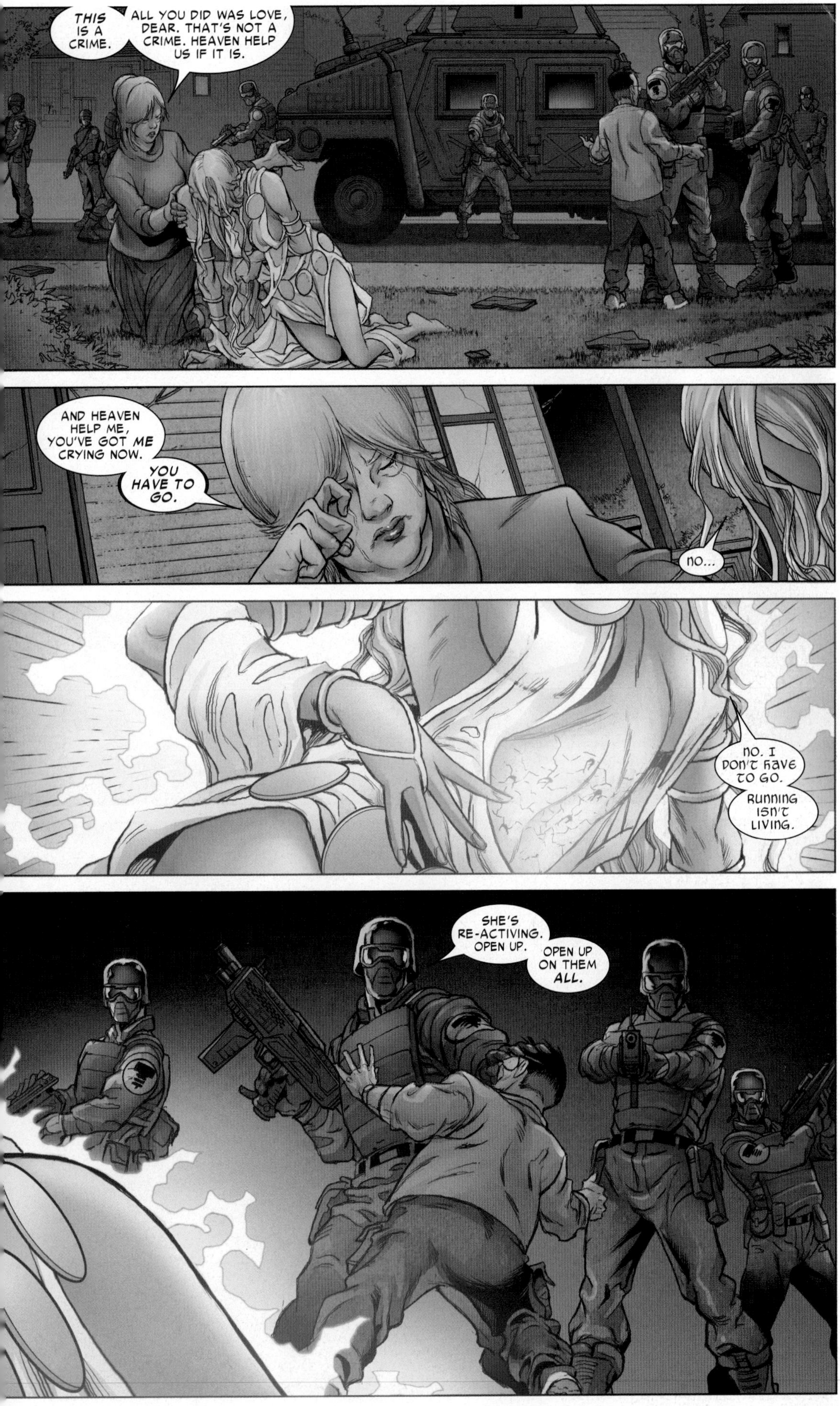
THIS IS A CRIME.
ALL YOU DID WAS LOVE, DEAR. THAT'S NOT A CRIME. HEAVEN HELP US IF IT IS.
AND HEAVEN HELP ME, YOU'VE GOT ME CRYING NOW.
YOU HAVE TO GO.
NO...
NO. I DON'T HAVE TO GO.
RUNNING ISN'T LIVING.
SHE'S RE-ACTIVING. OPEN UP.
OPEN UP ON THEM ALL.

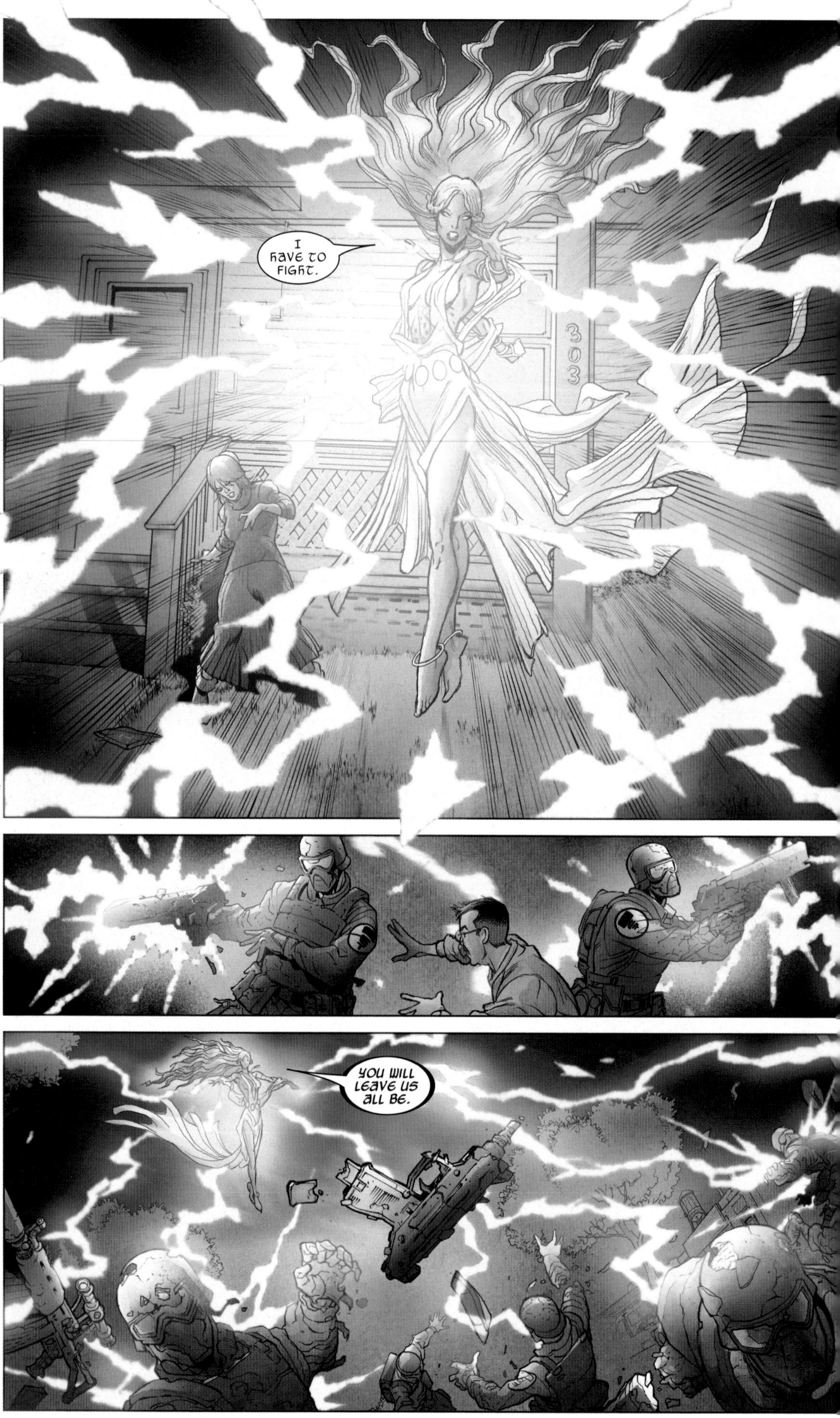
I HAVE TO FIGHT.
303
YOU WILL LEAVE US ALL BE.

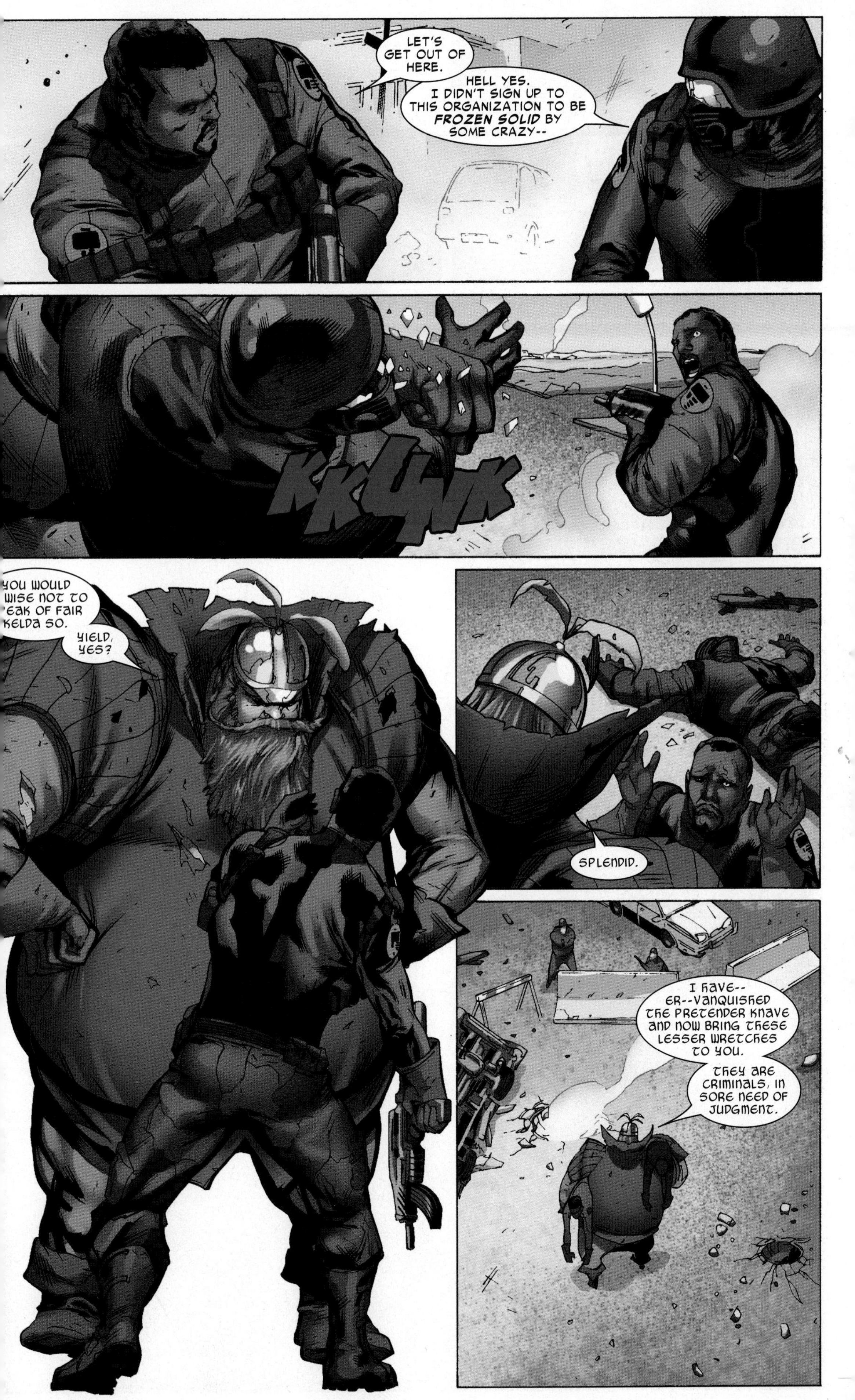
LET'S GET OUT OF HERE.
HELL YES. I DIDN'T SIGN UP TO THIS ORGANIZATION TO BE FROZEN SOLID BY SOME CRAZY--
KKLUNK
YOU WOULD WISE NOT TO EAK OF FAIR KELDA SO.
YIELD, YES?
SPLENDID.
I HAVE-- ER--VANQUISHED THE PRETENDER KNAVE AND NOW BRING THESE LESSER WRETCHES TO YOU.
THEY ARE CRIMINALS, IN SORE NEED OF JUDGMENT.

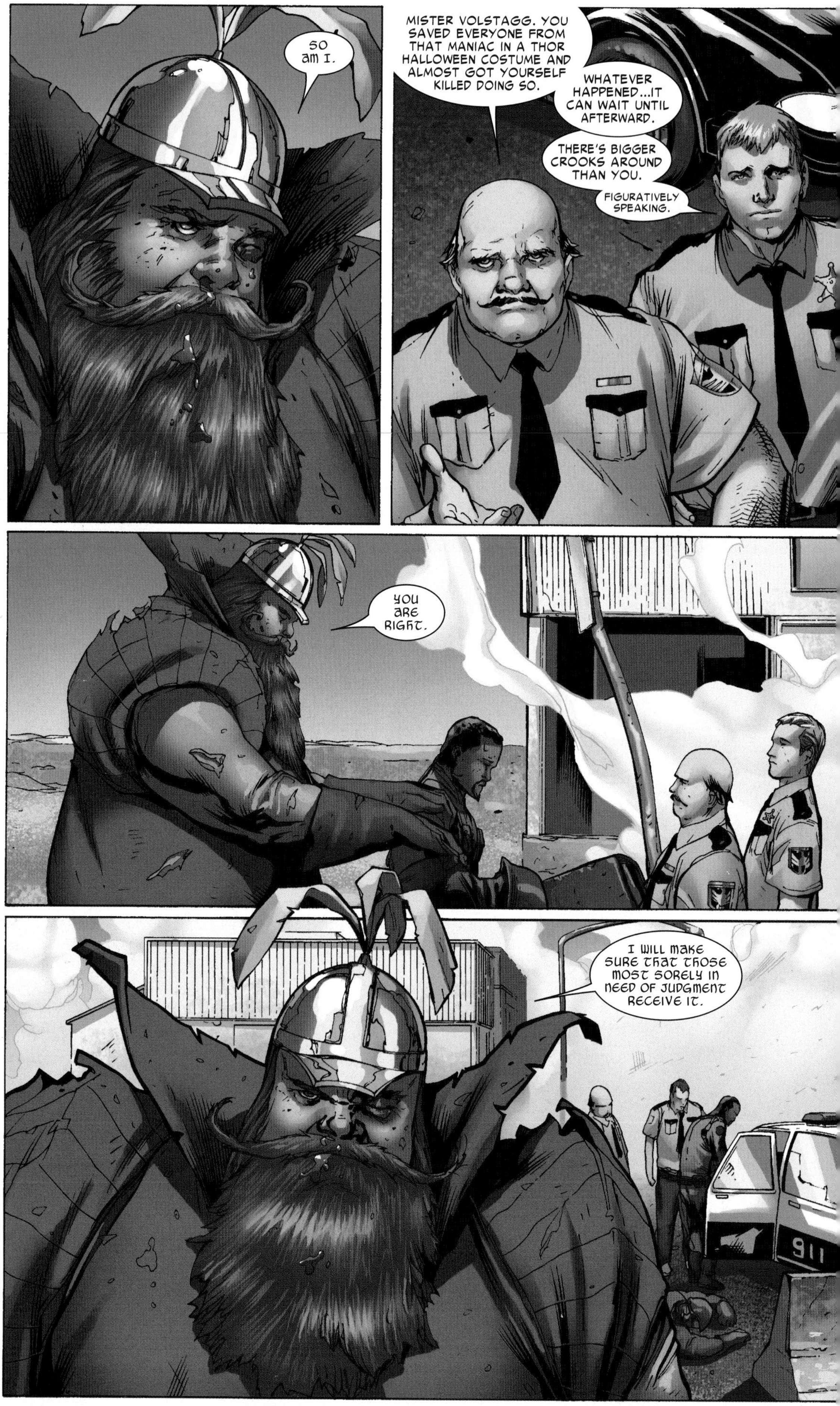
SO AM I.
MISTER VOLSTAGG. YOU SAVED EVERYONE FROM THAT MANIAC IN A THOR HALLOWEEN COSTUME AND ALMOST GOT YOURSELF KILLED DOING SO.
WHATEVER HAPPENED...IT CAN WAIT UNTIL AFTERWARD.
THERE'S BIGGER CROOKS AROUND THAN YOU.
FIGURATIVELY SPEAKING.
YOU ARE RIGHT.
I WILL MAKE SURE THAT THOSE MOST SORELY IN NEED OF JUDGMENT RECEIVE IT.
911

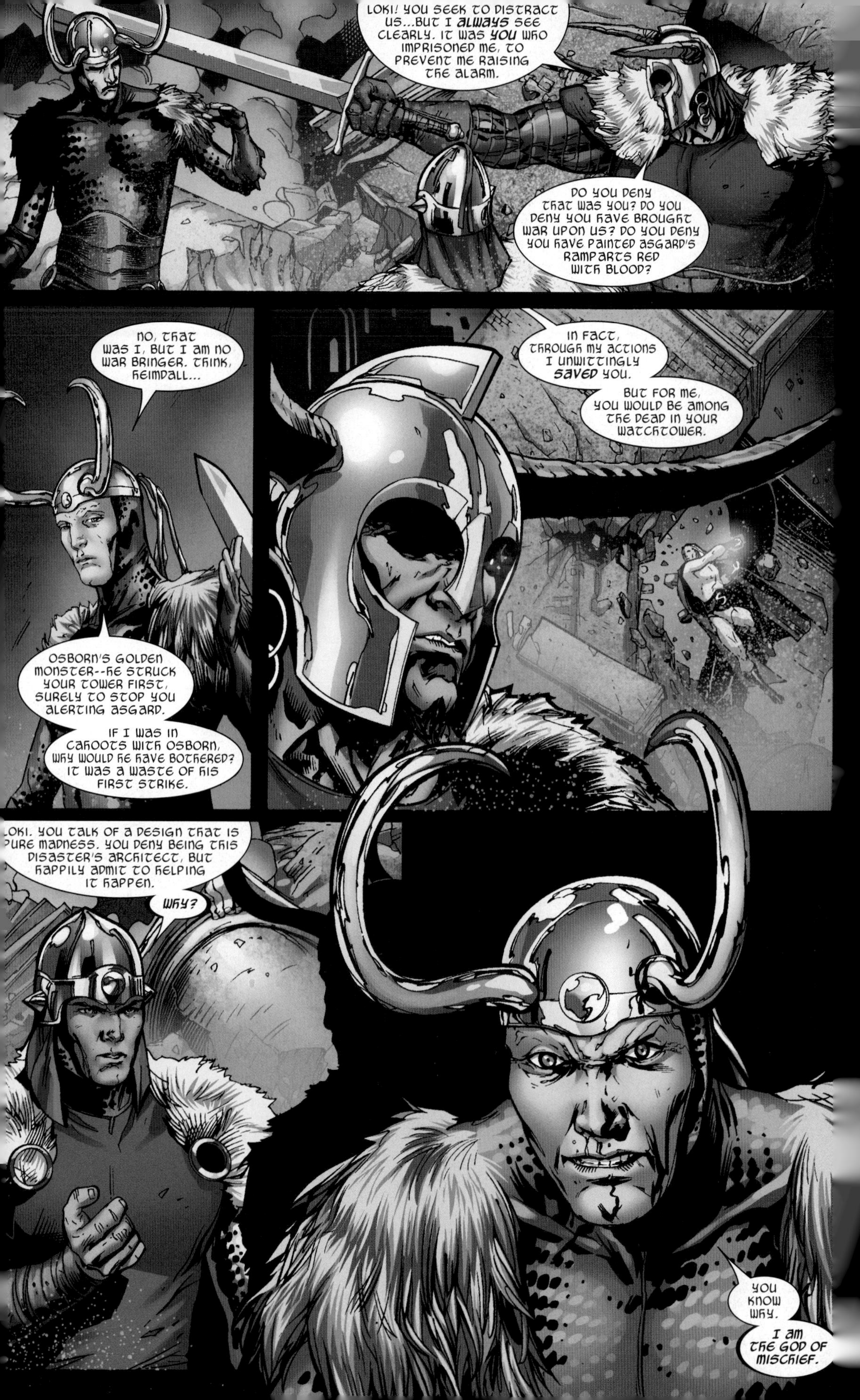
LOKI! YOU SEEK TO DISTRACT US...BUT I ALWAYS SEE CLEARLY. IT WAS YOU WHO IMPRISONED ME, TO PREVENT ME RAISING THE ALARM.
DO YOU DENY THAT WAS YOU? DO YOU DENY YOU HAVE BROUGHT WAR UPON US? DO YOU DENY YOU HAVE PAINTED ASGARD'S RAMPARTS RED WITH BLOOD?
NO, THAT WAS I, BUT I AM NO WAR BRINGER. THINK, HEIMDALL...
OSBORN'S GOLDEN MONSTER--HE STRUCK YOUR TOWER FIRST, SURELY TO STOP YOU ALERTING ASGARD.
IF I WAS IN CAHOOTS WITH OSBORN, WHY WOULD HE HAVE BOTHERED? IT WAS A WASTE OF HIS FIRST STRIKE.
IN FACT, THROUGH MY ACTIONS I UNWITTINGLY SAVED YOU.
BUT FOR ME, YOU WOULD BE AMONG THE DEAD IN YOUR WATCHTOWER.
LOKI. YOU TALK OF A DESIGN THAT IS PURE MADNESS. YOU DENY BEING THIS DISASTER'S ARCHITECT, BUT HAPPILY ADMIT TO HELPING IT HAPPEN.
WHY?
YOU KNOW WHY.
I AM THE GOD OF MISCHIEF.

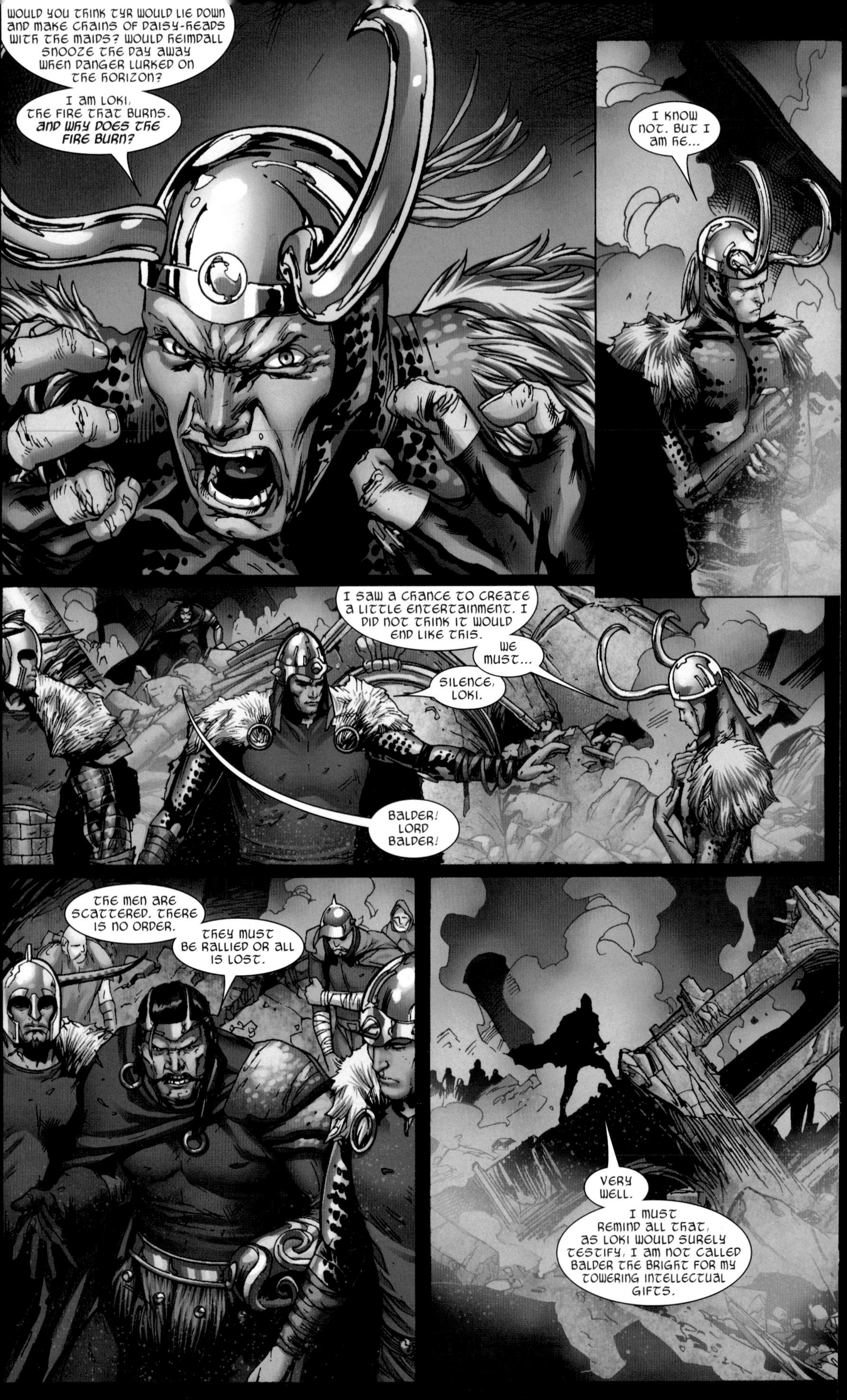

WOULD YOU THINK TYR WOULD LIE DOWN AND MAKE CHAINS OF DAISY-HEADS WITH THE MAIDS? WOULD HEIMDALL SNOOZE THE DAY AWAY WHEN DANGER LURKED ON THE HORIZON?
I AM LOKI, THE FIRE THAT BURNS. *AND WHY DOES THE FIRE BURN?*
I KNOW NOT. BUT I AM HE...
I SAW A CHANCE TO CREATE A LITTLE ENTERTAINMENT. I DID NOT THINK IT WOULD END LIKE THIS.
WE MUST...
SILENCE, LOKI.
BALDER! LORD BALDER!
THE MEN ARE SCATTERED. THERE IS NO ORDER.
THEY MUST BE RALLIED OR ALL IS LOST.
VERY WELL.
I MUST REMIND ALL THAT, AS LOKI WOULD SURELY TESTIFY, I AM NOT CALLED BALDER THE BRIGHT FOR MY TOWERING INTELLECTUAL GIFTS.

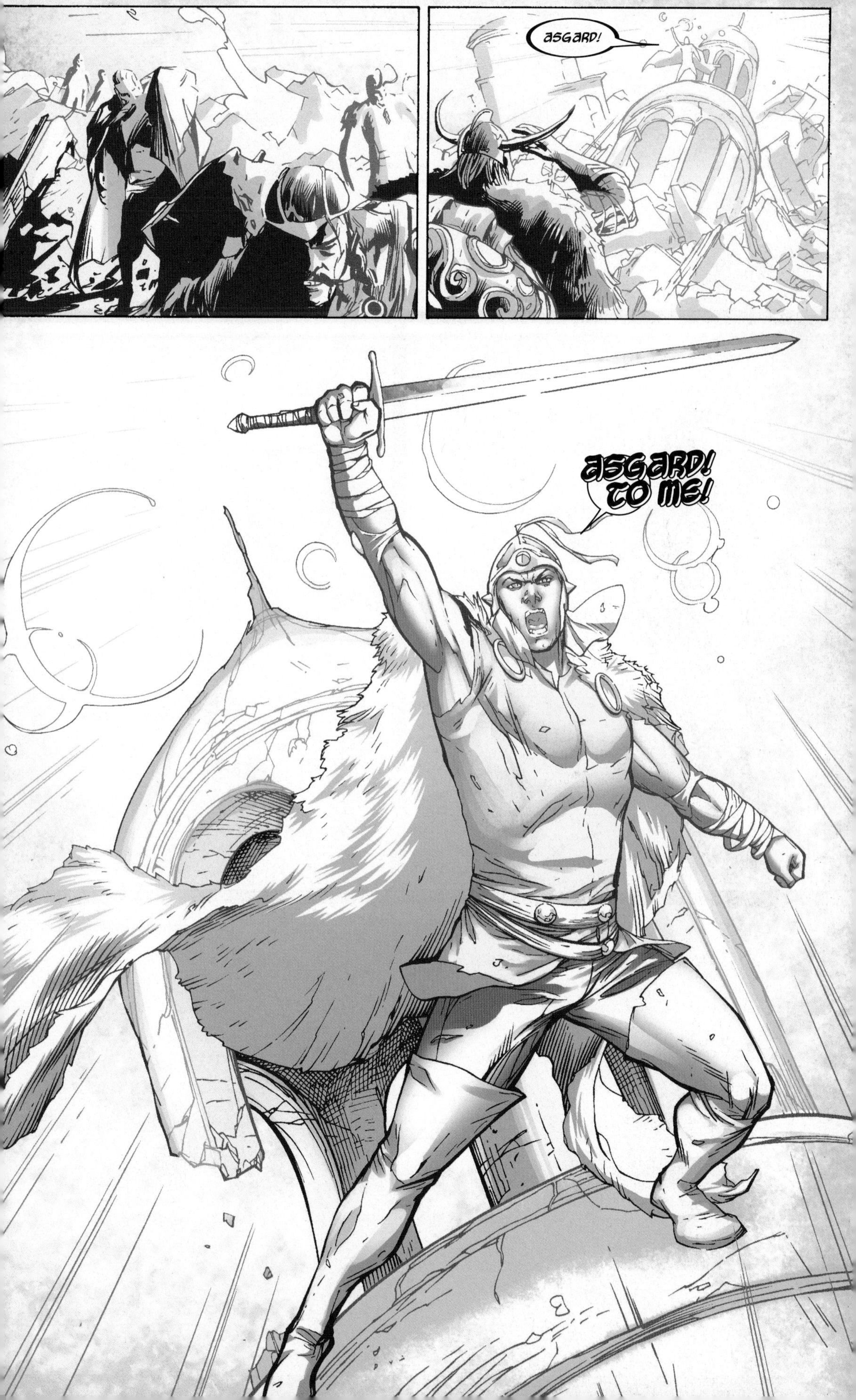
ASGARD!
ASGARD! TO ME!

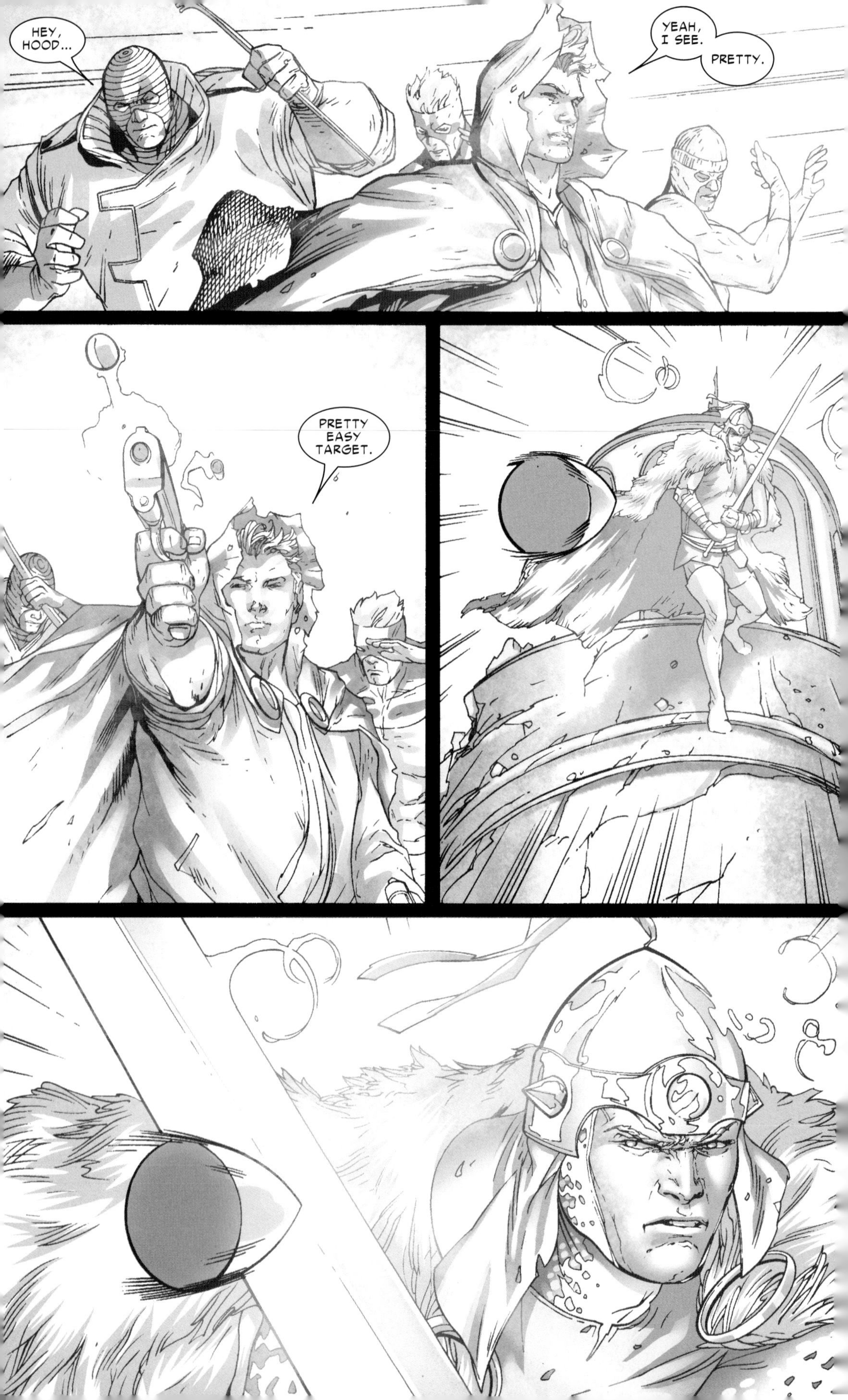
HEY, HOOD...
YEAH, I SEE.
PRETTY.
PRETTY EASY TARGET.

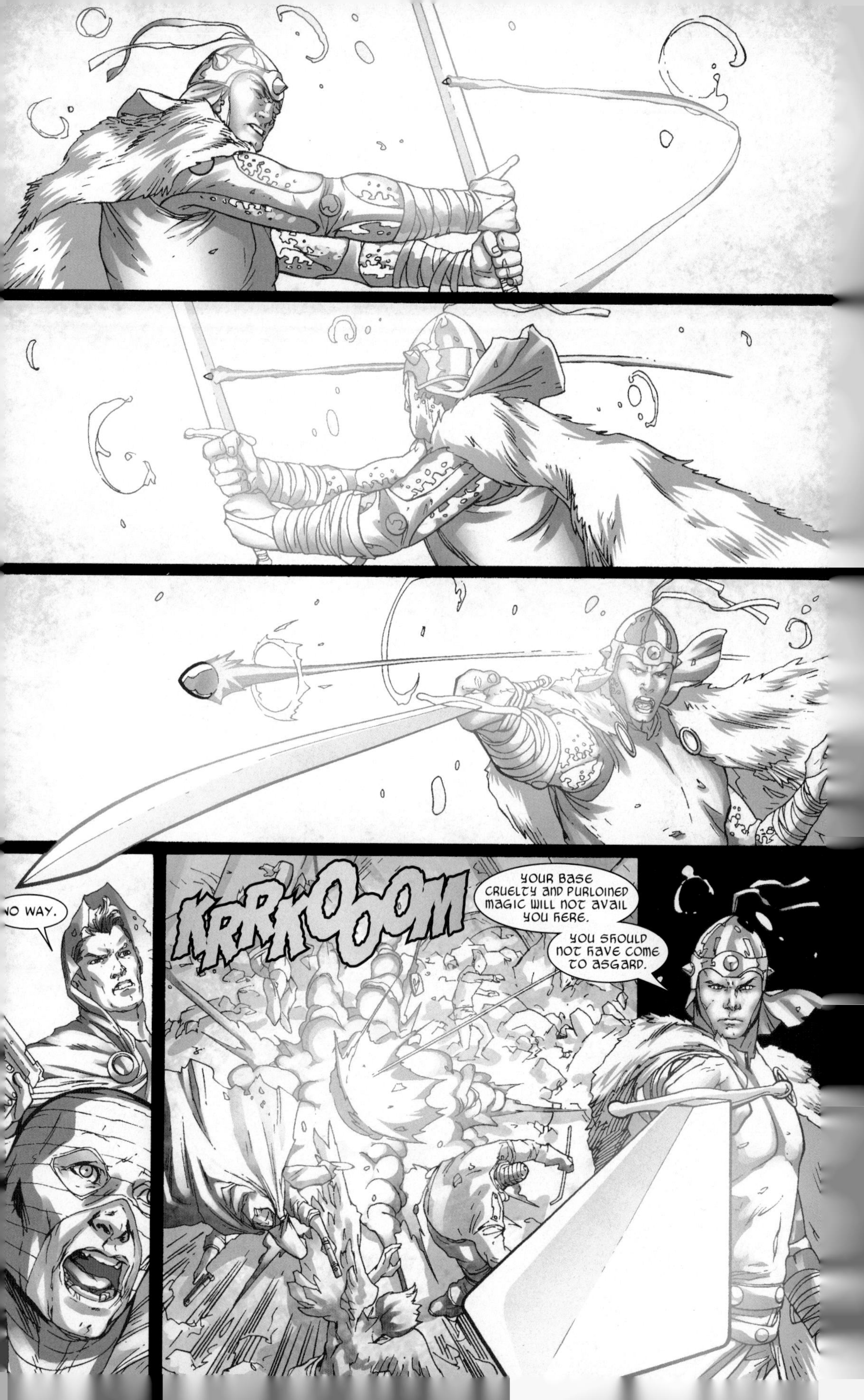
NO WAY.
KRRKOOOM
YOUR BASE CRUELTY AND PURLOINED MAGIC WILL NOT AVAIL YOU HERE.
YOU SHOULD NOT HAVE COME TO ASGARD.

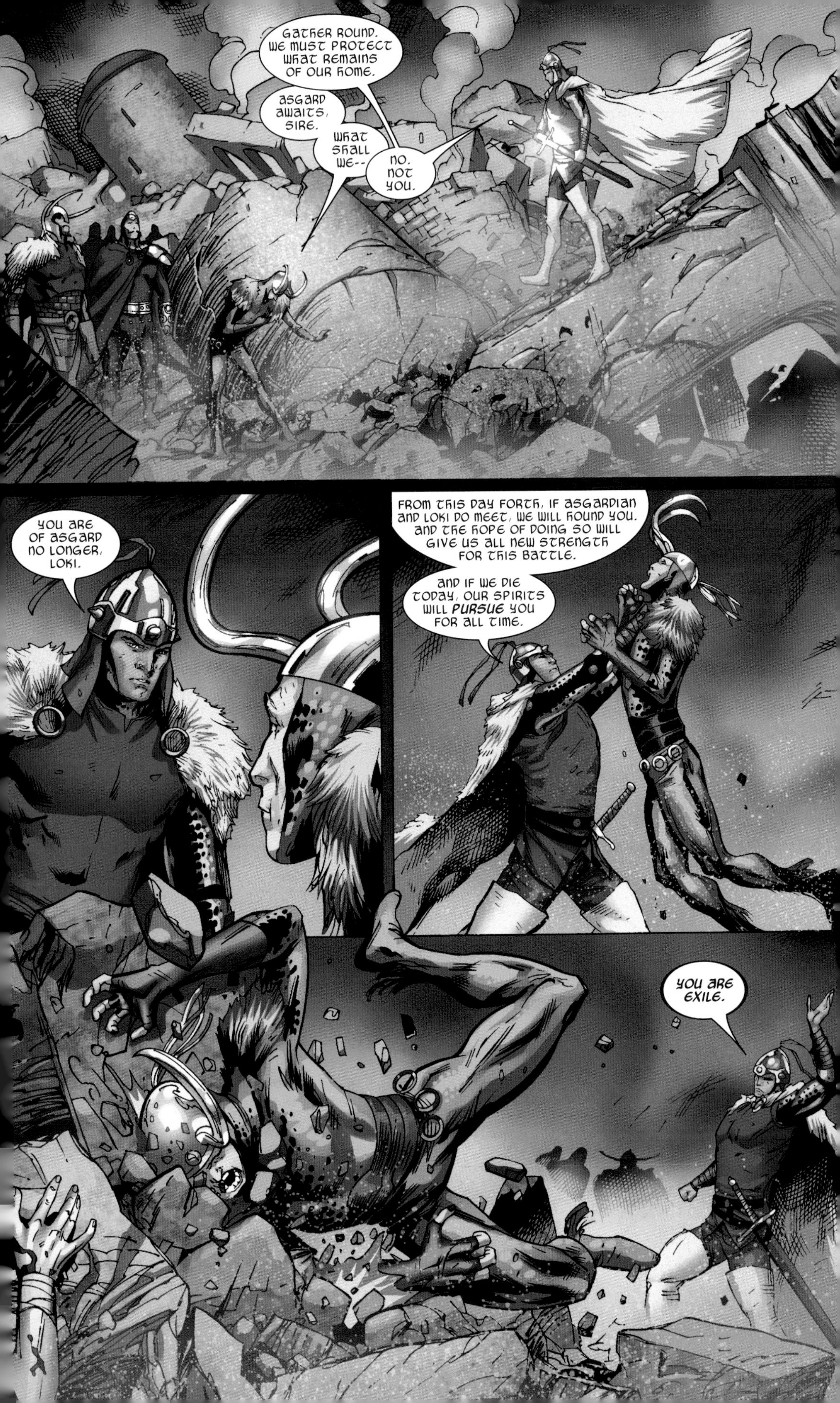
GATHER ROUND. WE MUST PROTECT WHAT REMAINS OF OUR HOME.
ASGARD AWAITS, SIRE.
WHAT SHALL WE--
NO. NOT YOU.
YOU ARE OF ASGARD NO LONGER, LOKI.
FROM THIS DAY FORTH, IF ASGARDIAN AND LOKI DO MEET, WE WILL HOUND YOU. AND THE HOPE OF DOING SO WILL GIVE US ALL NEW STRENGTH FOR THIS BATTLE.
AND IF WE DIE TODAY, OUR SPIRITS WILL PURSUE YOU FOR ALL TIME.
YOU ARE EXILE.

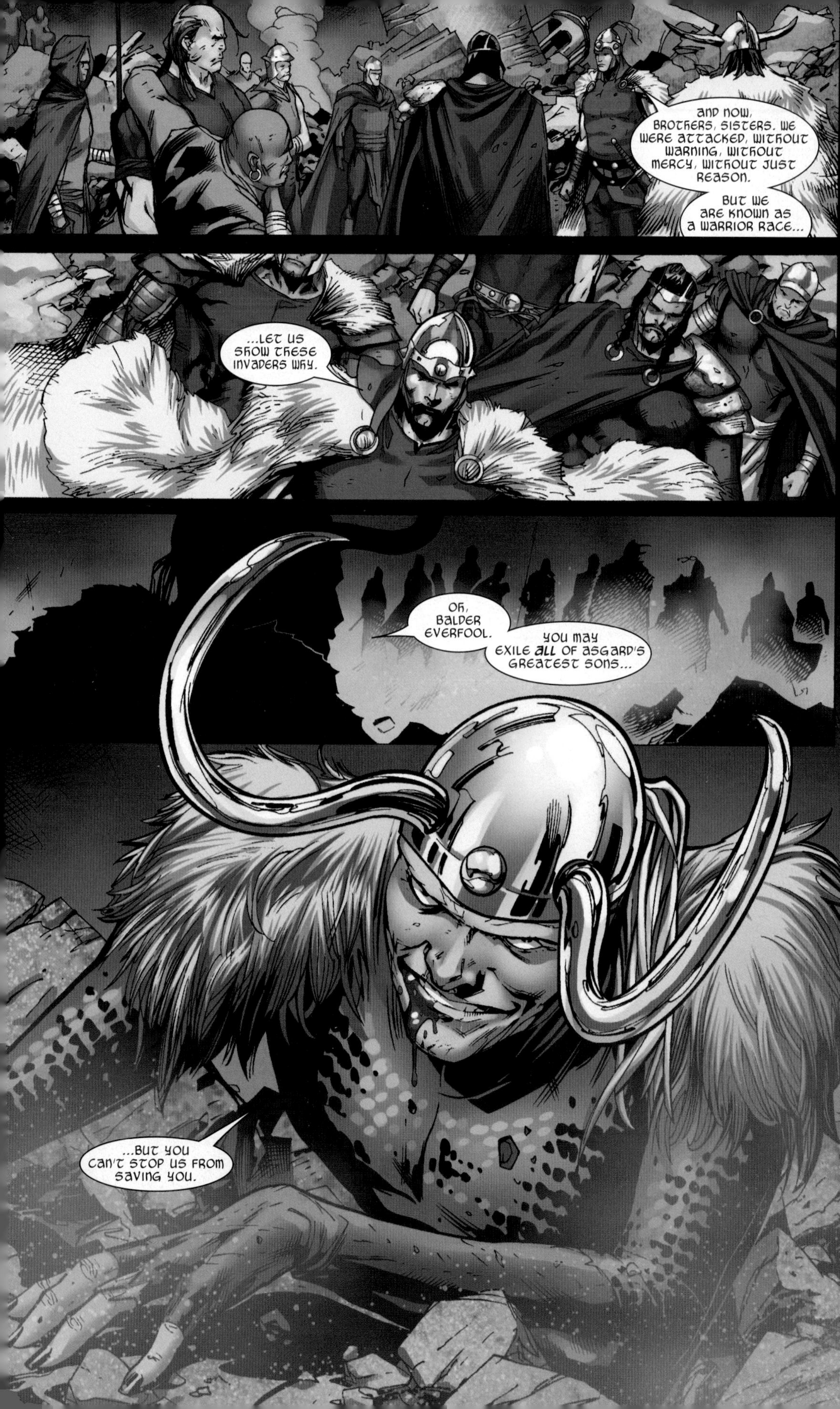
AND NOW, BROTHERS, SISTERS. WE WERE ATTACKED, WITHOUT WARNING, WITHOUT MERCY, WITHOUT JUST REASON.
BUT WE ARE KNOWN AS A WARRIOR RACE...
...LET US SHOW THESE INVADERS WHY.
OH, BALDER EVERFOOL.
YOU MAY EXILE ALL OF ASGARD'S GREATEST SONS...
...BUT YOU CAN'T STOP US FROM SAVING YOU.

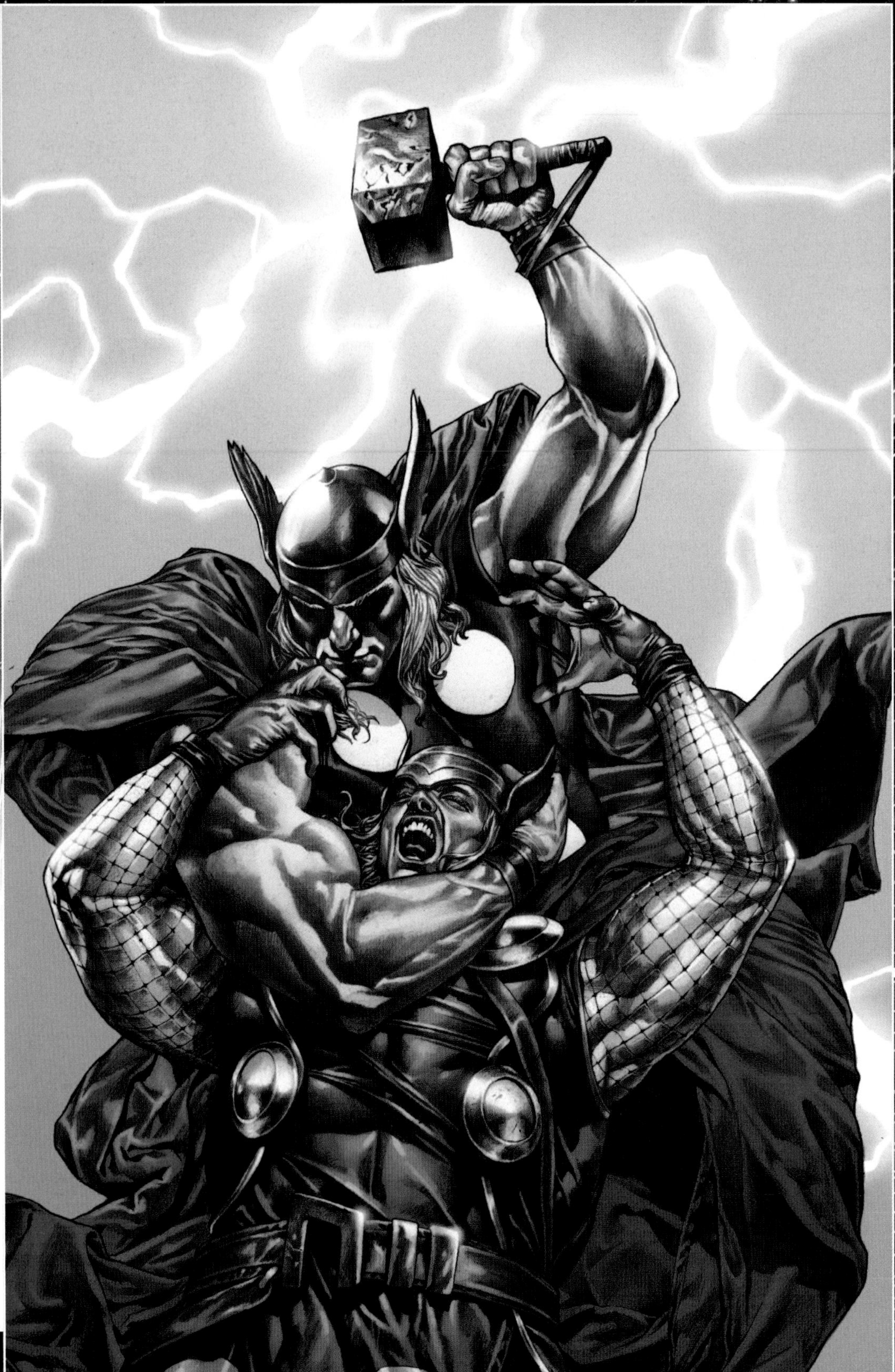

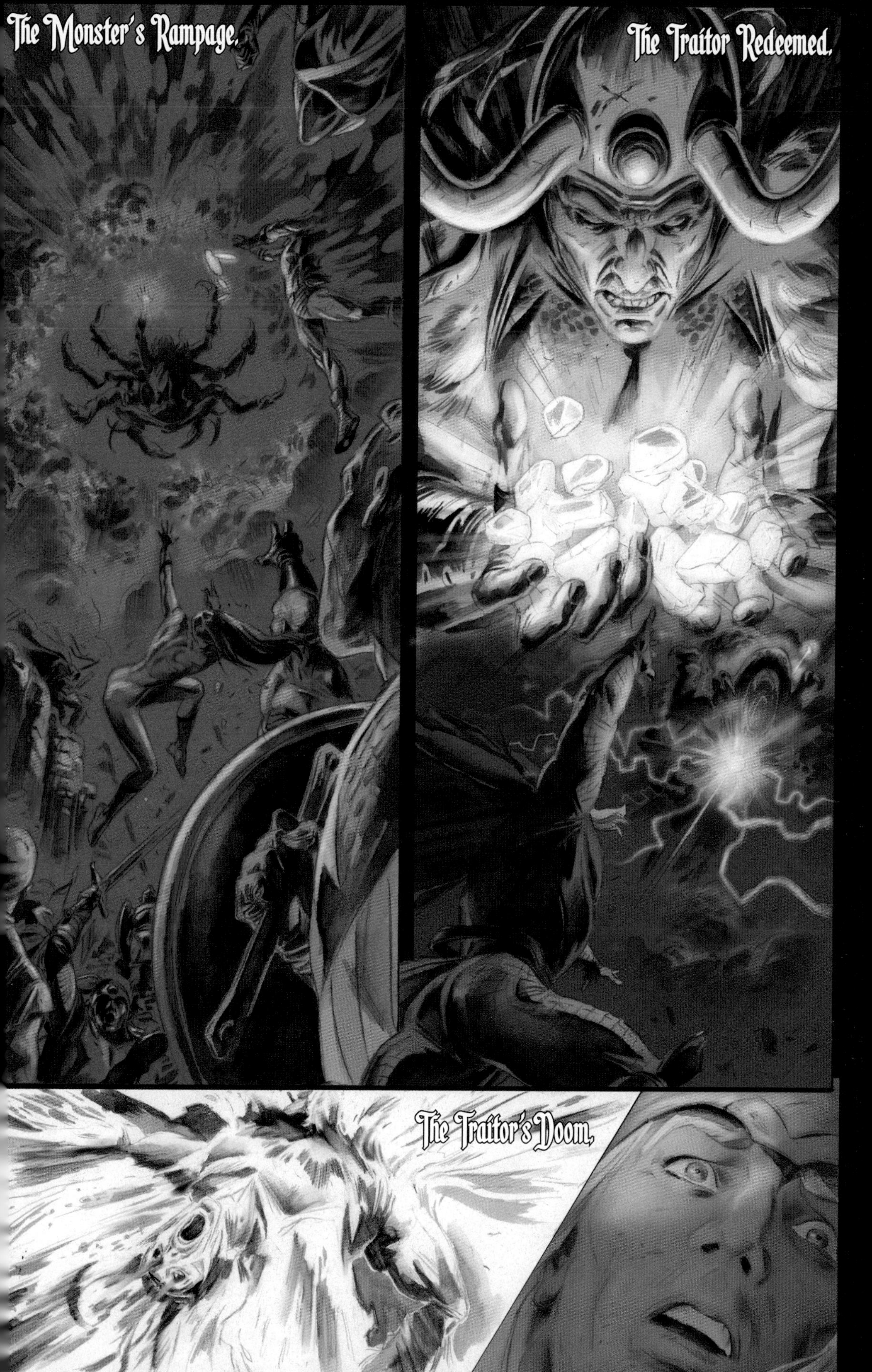

The Monster's Rampage.
The Traitor Redeemed.
The Traitor's Doom.

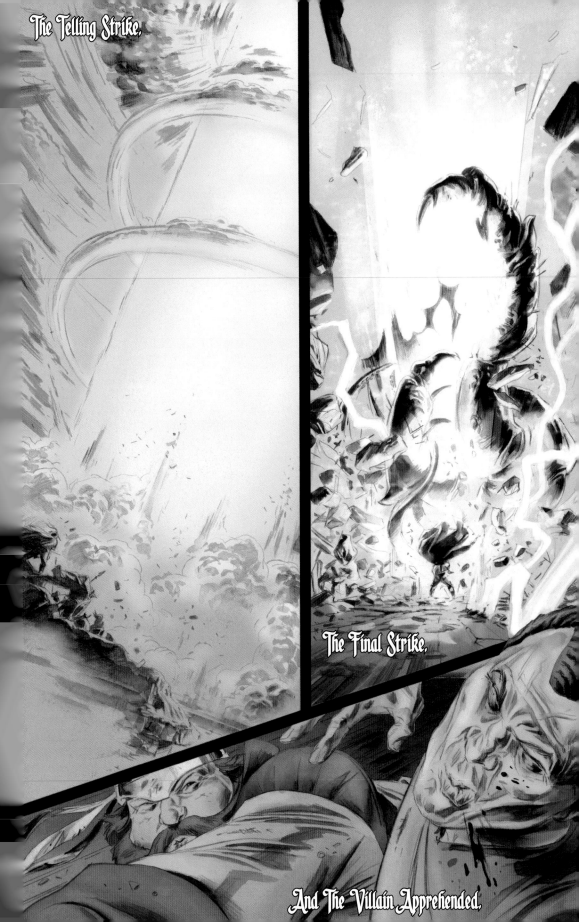

The Telling Strike,

The Final Strike,

And The Villain Apprehended.

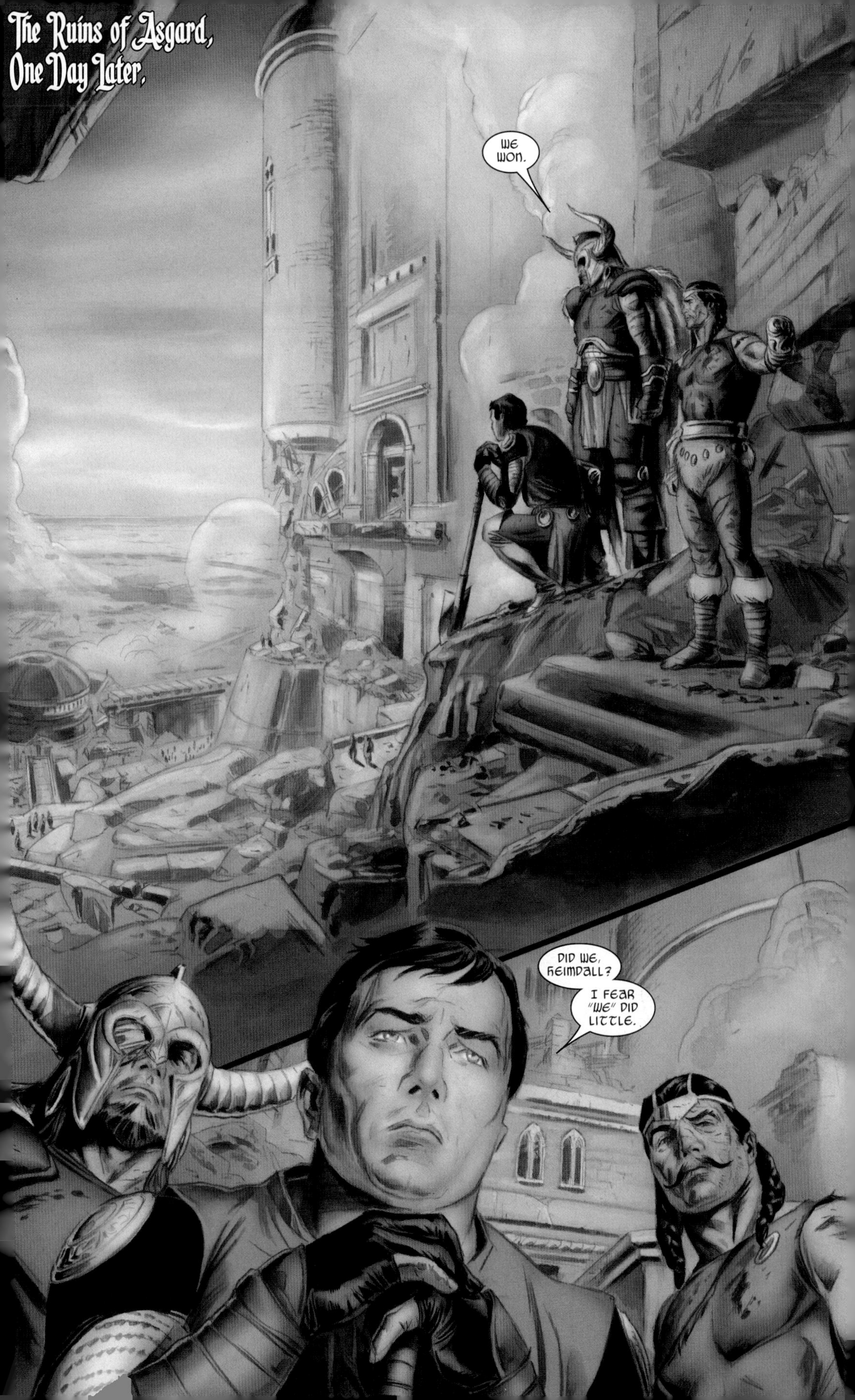
The Ruins of Asgard,
One Day Later,
WE WON.
DID WE, HEIMDALL?
I FEAR "WE" DID LITTLE.

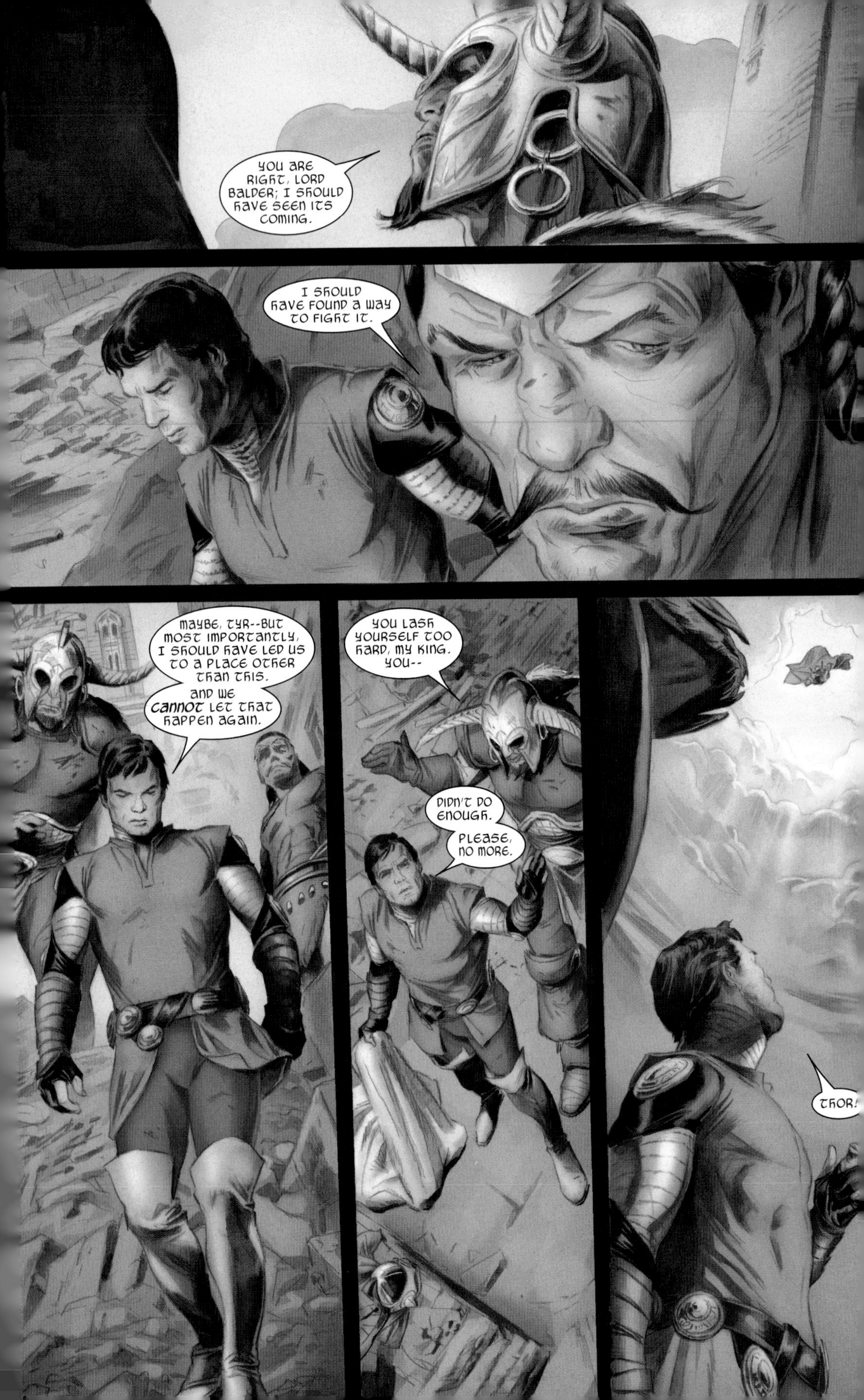
YOU ARE RIGHT, LORD BALDER; I SHOULD HAVE SEEN ITS COMING.
I SHOULD HAVE FOUND A WAY TO FIGHT IT.
MAYBE, TYR--BUT MOST IMPORTANTLY, I SHOULD HAVE LED US TO A PLACE OTHER THAN THIS.
AND WE CANNOT LET THAT HAPPEN AGAIN.
YOU LASH YOURSELF TOO HARD, MY KING. YOU--
DIDN'T DO ENOUGH.
PLEASE, NO MORE.
THOR!

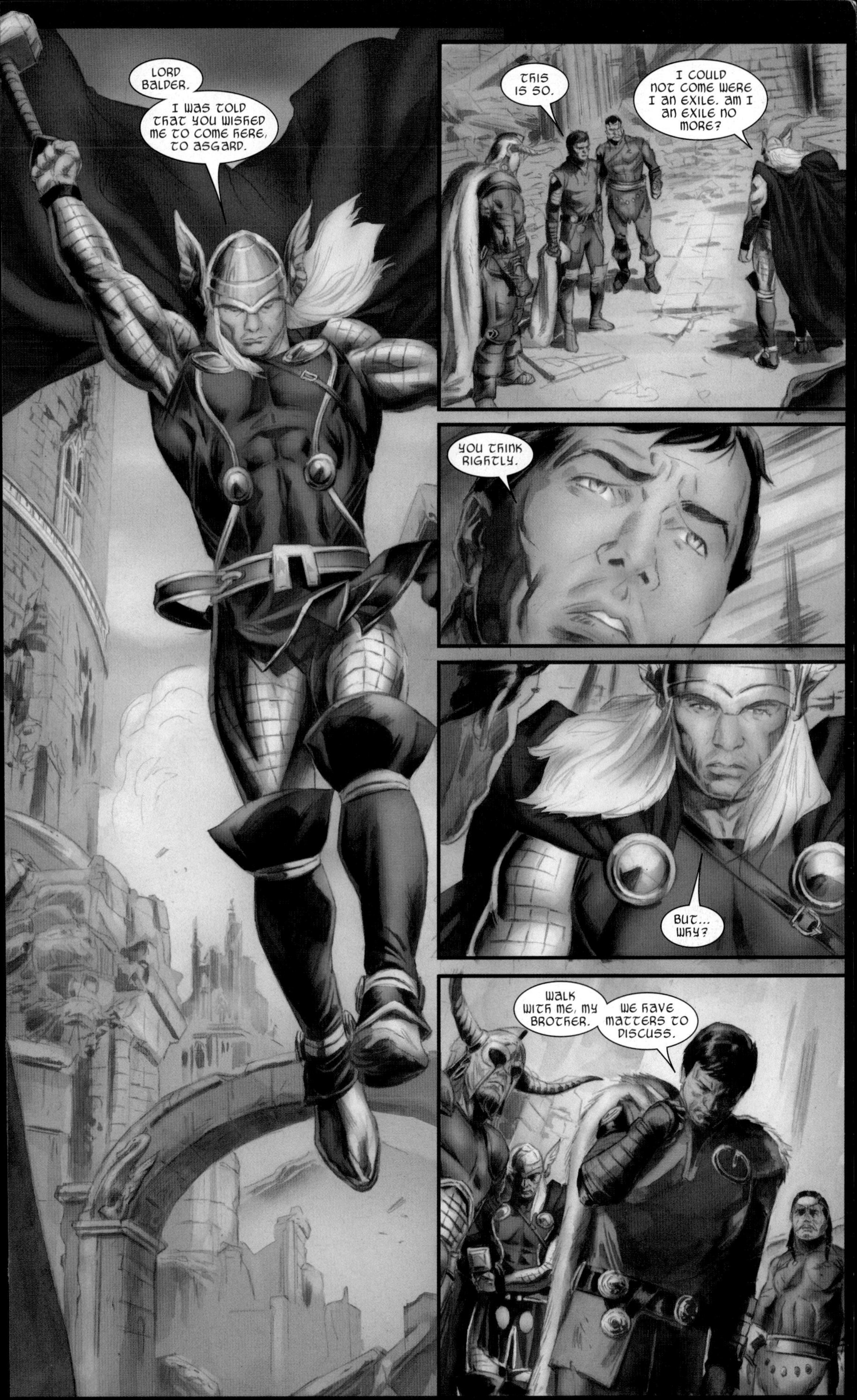
LORD BALDER.
I WAS TOLD THAT YOU WISHED ME TO COME HERE, TO ASGARD.
THIS IS SO.
I COULD NOT COME WERE I AN EXILE. AM I AN EXILE NO MORE?
YOU THINK RIGHTLY.
BUT... WHY?
WALK WITH ME, MY BROTHER.
WE HAVE MATTERS TO DISCUSS.

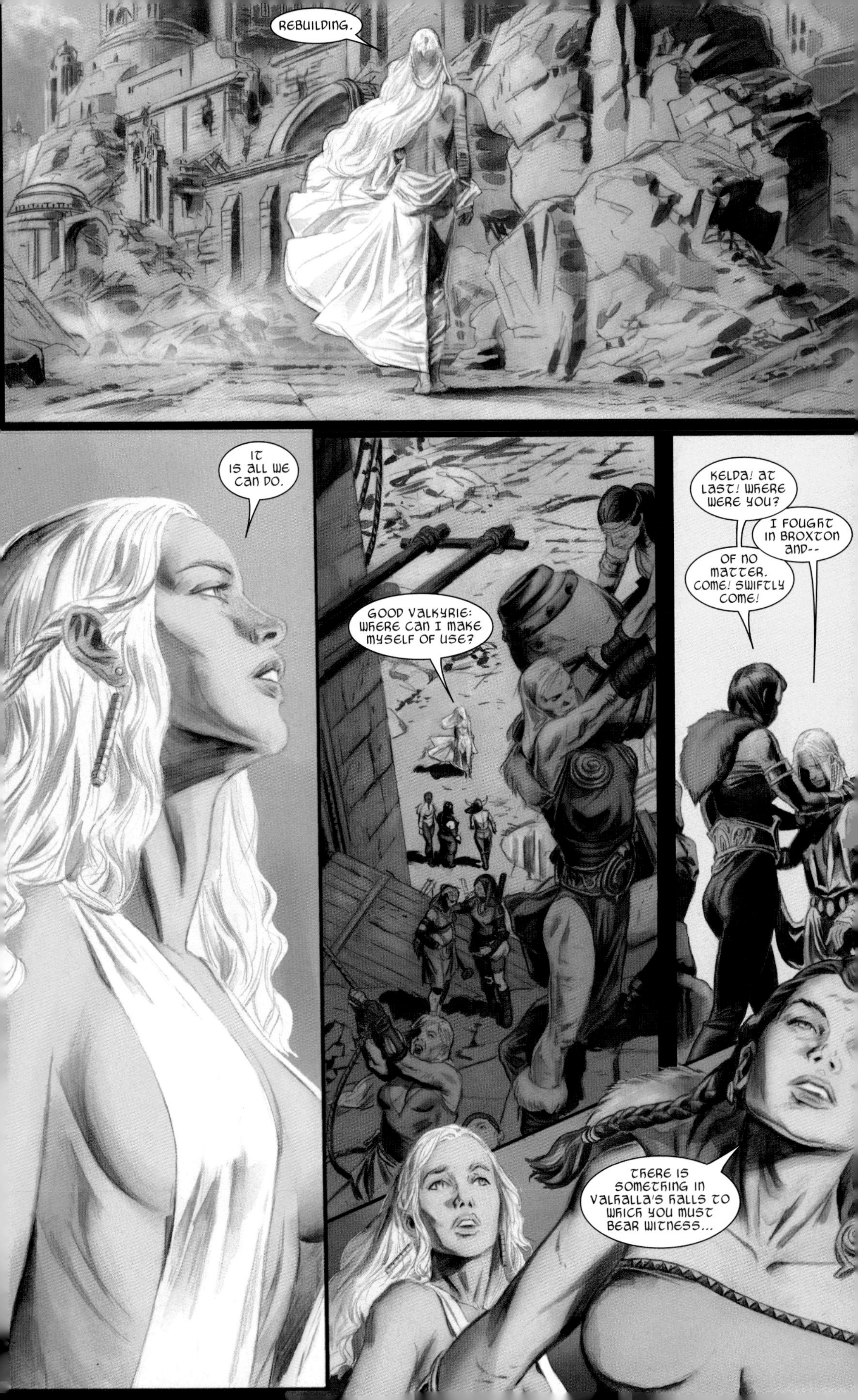
REBUILDING.
IT IS ALL WE CAN DO.
GOOD VALKYRIE: WHERE CAN I MAKE MYSELF OF USE?
KELDA! AT LAST! WHERE WERE YOU?
I FOUGHT IN BROXTON AND--
OF NO MATTER. COME! SWIFTLY COME!
THERE IS SOMETHING IN VALHALLA'S HALLS TO WHICH YOU MUST BEAR WITNESS...

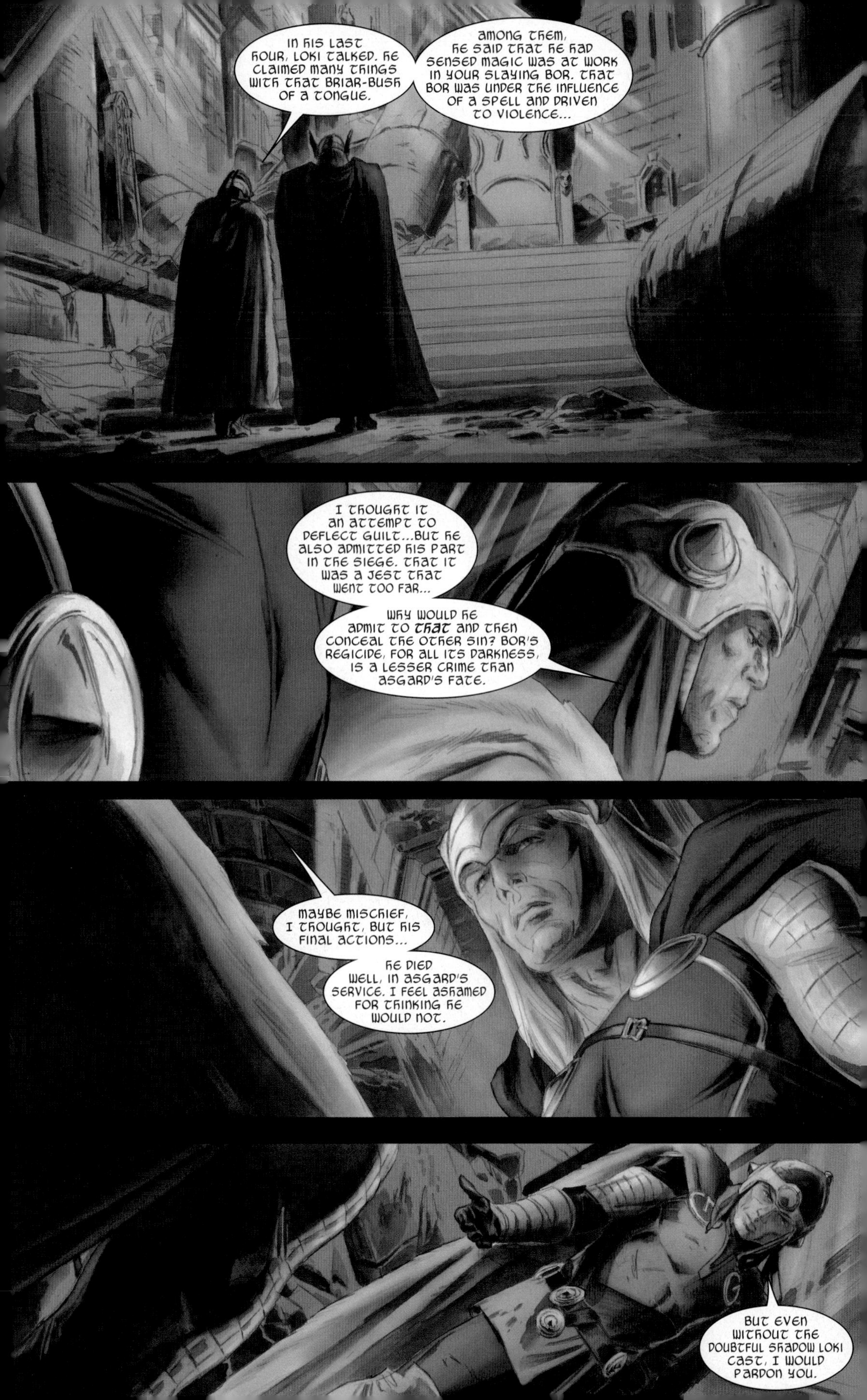
IN HIS LAST HOUR, LOKI TALKED. HE CLAIMED MANY THINGS WITH THAT BRIAR-BUSH OF A TONGUE.
AMONG THEM, HE SAID THAT HE HAD SENSED MAGIC WAS AT WORK IN YOUR SLAYING BOR. THAT BOR WAS UNDER THE INFLUENCE OF A SPELL AND DRIVEN TO VIOLENCE...
I THOUGHT IT AN ATTEMPT TO DEFLECT GUILT...BUT HE ALSO ADMITTED HIS PART IN THE SIEGE. THAT IT WAS A JEST THAT WENT TOO FAR...
WHY WOULD HE ADMIT TO *THAT* AND THEN CONCEAL THE OTHER SIN? BOR'S REGICIDE, FOR ALL ITS DARKNESS, IS A LESSER CRIME THAN ASGARD'S FATE.
MAYBE MISCHIEF, I THOUGHT, BUT HIS FINAL ACTIONS...
HE DIED WELL, IN ASGARD'S SERVICE. I FEEL ASHAMED FOR THINKING HE WOULD NOT.
BUT EVEN WITHOUT THE DOUBTFUL SHADOW LOKI CAST, I WOULD PARDON YOU.

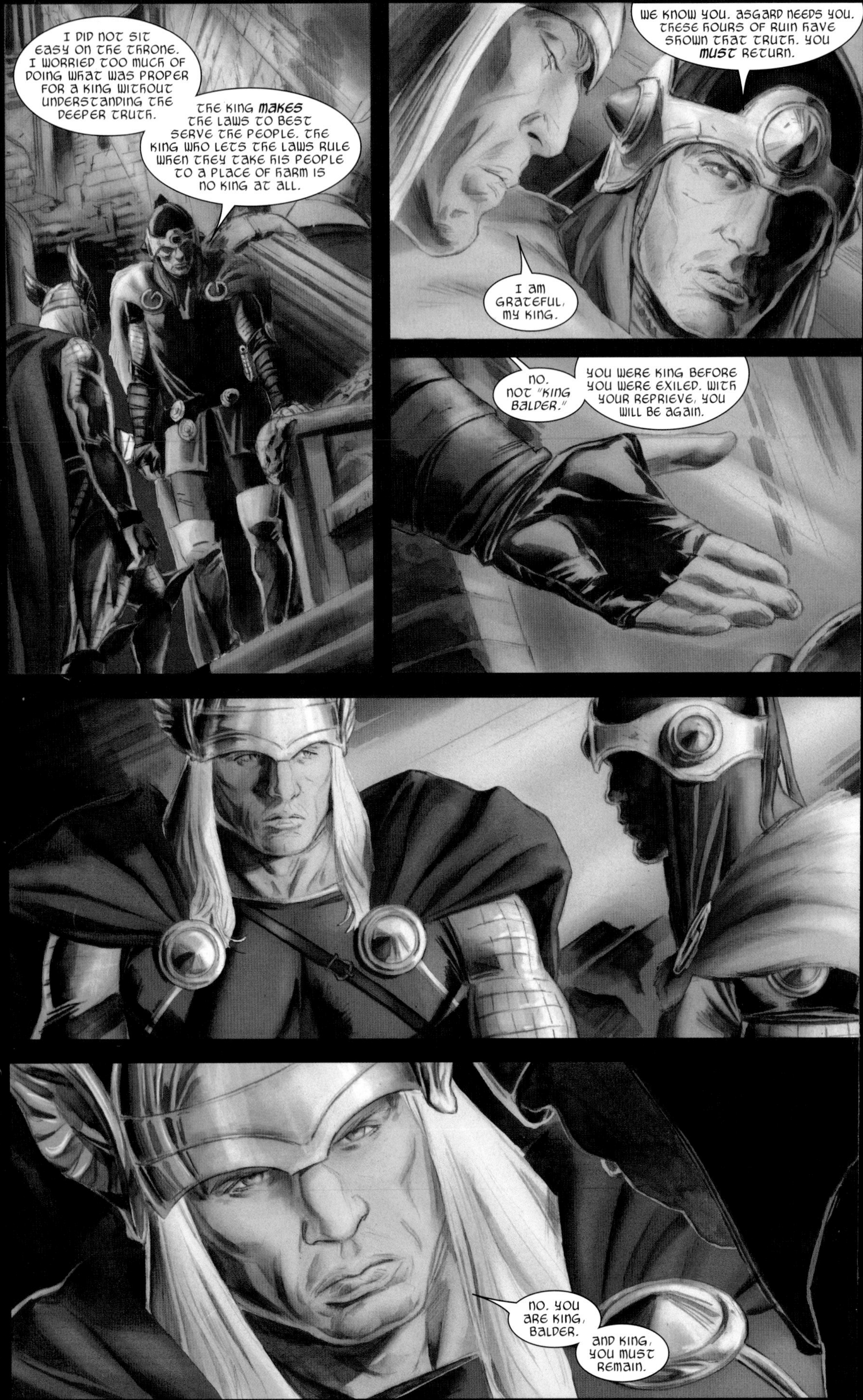
I DID NOT SIT EASY ON THE THRONE. I WORRIED TOO MUCH OF DOING WHAT WAS PROPER FOR A KING WITHOUT UNDERSTANDING THE DEEPER TRUTH.
THE KING **MAKES** THE LAWS TO BEST SERVE THE PEOPLE. THE KING WHO LETS THE LAWS RULE WHEN THEY TAKE HIS PEOPLE TO A PLACE OF HARM IS NO KING AT ALL.
WE KNOW YOU. ASGARD NEEDS YOU. THESE HOURS OF RUIN HAVE SHOWN THAT TRUTH. YOU **MUST** RETURN.
I AM GRATEFUL, MY KING.
NO. NOT "KING BALDER."
YOU WERE KING BEFORE YOU WERE EXILED. WITH YOUR REPRIEVE, YOU WILL BE AGAIN.
NO. YOU ARE KING, BALDER.
AND KING, YOU MUST REMAIN.

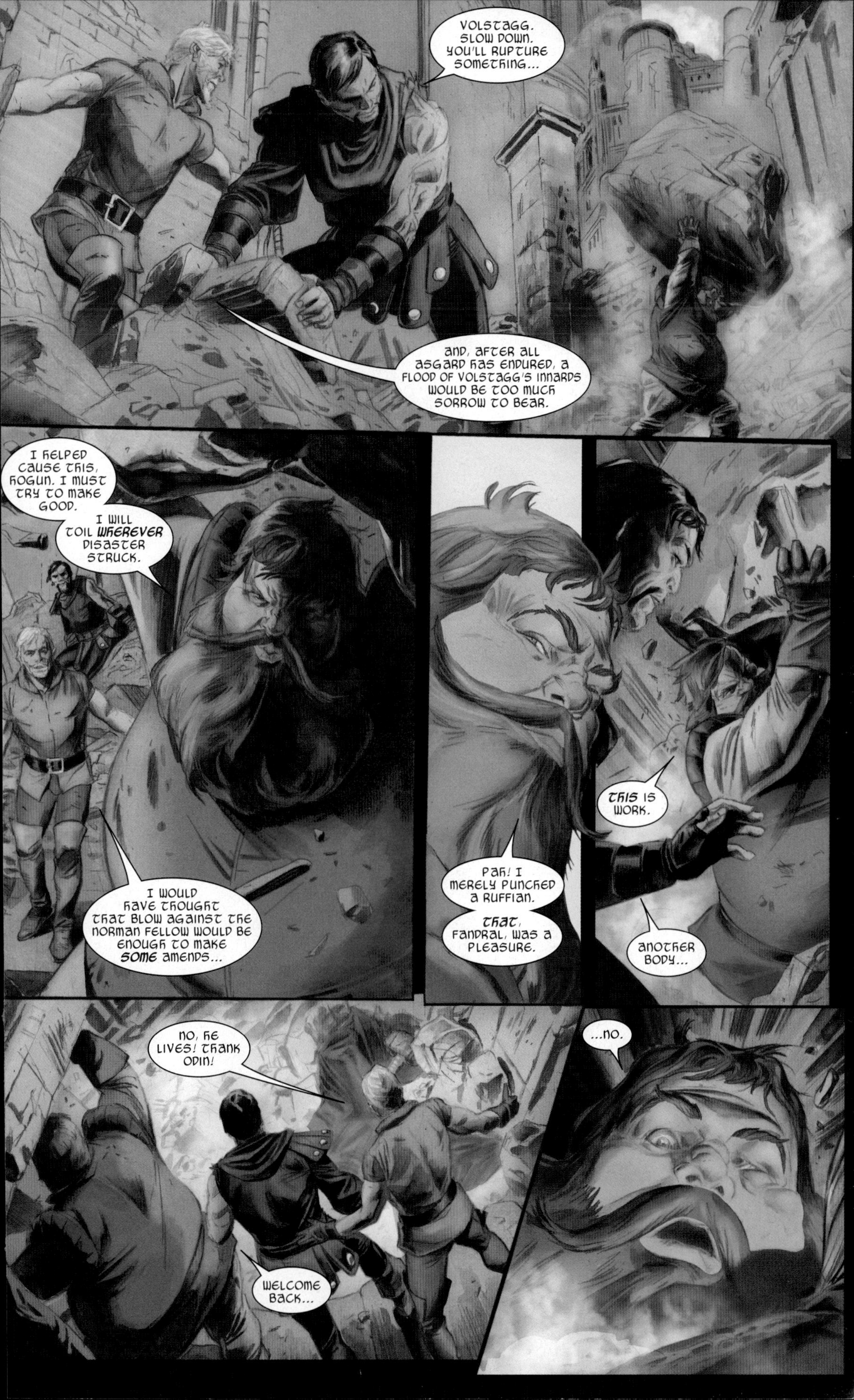
VOLSTAGG. SLOW DOWN. YOU'LL RUPTURE SOMETHING...
AND, AFTER ALL ASGARD HAS ENDURED, A FLOOD OF VOLSTAGG'S INNARDS WOULD BE TOO MUCH SORROW TO BEAR.
I HELPED CAUSE THIS, HOGUN. I MUST TRY TO MAKE GOOD.
I WILL TOIL **WHEREVER** DISASTER STRUCK.
I WOULD HAVE THOUGHT THAT BLOW AGAINST THE NORMAN FELLOW WOULD BE ENOUGH TO MAKE **SOME** AMENDS...
PAH! I MERELY PUNCHED A RUFFIAN.
THAT, FANDRAL, WAS A PLEASURE.
THIS IS WORK.
ANOTHER BODY...
NO, HE LIVES! THANK ODIN!
WELCOME BACK...
...NO.

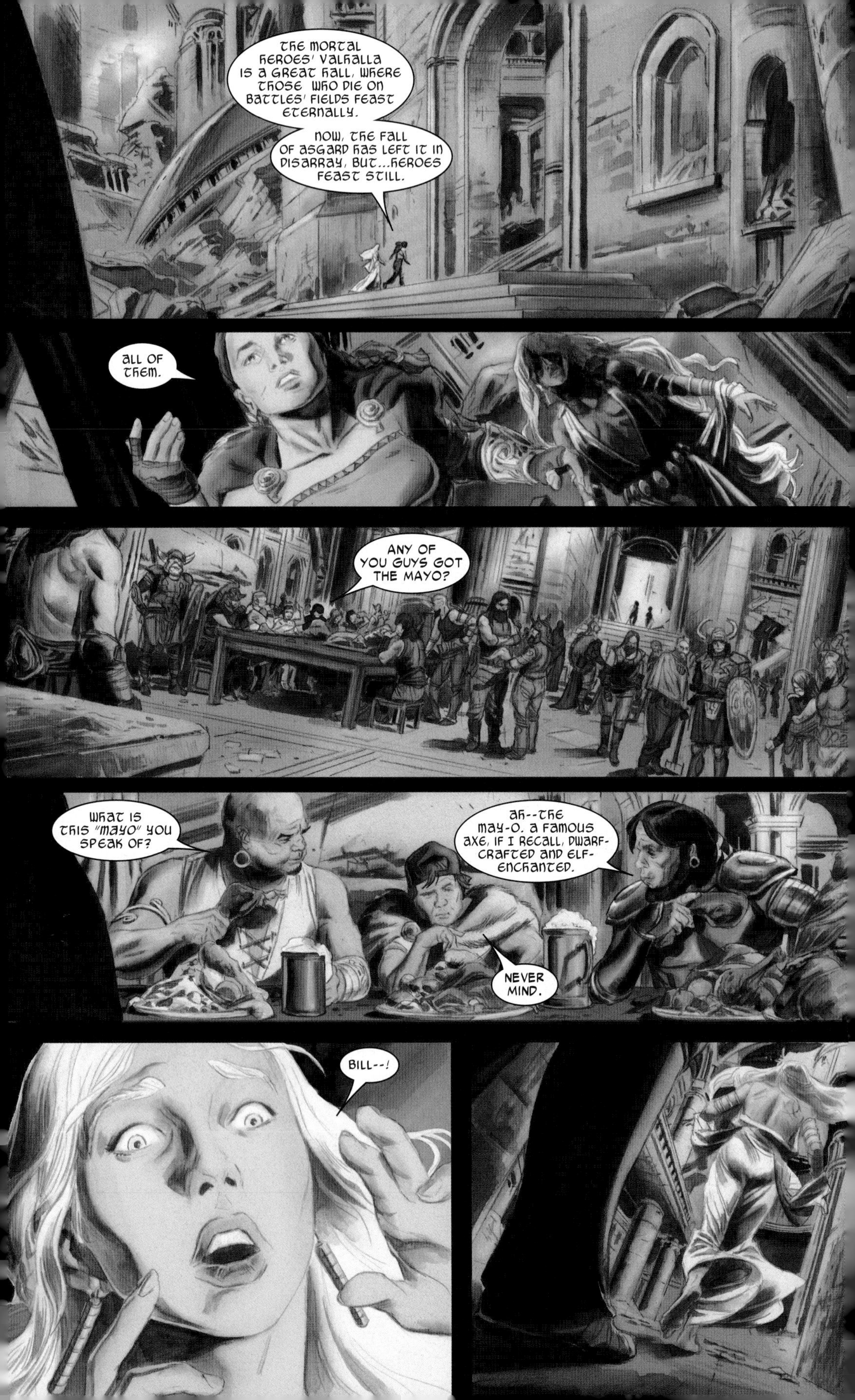
THE MORTAL HEROES' VALHALLA IS A GREAT HALL, WHERE THOSE WHO DIE ON BATTLES' FIELDS FEAST ETERNALLY.
NOW, THE FALL OF ASGARD HAS LEFT IT IN DISARRAY, BUT...HEROES FEAST STILL.
ALL OF THEM.
ANY OF YOU GUYS GOT THE MAYO?
WHAT IS THIS "MAYO" YOU SPEAK OF?
AH--THE MAY-O. A FAMOUS AXE, IF I RECALL, DWARF-CRAFTED AND ELF-ENCHANTED.
NEVER MIND.
BILL--!

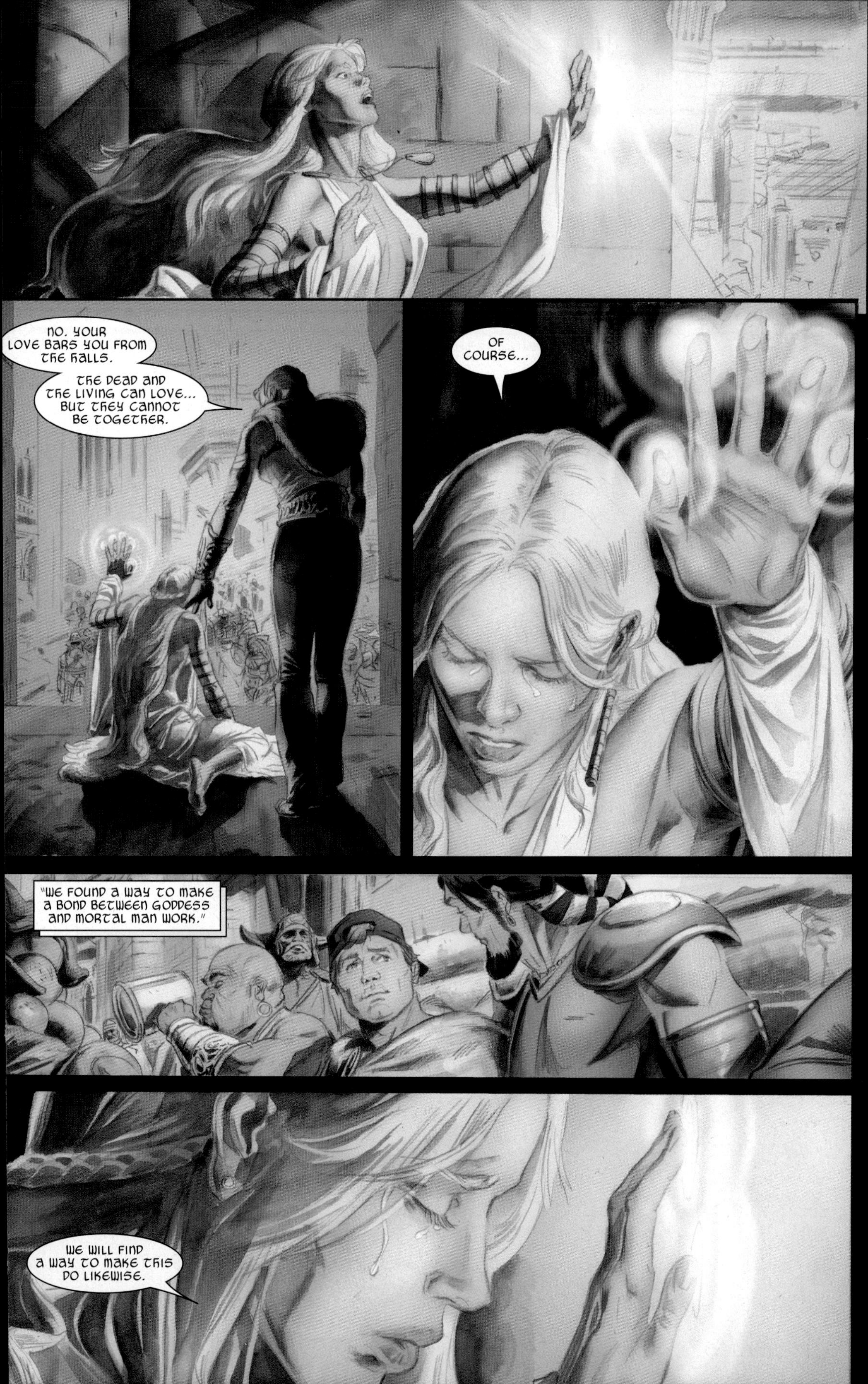
NO. YOUR LOVE BARS YOU FROM THE HALLS.
THE DEAD AND THE LIVING CAN LOVE... BUT THEY CANNOT BE TOGETHER.
OF COURSE...
"WE FOUND A WAY TO MAKE A BOND BETWEEN GODDESS AND MORTAL MAN WORK."
WE WILL FIND A WAY TO MAKE THIS DO LIKEWISE.

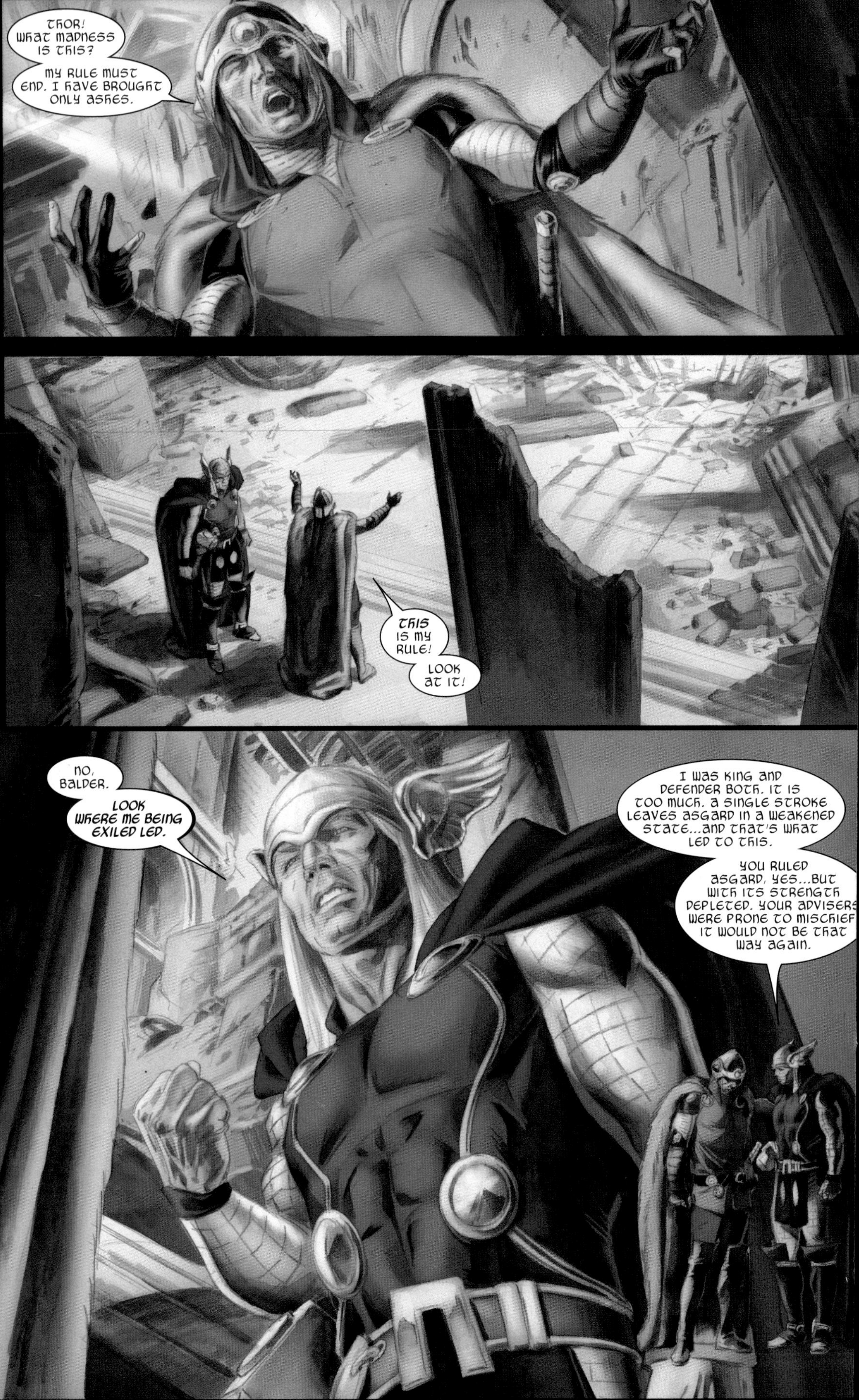
THOR! WHAT MADNESS IS THIS?
MY RULE MUST END. I HAVE BROUGHT ONLY ASHES.
THIS IS MY RULE!
LOOK AT IT!
NO, BALDER.
LOOK WHERE ME BEING EXILED LED.
I WAS KING AND DEFENDER BOTH. IT IS TOO MUCH. A SINGLE STROKE LEAVES ASGARD IN A WEAKENED STATE...AND THAT'S WHAT LED TO THIS.
YOU RULED ASGARD, YES...BUT WITH ITS STRENGTH DEPLETED. YOUR ADVISERS WERE PRONE TO MISCHIEF. IT WOULD NOT BE THAT WAY AGAIN.

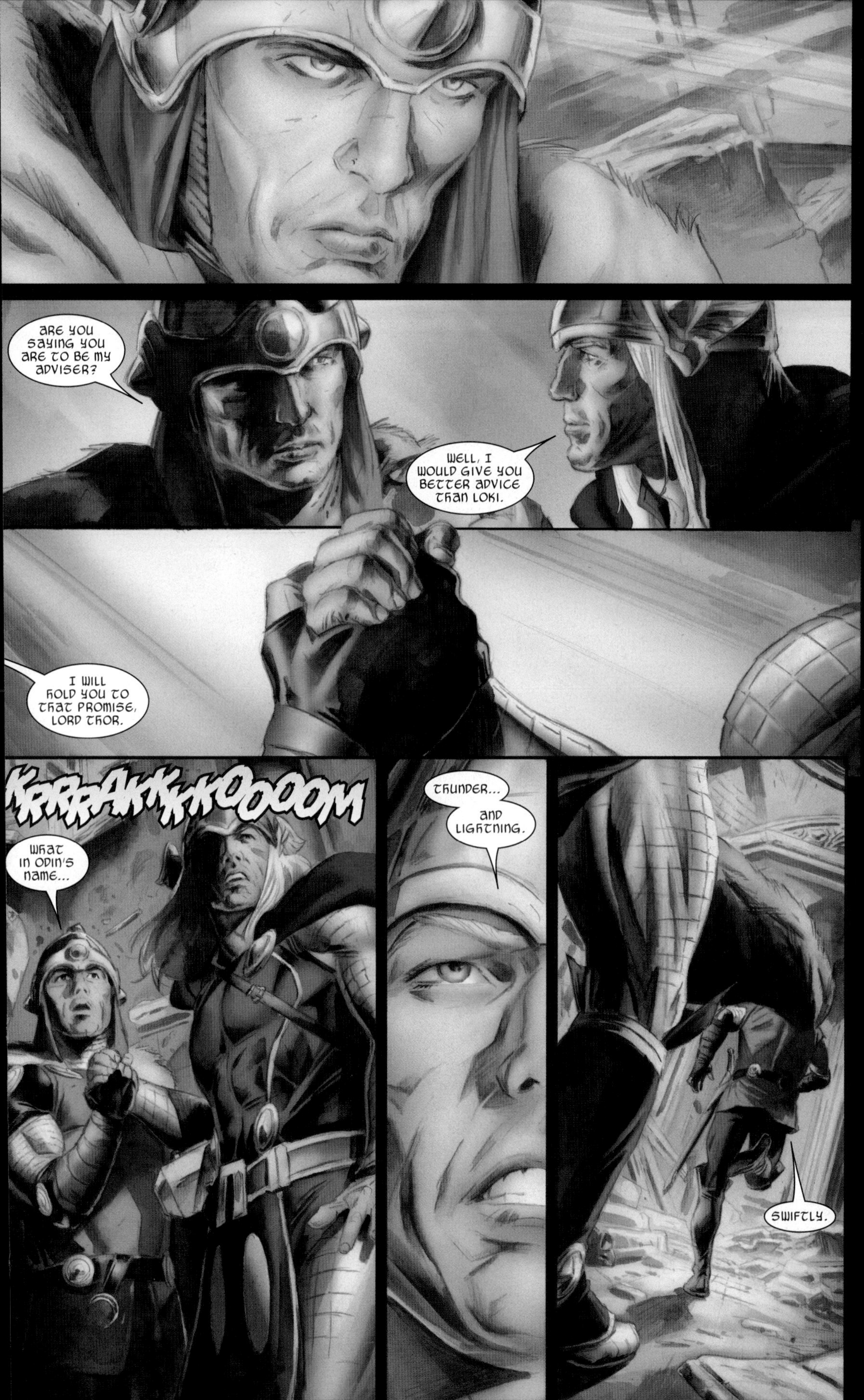
ARE YOU SAYING YOU ARE TO BE MY ADVISER?
WELL, I WOULD GIVE YOU BETTER ADVICE THAN LOKI.
I WILL HOLD YOU TO THAT PROMISE, LORD THOR.
KRRRAKKKKOOOOOM
WHAT IN ODIN'S NAME...
THUNDER...
AND LIGHTNING.
SWIFTLY.

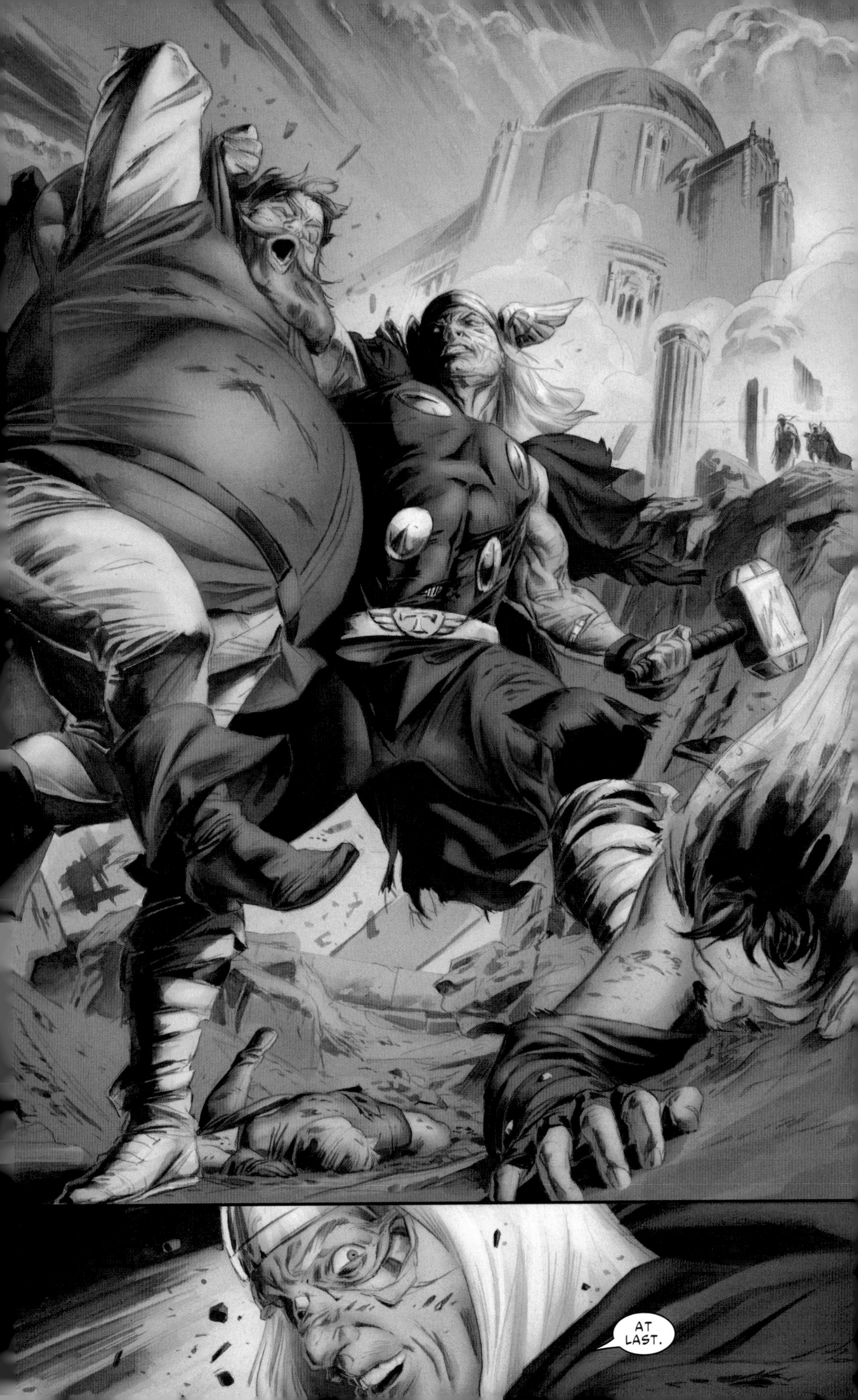
AT LAST.

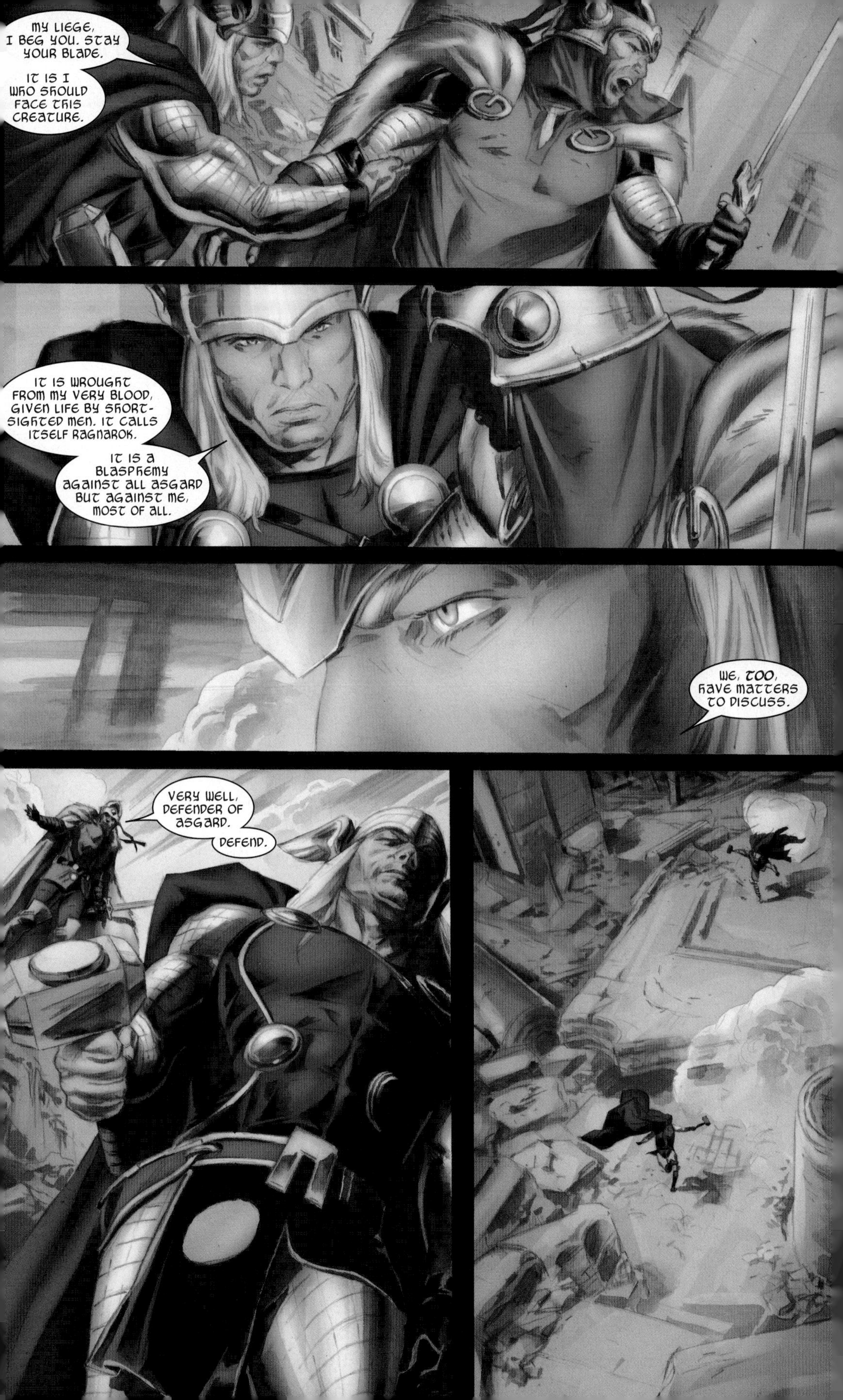
MY LIEGE, I BEG YOU. STAY YOUR BLADE.
IT IS I WHO SHOULD FACE THIS CREATURE.
IT IS WROUGHT FROM MY VERY BLOOD, GIVEN LIFE BY SHORT-SIGHTED MEN. IT CALLS ITSELF RAGNAROK.
IT IS A BLASPHEMY AGAINST ALL ASGARD BUT AGAINST ME, MOST OF ALL.
WE, TOO, HAVE MATTERS TO DISCUSS.
VERY WELL, DEFENDER OF ASGARD.
DEFEND.

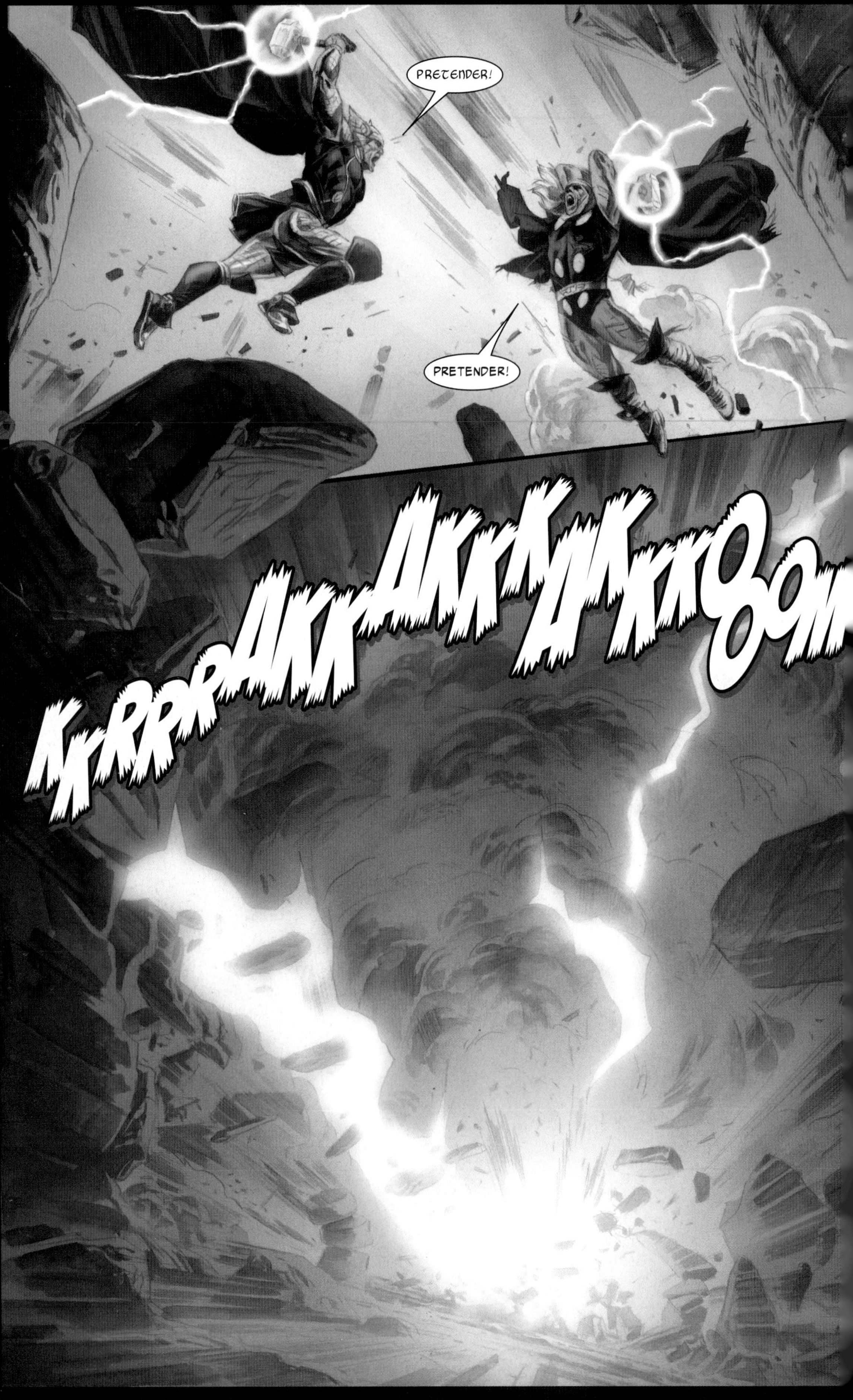
PRETENDER!
PRETENDER!
KKRRRRAKKKAKKKKAKKKKOOOM

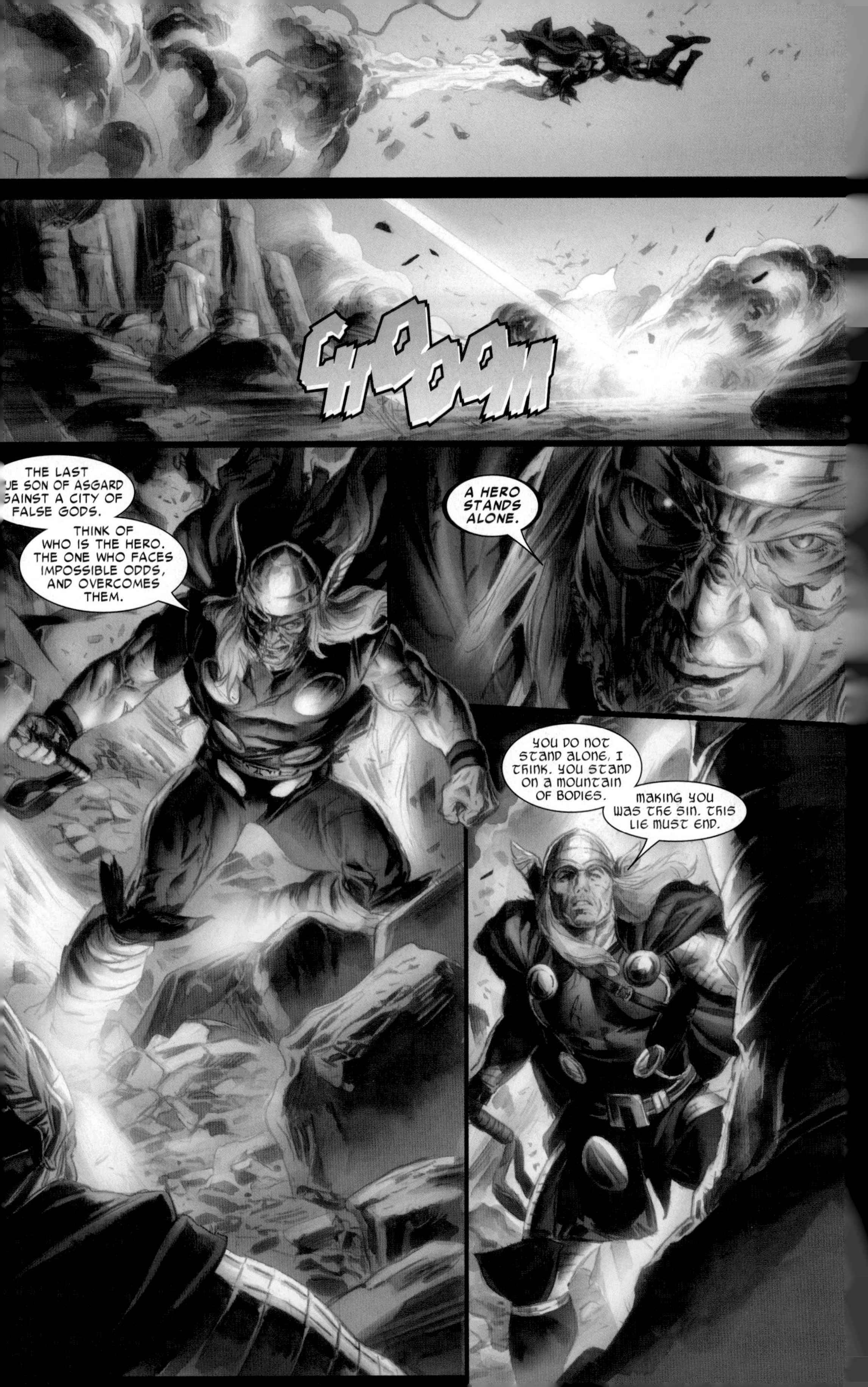
CHOOOM
THE LAST UE SON OF ASGARD GAINST A CITY OF FALSE GODS.
THINK OF WHO IS THE HERO. THE ONE WHO FACES IMPOSSIBLE ODDS, AND OVERCOMES THEM.
A HERO STANDS ALONE.
YOU DO NOT STAND ALONE, I THINK. YOU STAND ON A MOUNTAIN OF BODIES.
MAKING YOU WAS THE SIN. THIS LIE MUST END.

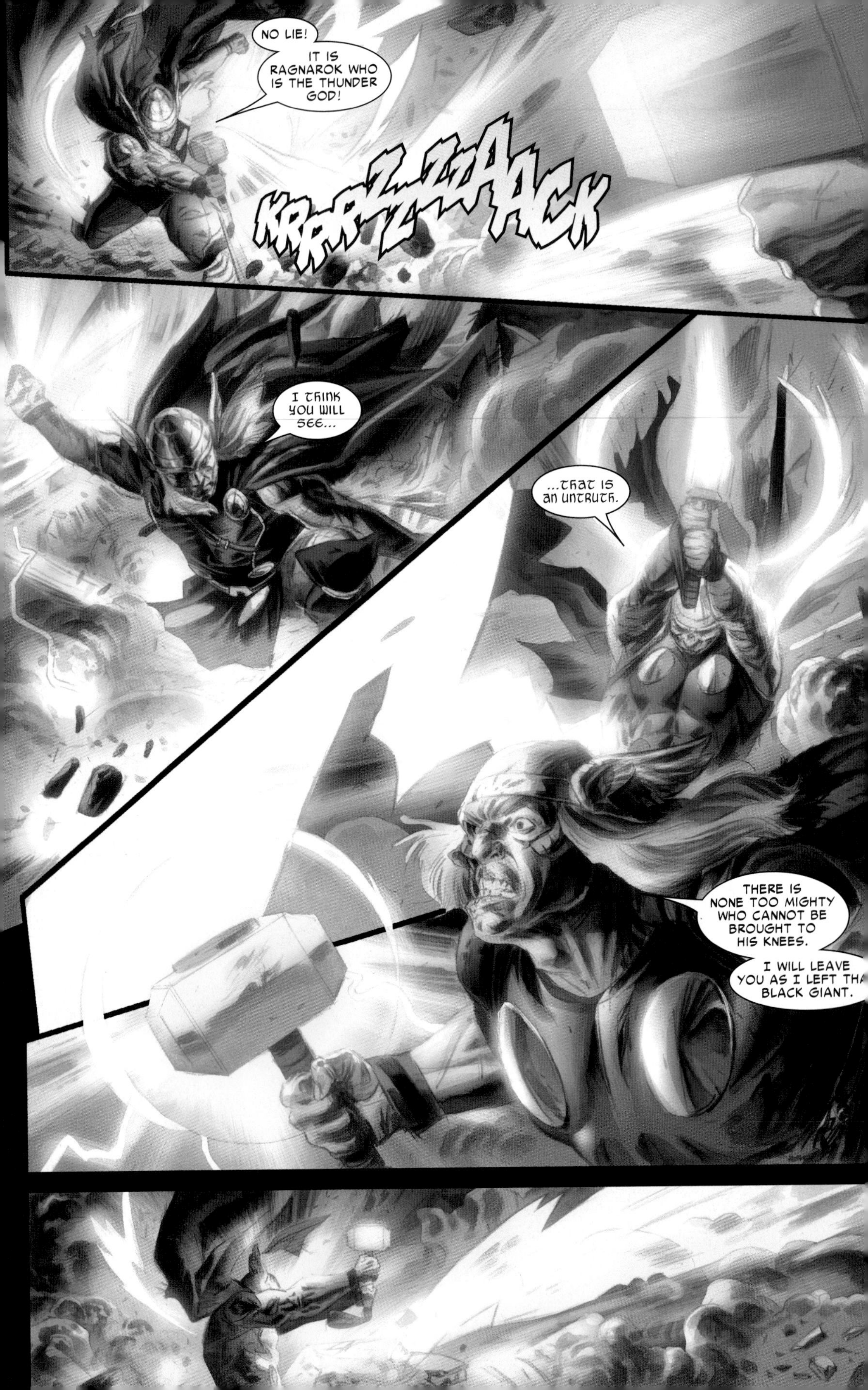
NO LIE!
IT IS RAGNAROK WHO IS THE THUNDER GOD!
KRRRZZZAACK
I THINK YOU WILL SEE...
...THAT IS AN UNTRUTH.
THERE IS NONE TOO MIGHTY WHO CANNOT BE BROUGHT TO HIS KNEES.
I WILL LEAVE YOU AS I LEFT THA BLACK GIANT.

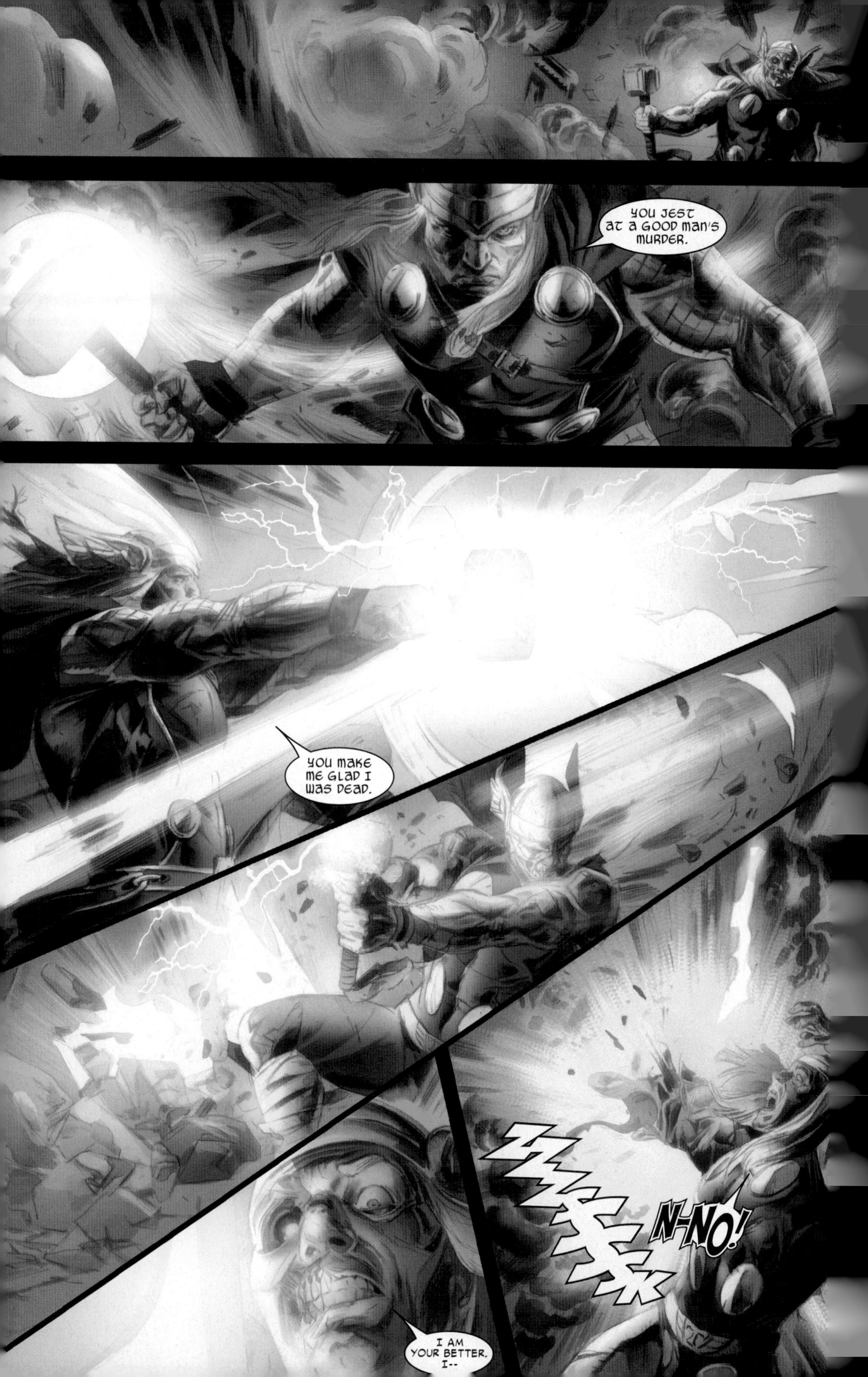
YOU JEST AT A GOOD MAN'S MURDER.
YOU MAKE ME GLAD I WAS DEAD.
ZZZZZZK
N-NO!
I AM YOUR BETTER. I--

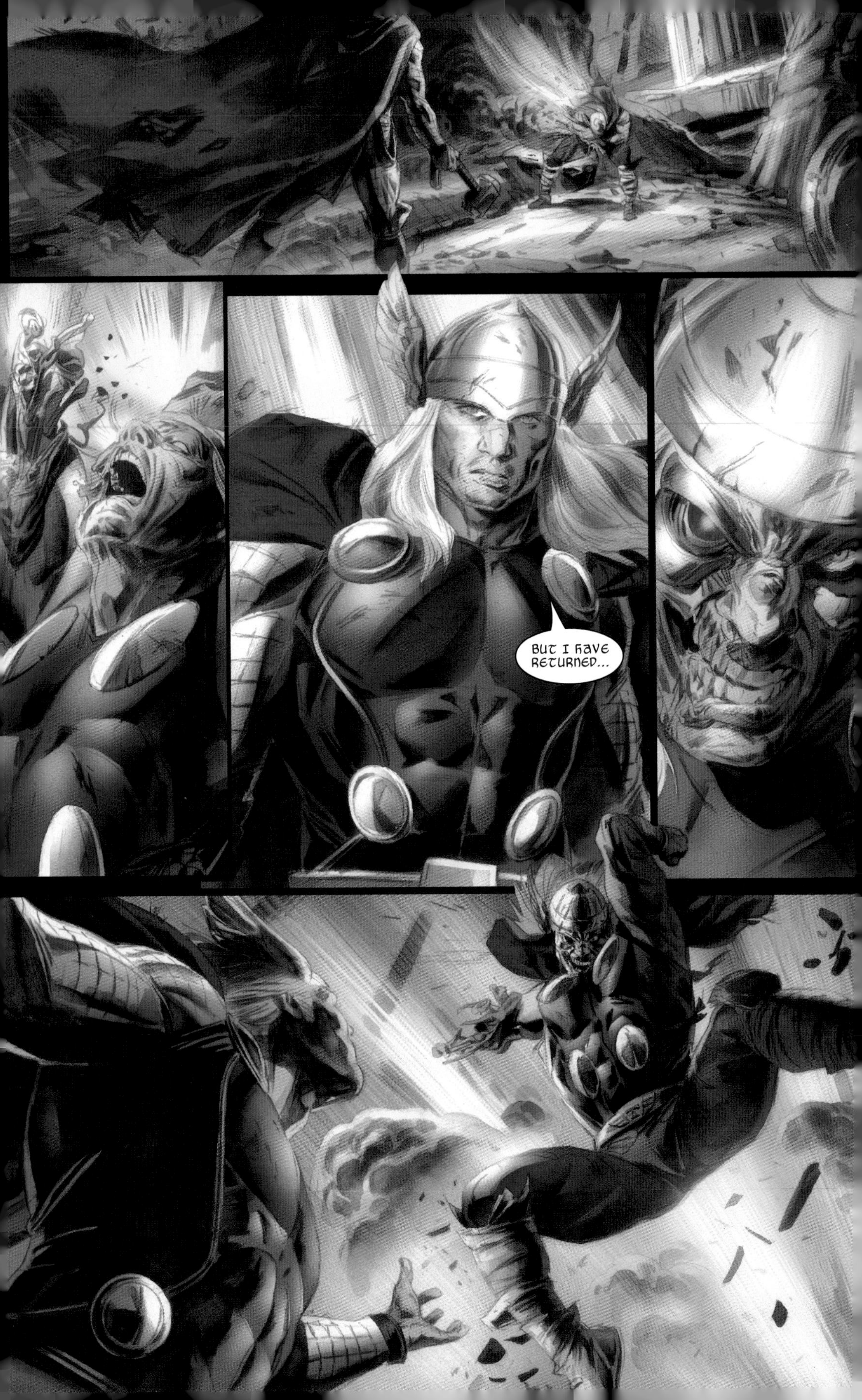
BUT I HAVE RETURNED...

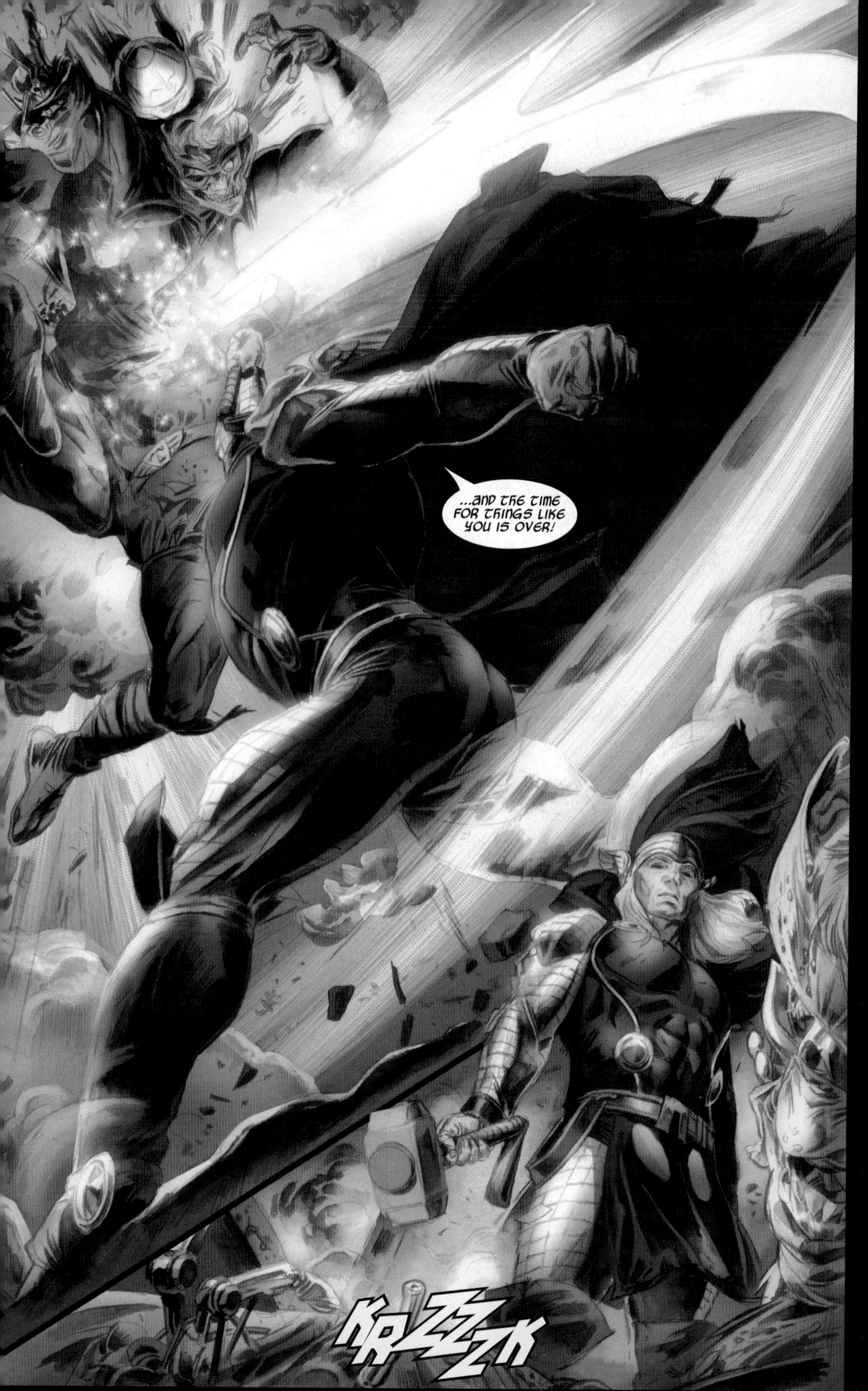
...AND THE TIME FOR THINGS LIKE YOU IS OVER!
KRZZZK

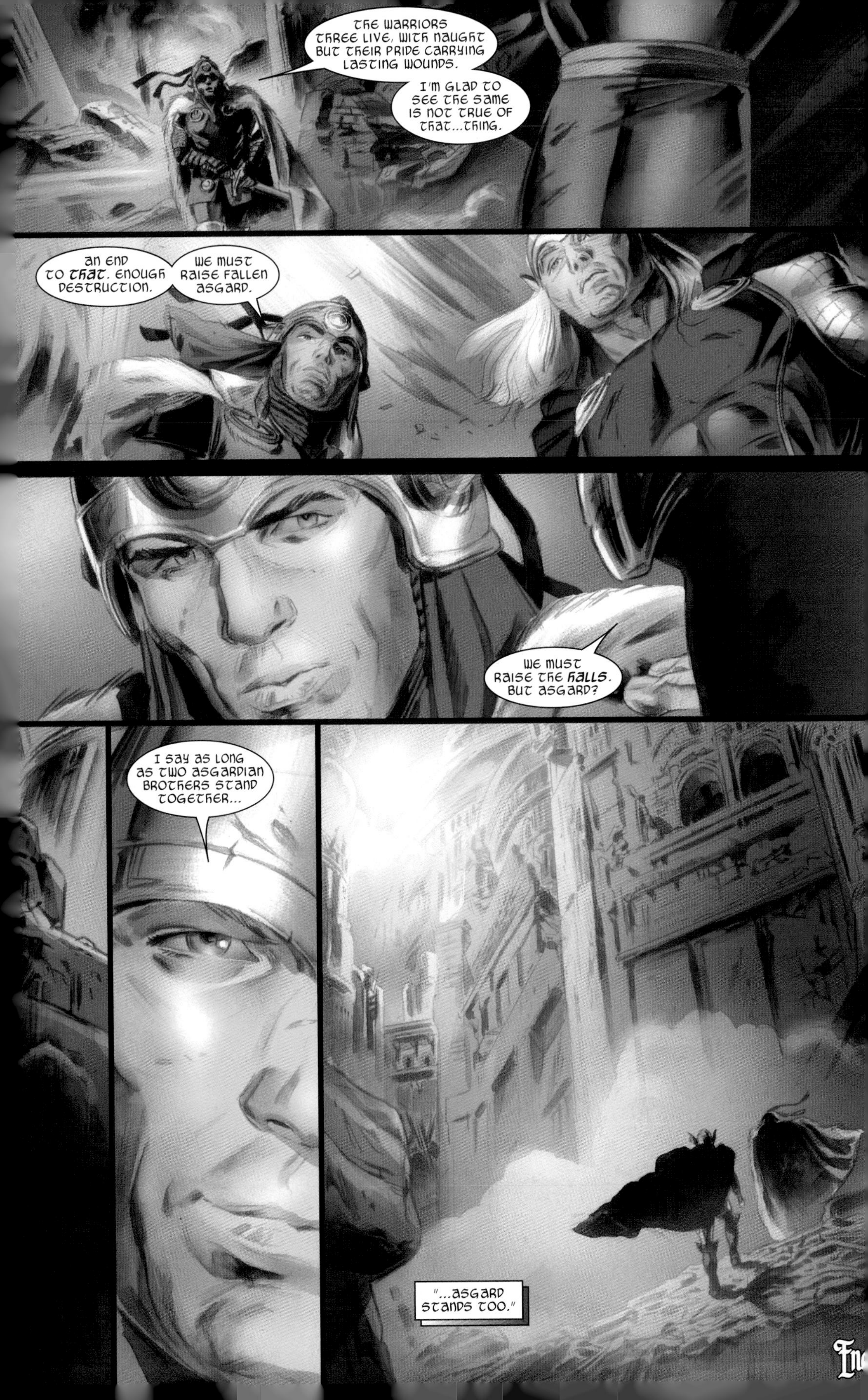
THE WARRIORS THREE LIVE, WITH NAUGHT BUT THEIR PRIDE CARRYING LASTING WOUNDS.
I'M GLAD TO SEE THE SAME IS NOT TRUE OF THAT...THING.
AN END TO *THAT*. ENOUGH DESTRUCTION.
WE MUST RAISE FALLEN ASGARD.
WE MUST RAISE THE **HALLS**. BUT ASGARD?
I SAY AS LONG AS TWO ASGARDIAN BROTHERS STAND TOGETHER...
"...ASGARD STANDS TOO."

THOR #609 IRON MAN BY DESIGN VARIANT

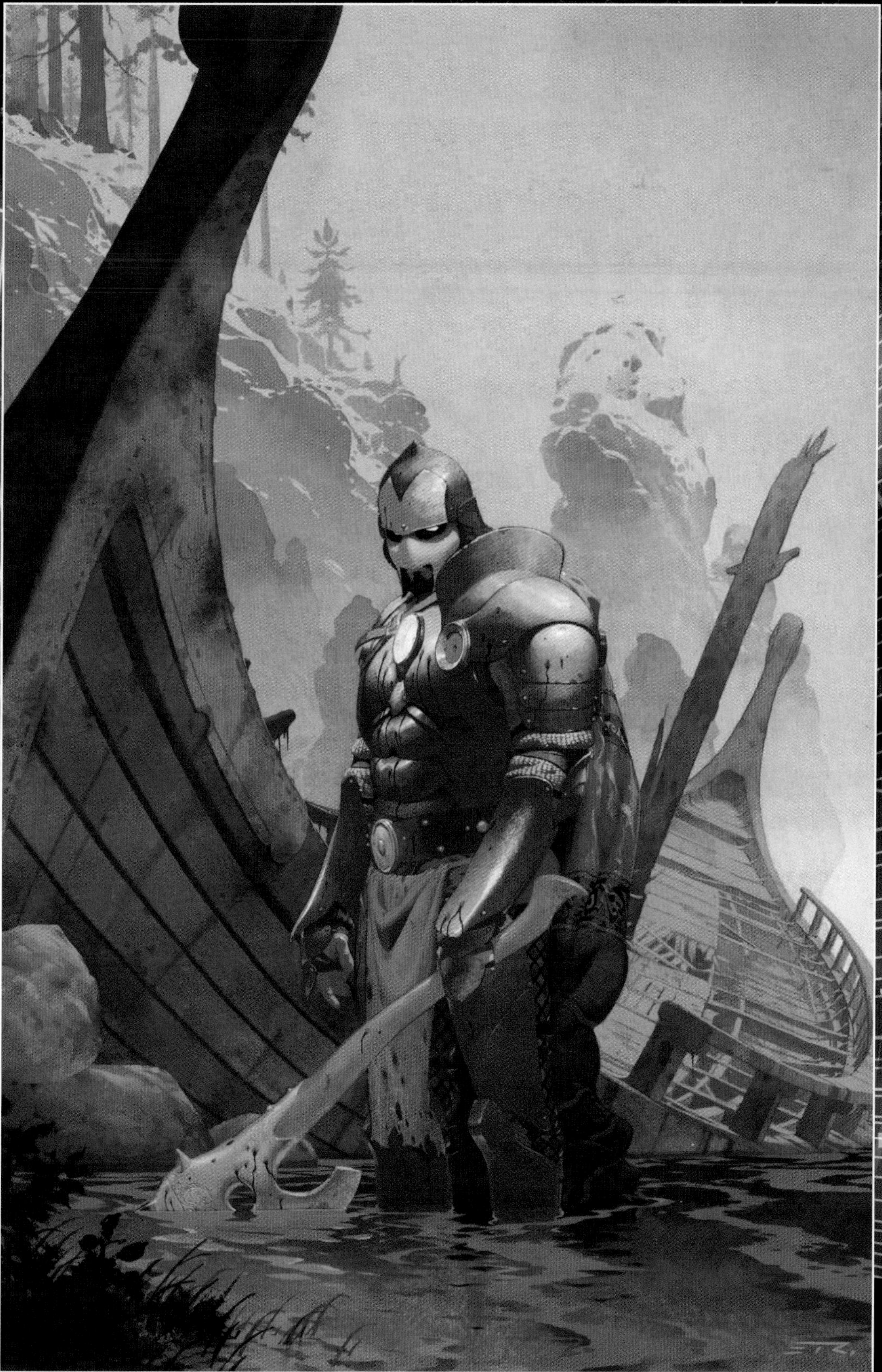

BY **ESAD RIBIC**

THOR #610 HEROIC AGE VARIANT

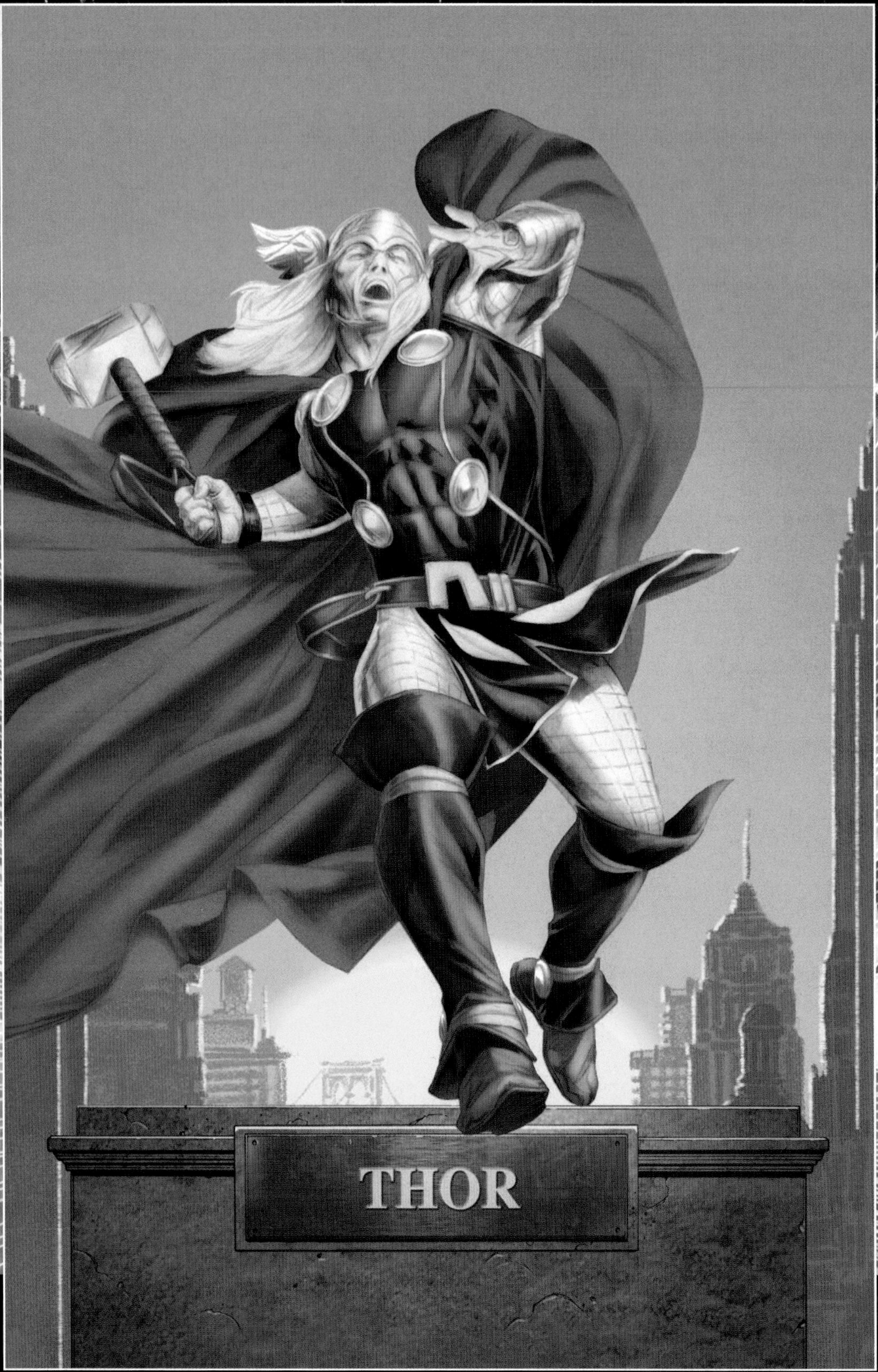
THOR

BY **DOUG BRAITHWAITE** & **ANDY TROY**

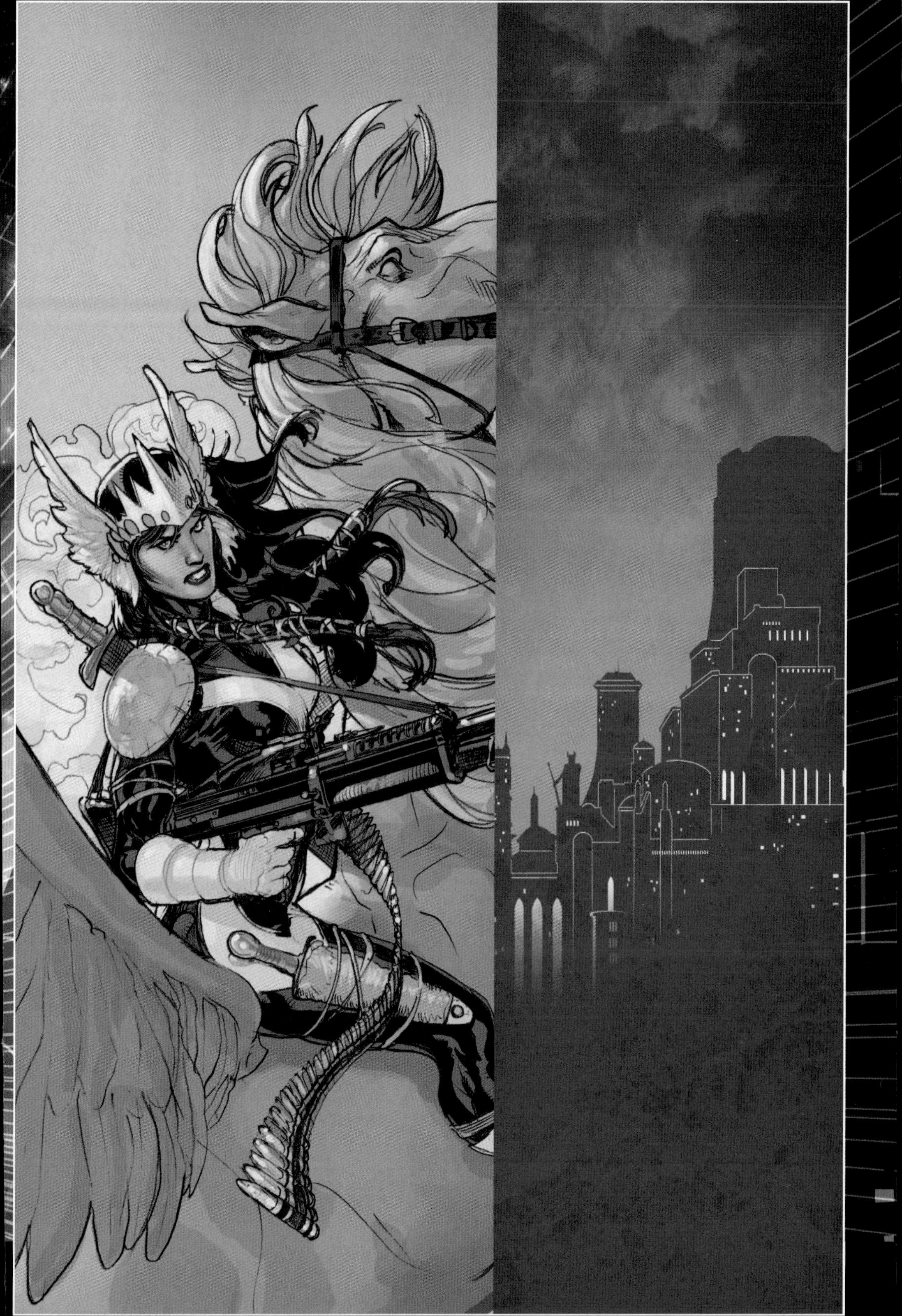

PREVIOUSLY IN

NEW MUTANTS

When Norman Obsorn, leader of the Dark Avengers, waged war on the X-Men, team leader Cyclops created a plan for fighting back. A key component of his strategy involved Dani Moonstar—depowered mutant and former Asgardian Valkyrie. Moonstar went to Hela, Asgardian goddess of death, and made a bargain with her: Hela would imbue Moonstar with the power of a Valkyrie once more so that she could repel the Dark Avengers' attack on the X-Men, but in turn, Moonstar would be indebted to the goddess.

"HEL'S VALKYRIE"

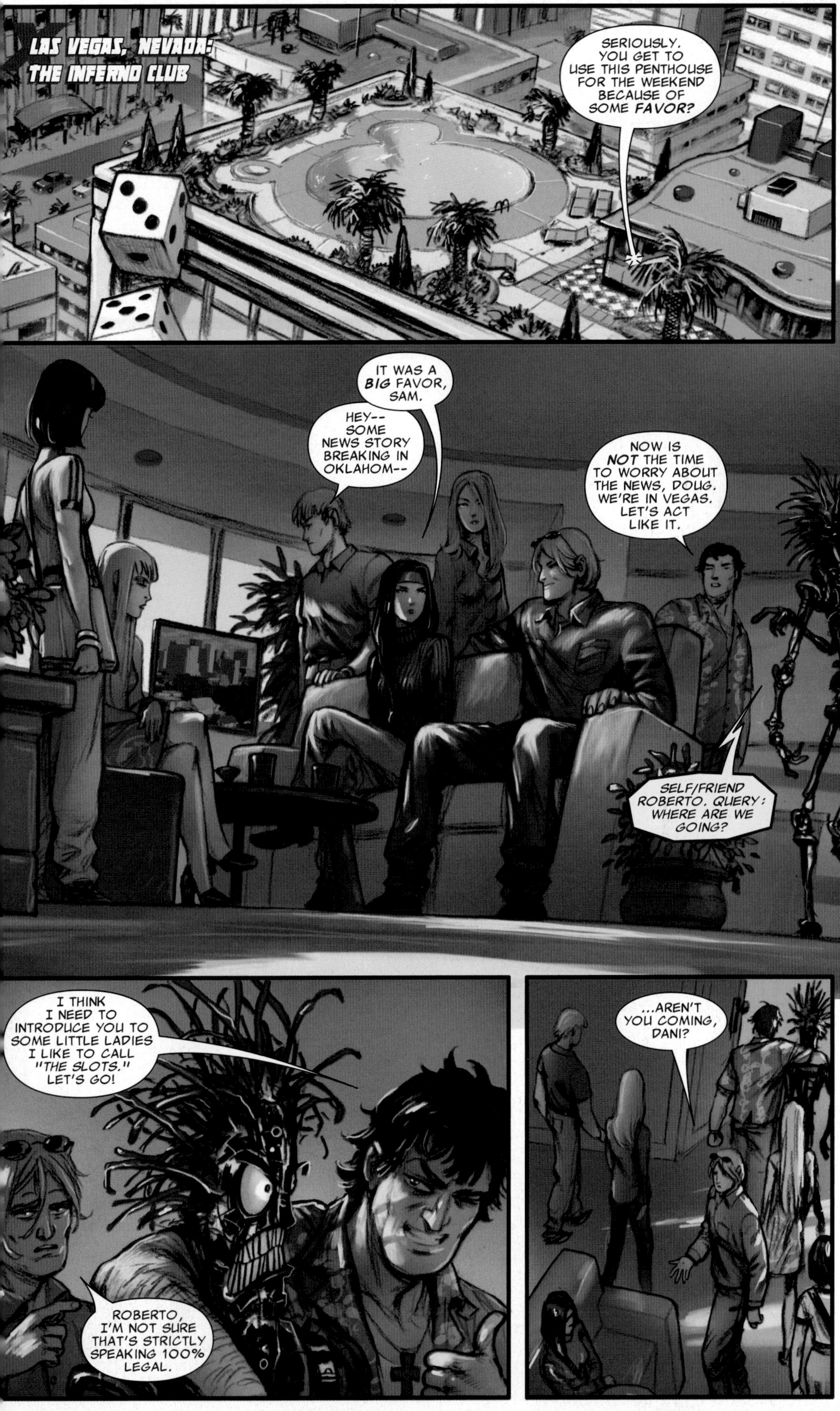
LAS VEGAS, NEVADA: THE INFERNO CLUB
SERIOUSLY. YOU GET TO USE THIS PENTHOUSE FOR THE WEEKEND BECAUSE OF SOME FAVOR?
IT WAS A BIG FAVOR, SAM.
HEY-- SOME NEWS STORY BREAKING IN OKLAHOM--
NOW IS NOT THE TIME TO WORRY ABOUT THE NEWS, DOUG. WE'RE IN VEGAS. LET'S ACT LIKE IT.
SELF/FRIEND ROBERTO. QUERY: WHERE ARE WE GOING?
I THINK I NEED TO INTRODUCE YOU TO SOME LITTLE LADIES I LIKE TO CALL "THE SLOTS." LET'S GO!
ROBERTO, I'M NOT SURE THAT'S STRICTLY SPEAKING 100% LEGAL.
...AREN'T YOU COMING, DANI?

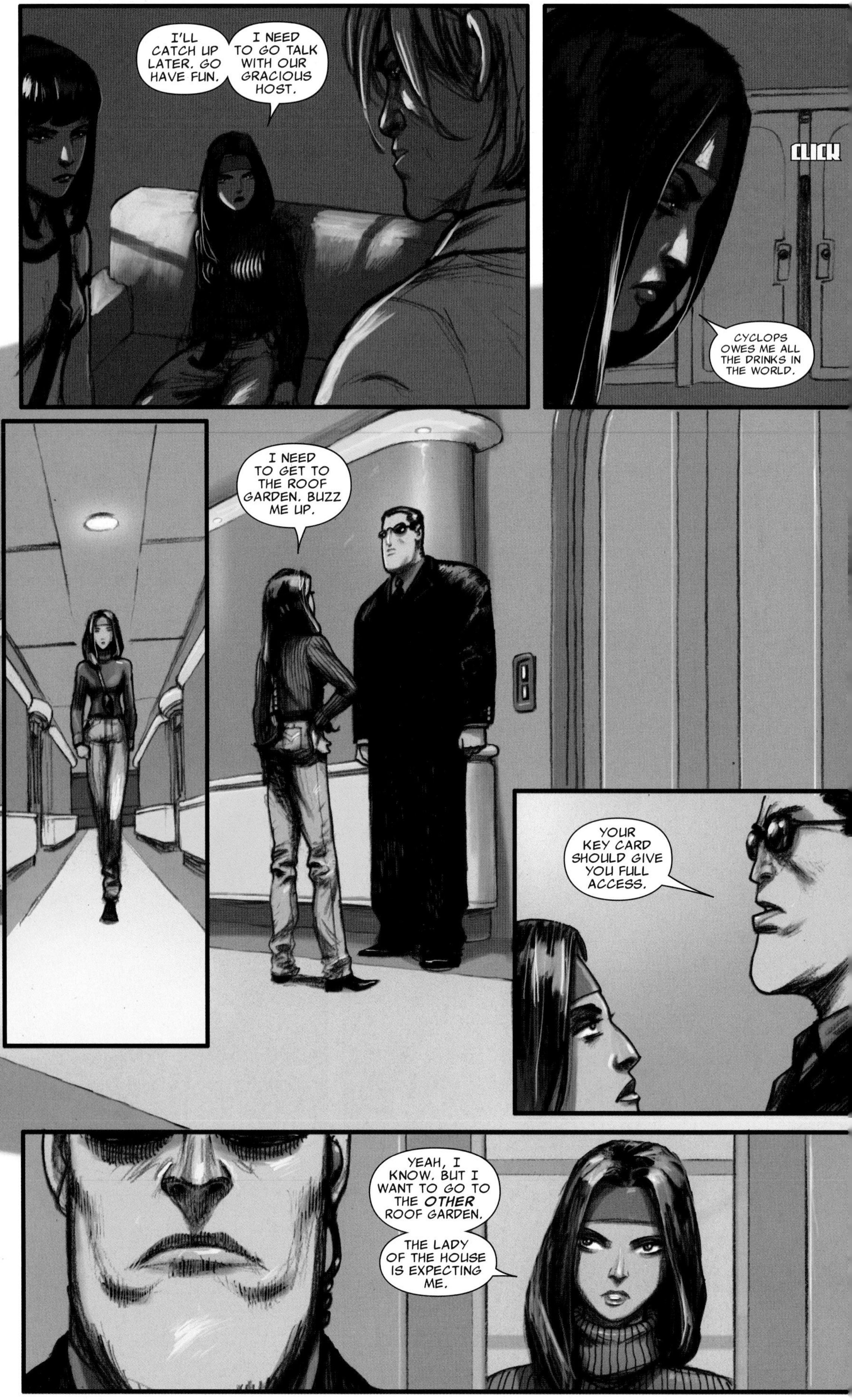
I'LL CATCH UP LATER. GO HAVE FUN.
I NEED TO GO TALK WITH OUR GRACIOUS HOST.
CLICK
CYCLOPS OWES ME ALL THE DRINKS IN THE WORLD.
I NEED TO GET TO THE ROOF GARDEN. BUZZ ME UP.
YOUR KEY CARD SHOULD GIVE YOU FULL ACCESS.
YEAH, I KNOW. BUT I WANT TO GO TO THE *OTHER* ROOF GARDEN.
THE LADY OF THE HOUSE IS EXPECTING ME.

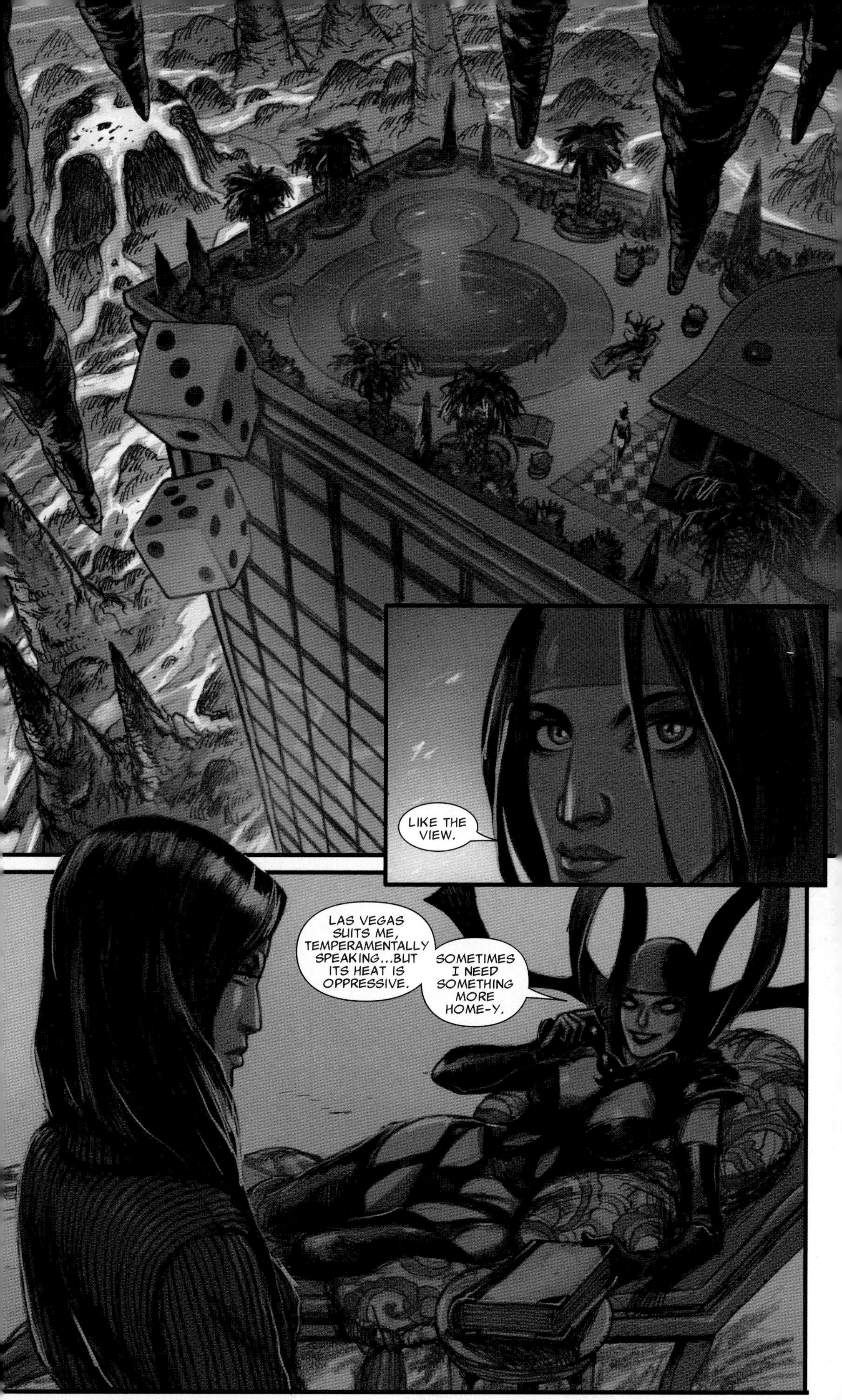
LIKE THE VIEW.
LAS VEGAS SUITS ME, TEMPERAMENTALLY SPEAKING...BUT ITS HEAT IS OPPRESSIVE.
SOMETIMES I NEED SOMETHING MORE HOME-Y.

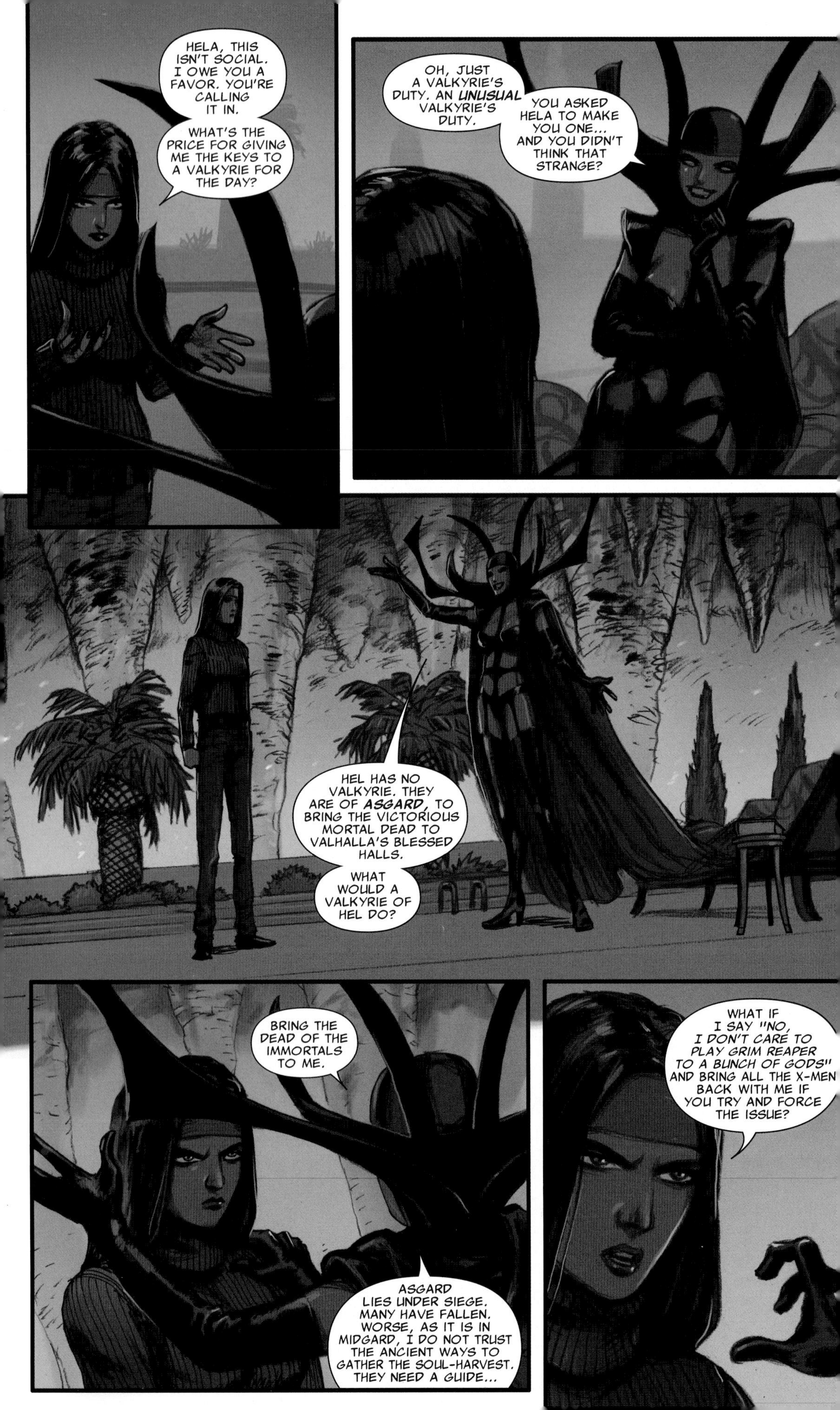
HELA, THIS ISN'T SOCIAL. I OWE YOU A FAVOR. YOU'RE CALLING IT IN.
WHAT'S THE PRICE FOR GIVING ME THE KEYS TO A VALKYRIE FOR THE DAY?
OH, JUST A VALKYRIE'S DUTY. AN UNUSUAL VALKYRIE'S DUTY.
YOU ASKED HELA TO MAKE YOU ONE... AND YOU DIDN'T THINK THAT STRANGE?
HEL HAS NO VALKYRIE. THEY ARE OF ASGARD, TO BRING THE VICTORIOUS MORTAL DEAD TO VALHALLA'S BLESSED HALLS.
WHAT WOULD A VALKYRIE OF HEL DO?
BRING THE DEAD OF THE IMMORTALS TO ME.
ASGARD LIES UNDER SIEGE. MANY HAVE FALLEN. WORSE, AS IT IS IN MIDGARD, I DO NOT TRUST THE ANCIENT WAYS TO GATHER THE SOUL-HARVEST. THEY NEED A GUIDE...
WHAT IF I SAY "NO, I DON'T CARE TO PLAY GRIM REAPER TO A BUNCH OF GODS" AND BRING ALL THE X-MEN BACK WITH ME IF YOU TRY AND FORCE THE ISSUE?

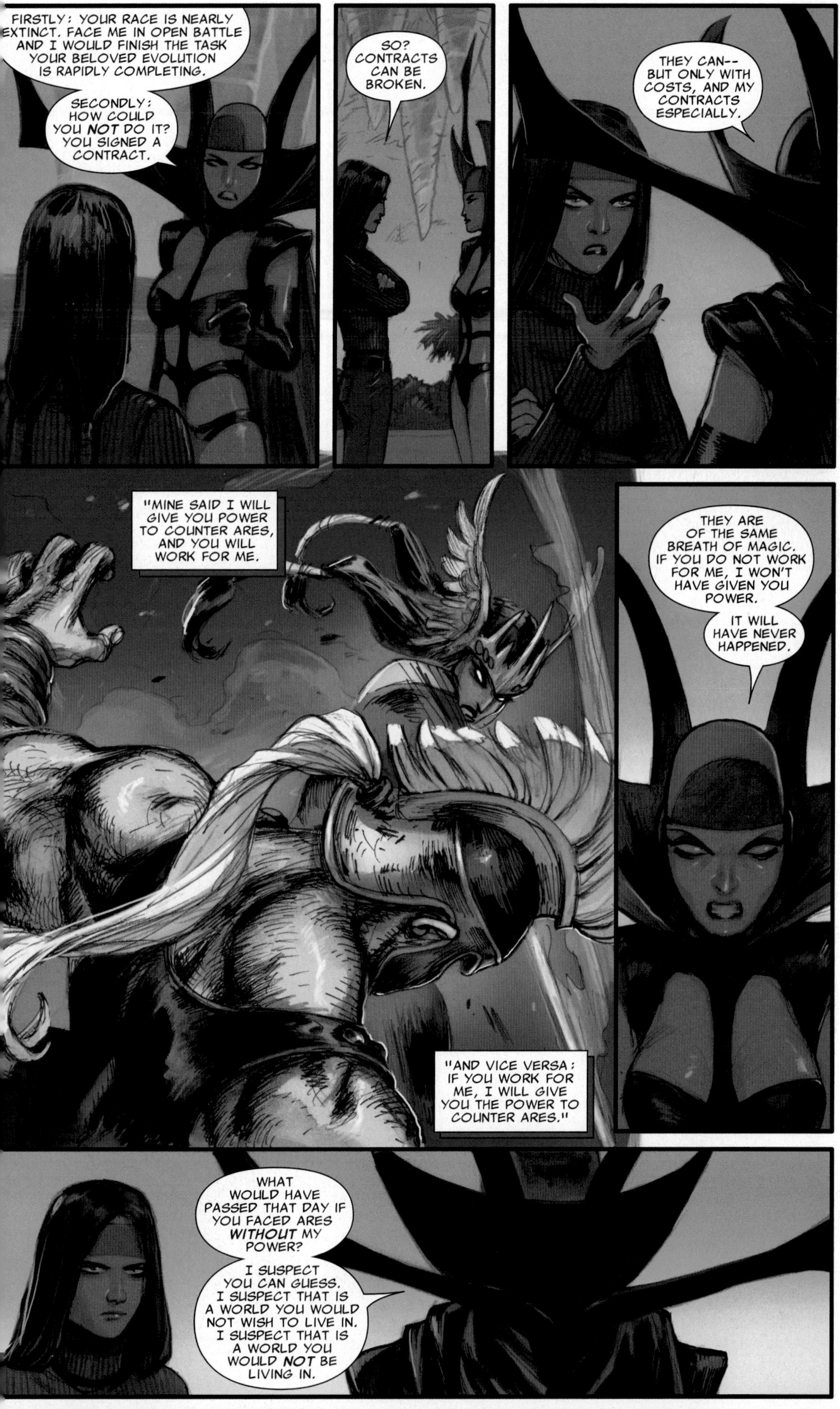
FIRSTLY: YOUR RACE IS NEARLY EXTINCT. FACE ME IN OPEN BATTLE AND I WOULD FINISH THE TASK YOUR BELOVED EVOLUTION IS RAPIDLY COMPLETING.
SECONDLY: HOW COULD YOU **NOT** DO IT? YOU SIGNED A CONTRACT.
SO? CONTRACTS CAN BE BROKEN.
THEY CAN-- BUT ONLY WITH COSTS, AND MY CONTRACTS ESPECIALLY.
"MINE SAID I WILL GIVE YOU POWER TO COUNTER ARES, AND YOU WILL WORK FOR ME.
THEY ARE OF THE SAME BREATH OF MAGIC. IF YOU DO NOT WORK FOR ME, I WON'T HAVE GIVEN YOU POWER.
IT WILL HAVE NEVER HAPPENED.
"AND VICE VERSA: IF YOU WORK FOR ME, I WILL GIVE YOU THE POWER TO COUNTER ARES."
WHAT WOULD HAVE PASSED THAT DAY IF YOU FACED ARES **WITHOUT** MY POWER?
I SUSPECT YOU CAN GUESS. I SUSPECT THAT IS A WORLD YOU WOULD NOT WISH TO LIVE IN. I SUSPECT THAT IS A WORLD YOU WOULD **NOT** BE LIVING IN.

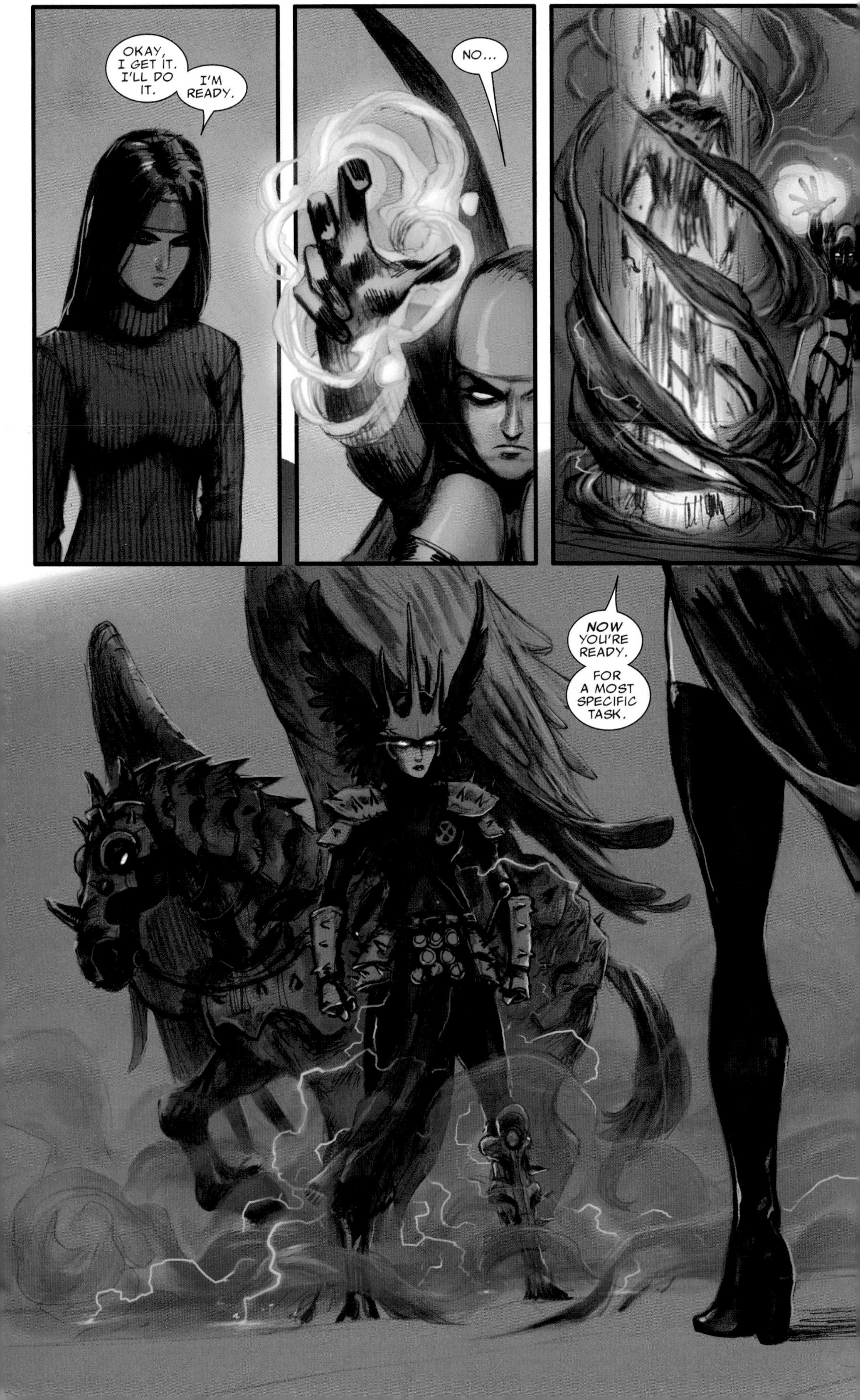

OKAY, I GET IT. I'LL DO IT.
I'M READY.
NO...
NOW YOU'RE READY.
FOR A MOST SPECIFIC TASK.

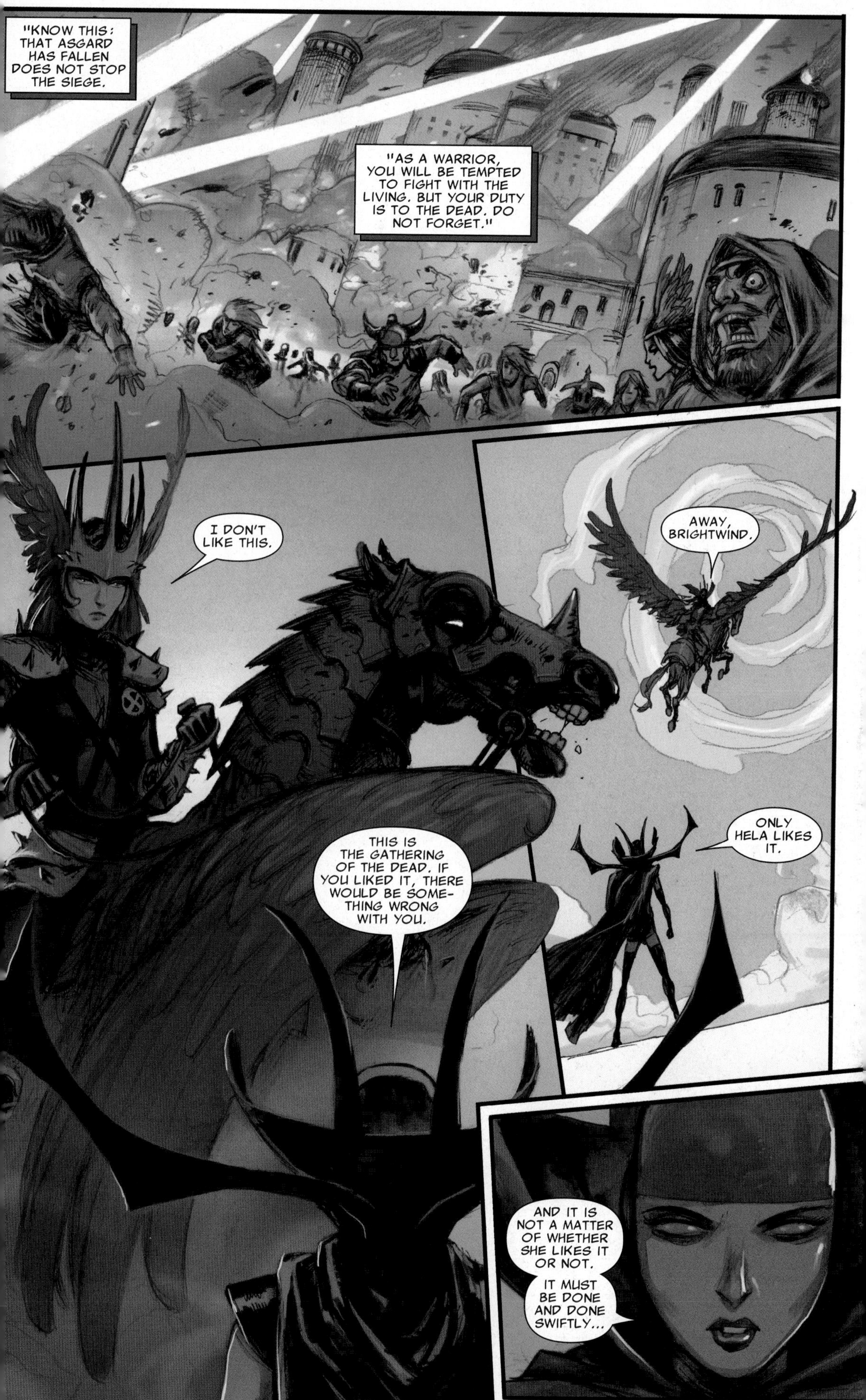
"KNOW THIS: THAT ASGARD HAS FALLEN DOES NOT STOP THE SIEGE.
"AS A WARRIOR, YOU WILL BE TEMPTED TO FIGHT WITH THE LIVING. BUT YOUR DUTY IS TO THE DEAD. DO NOT FORGET."
I DON'T LIKE THIS.
THIS IS THE GATHERING OF THE DEAD. IF YOU LIKED IT, THERE WOULD BE SOME-THING WRONG WITH YOU.
AWAY, BRIGHTWIND.
ONLY HELA LIKES IT.
AND IT IS NOT A MATTER OF WHETHER SHE LIKES IT OR NOT.
IT MUST BE DONE AND DONE SWIFTLY...

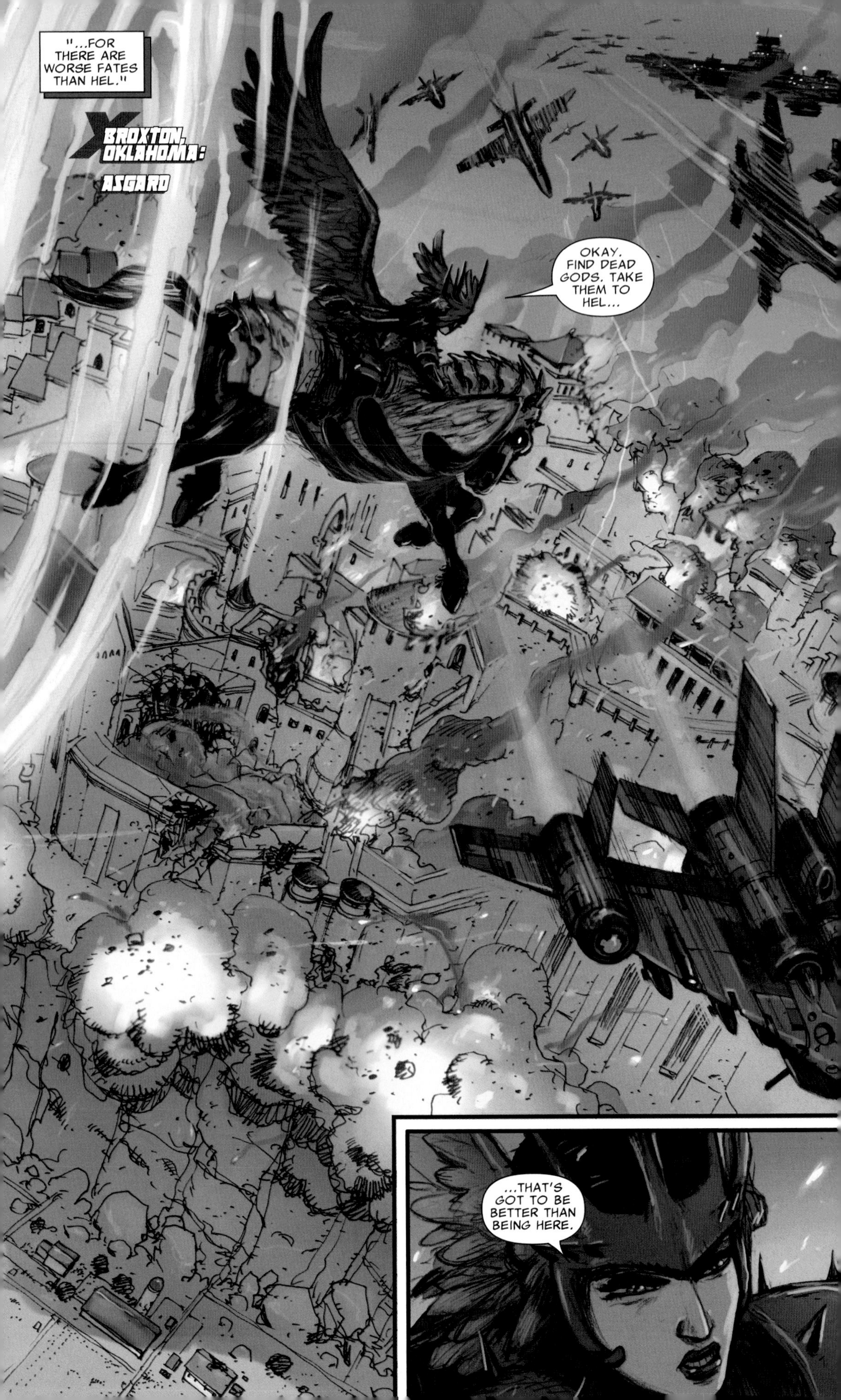
"...FOR THERE ARE WORSE FATES THAN HEL."
BROXTON, OKLAHOMA:
ASGARD
OKAY. FIND DEAD GODS. TAKE THEM TO HEL...
...THAT'S GOT TO BE BETTER THAN BEING HERE.

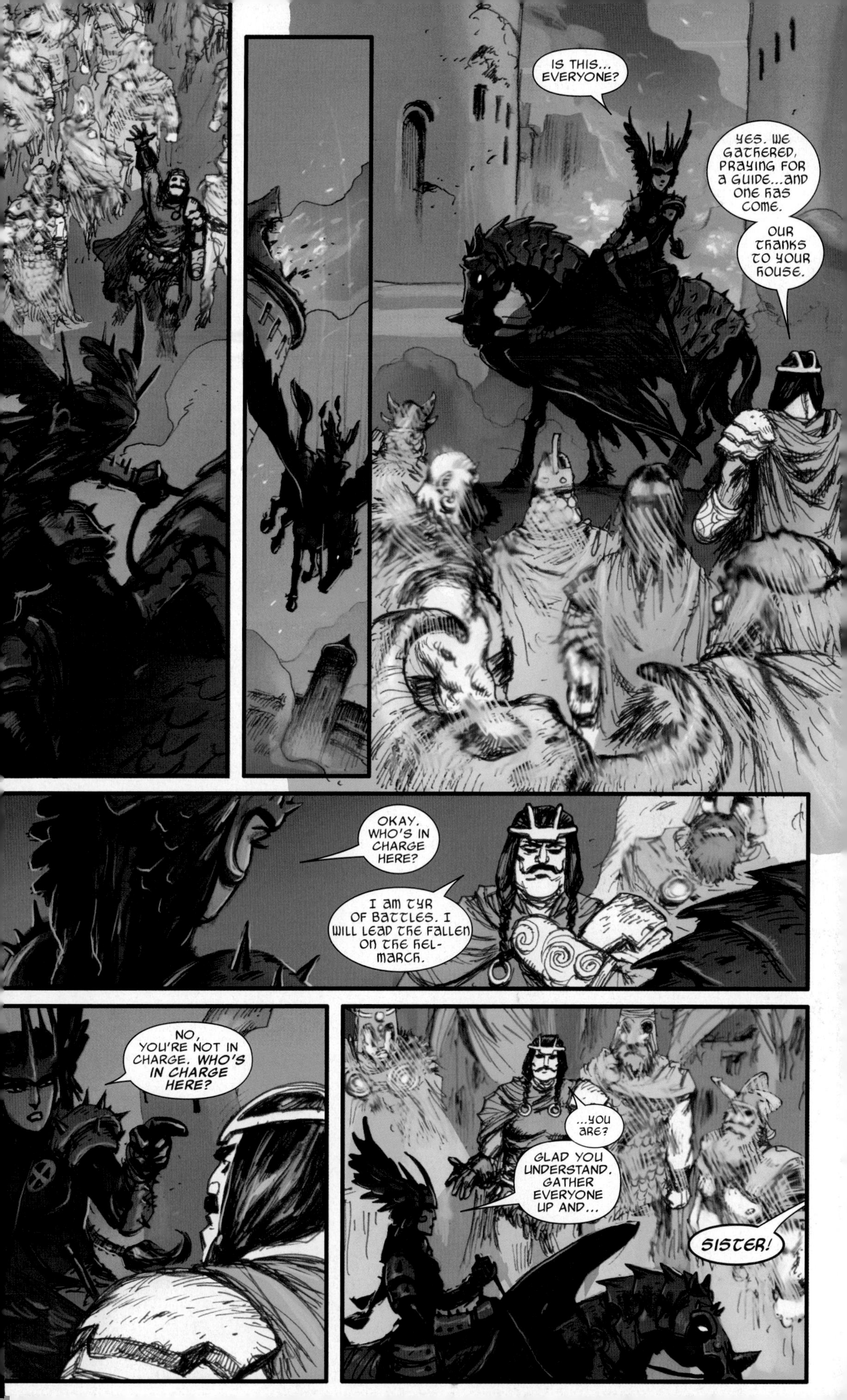
IS THIS... EVERYONE?
YES. WE GATHERED, PRAYING FOR A GUIDE...AND ONE HAS COME.
OUR THANKS TO YOUR HOUSE.
OKAY. WHO'S IN CHARGE HERE?
I AM TYR OF BATTLES. I WILL LEAD THE FALLEN ON THE HEL-MARCH.
NO, YOU'RE NOT IN CHARGE. WHO'S IN CHARGE HERE?
...YOU ARE?
GLAD YOU UNDERSTAND. GATHER EVERYONE UP AND...
SISTER!

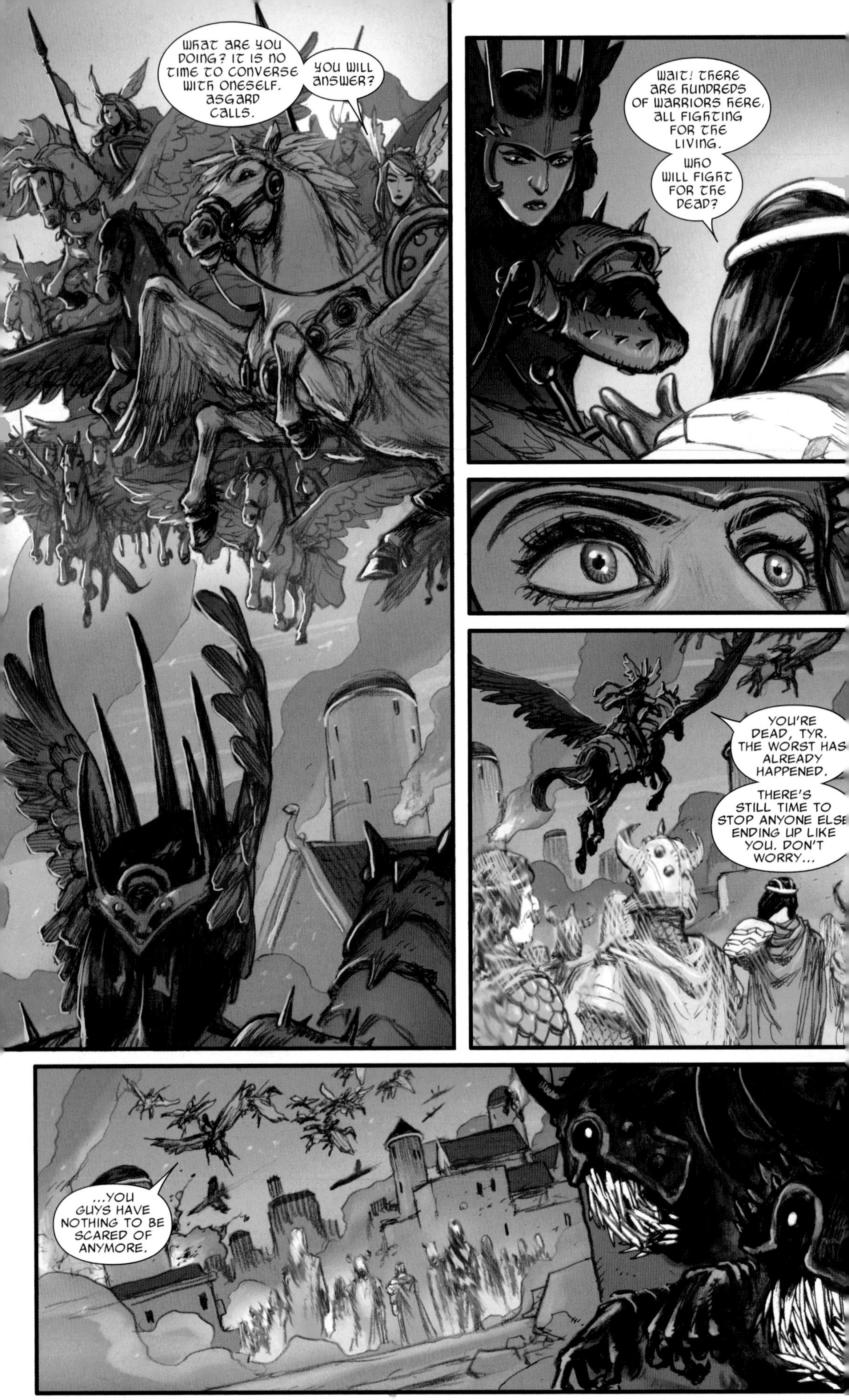
WHAT ARE YOU DOING? IT IS NO TIME TO CONVERSE WITH ONESELF. ASGARD CALLS.
YOU WILL ANSWER?
WAIT! THERE ARE HUNDREDS OF WARRIORS HERE, ALL FIGHTING FOR THE LIVING.
WHO WILL FIGHT FOR THE DEAD?
YOU'RE DEAD, TYR. THE WORST HAS ALREADY HAPPENED.
THERE'S STILL TIME TO STOP ANYONE ELSE ENDING UP LIKE YOU. DON'T WORRY...
...YOU GUYS HAVE NOTHING TO BE SCARED OF ANYMORE.

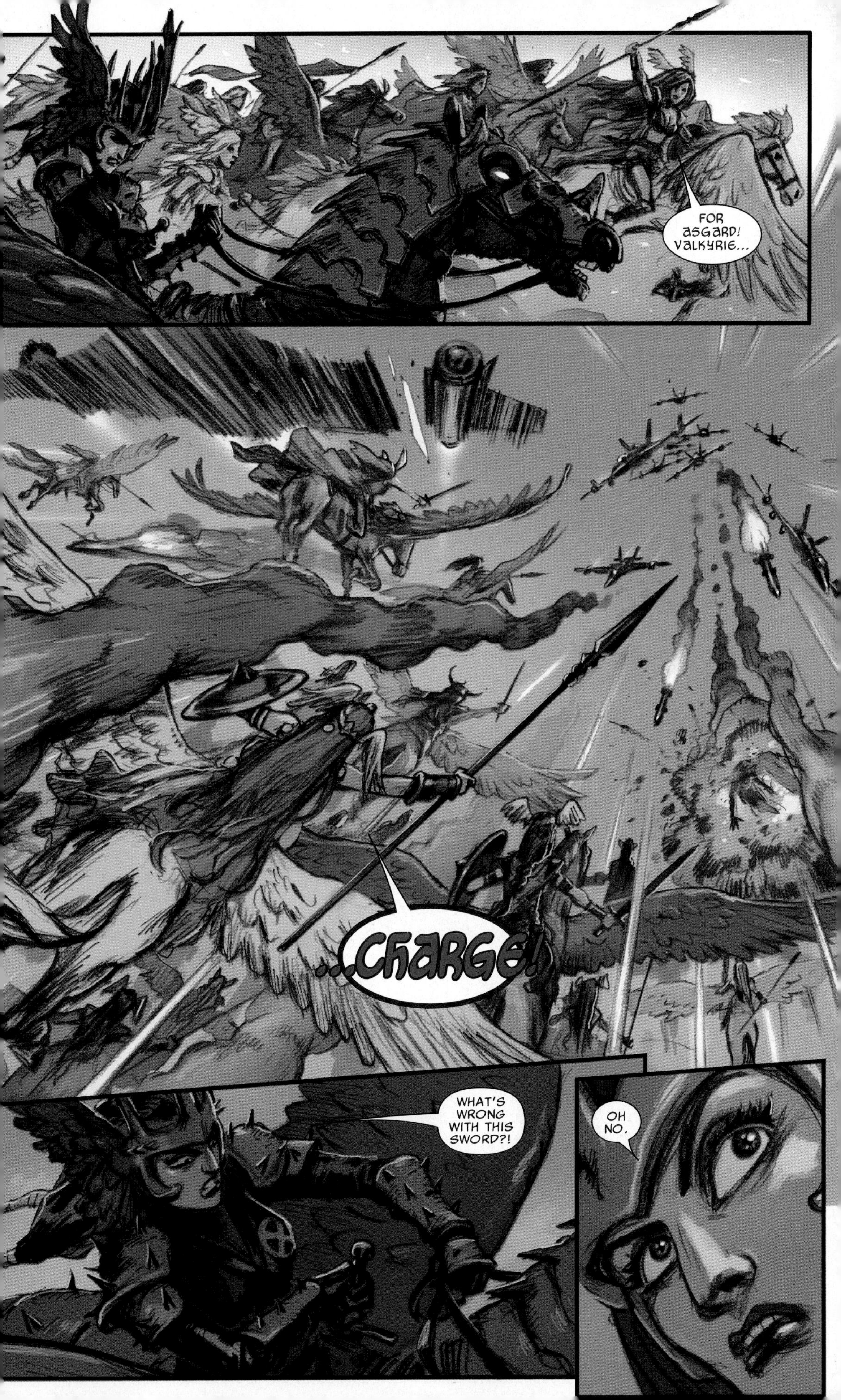
FOR ASGARD! VALKYRIE...
...CHARGE!
WHAT'S WRONG WITH THIS SWORD?!
OH NO.

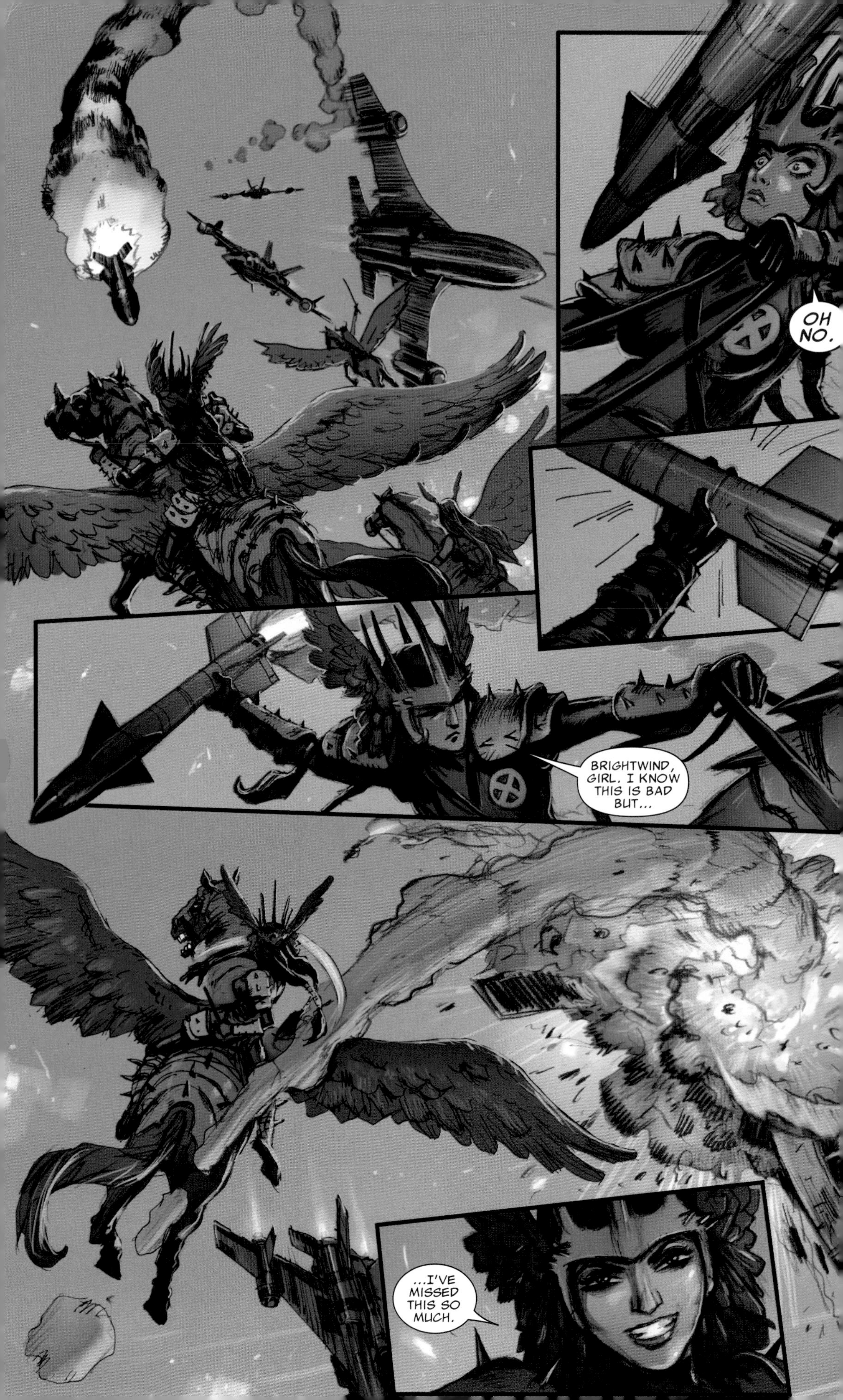

OH NO.
BRIGHTWIND, GIRL. I KNOW THIS IS BAD BUT...
...I'VE MISSED THIS SO MUCH.

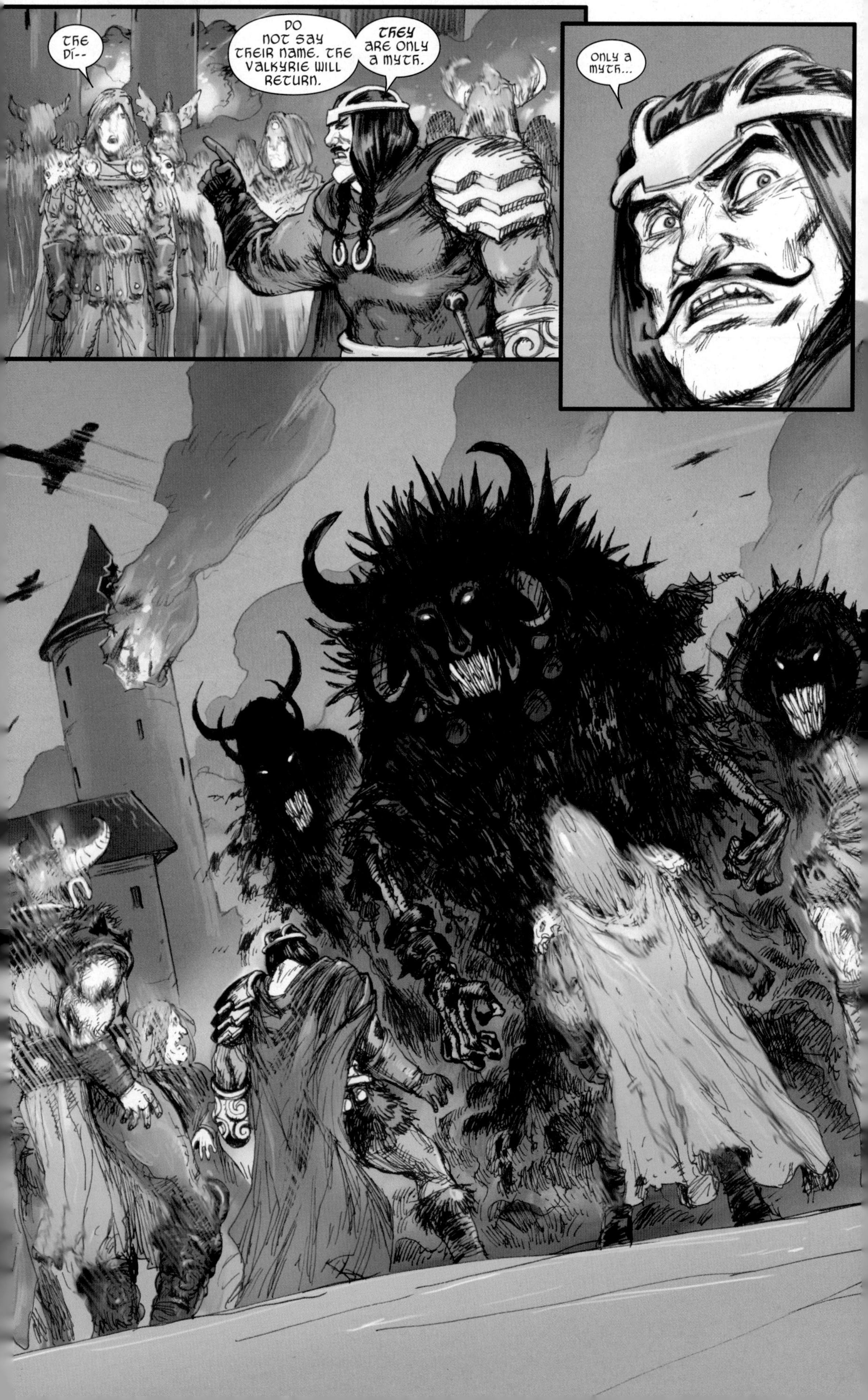
THE DI--
DO NOT SAY THEIR NAME. THE VALKYRIE WILL RETURN.
THEY ARE ONLY A MYTH.
ONLY A MYTH...

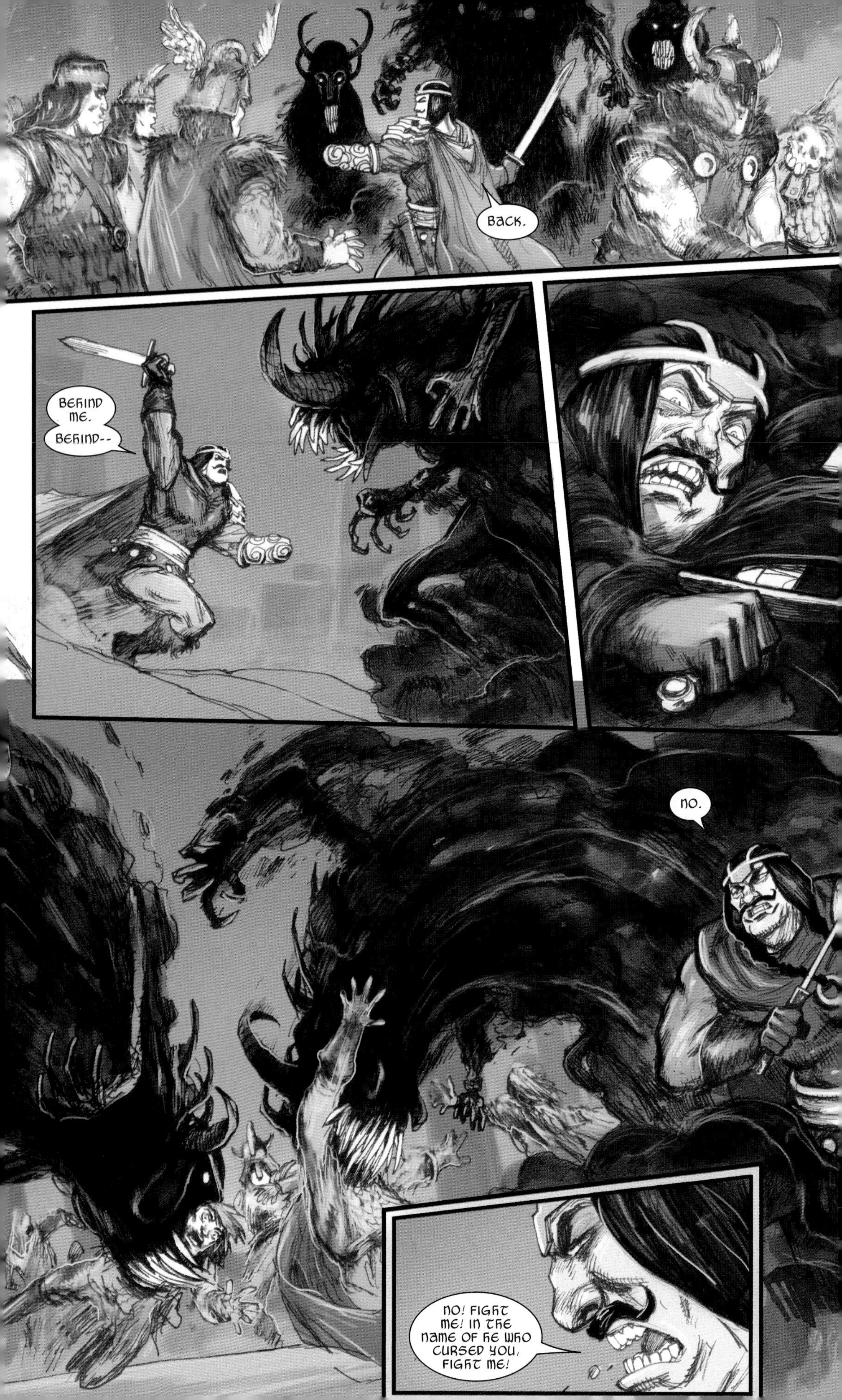
BACK.
BEHIND ME.
BEHIND--
NO.
NO! FIGHT ME! IN THE NAME OF HE WHO CURSED YOU, FIGHT ME!

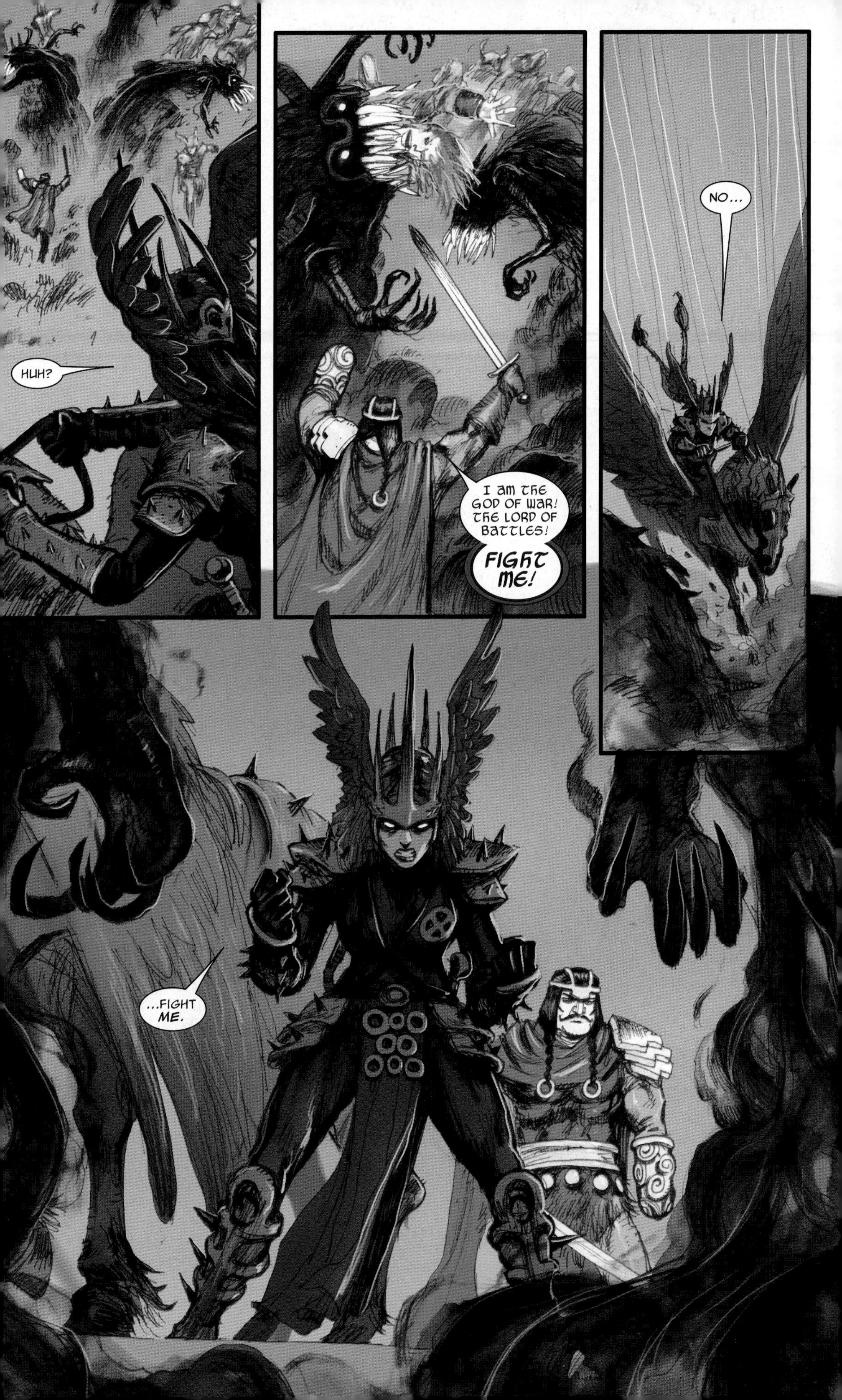
HUH?
I AM THE GOD OF WAR! THE LORD OF BATTLES!
FIGHT ME!
NO...
...FIGHT ME.

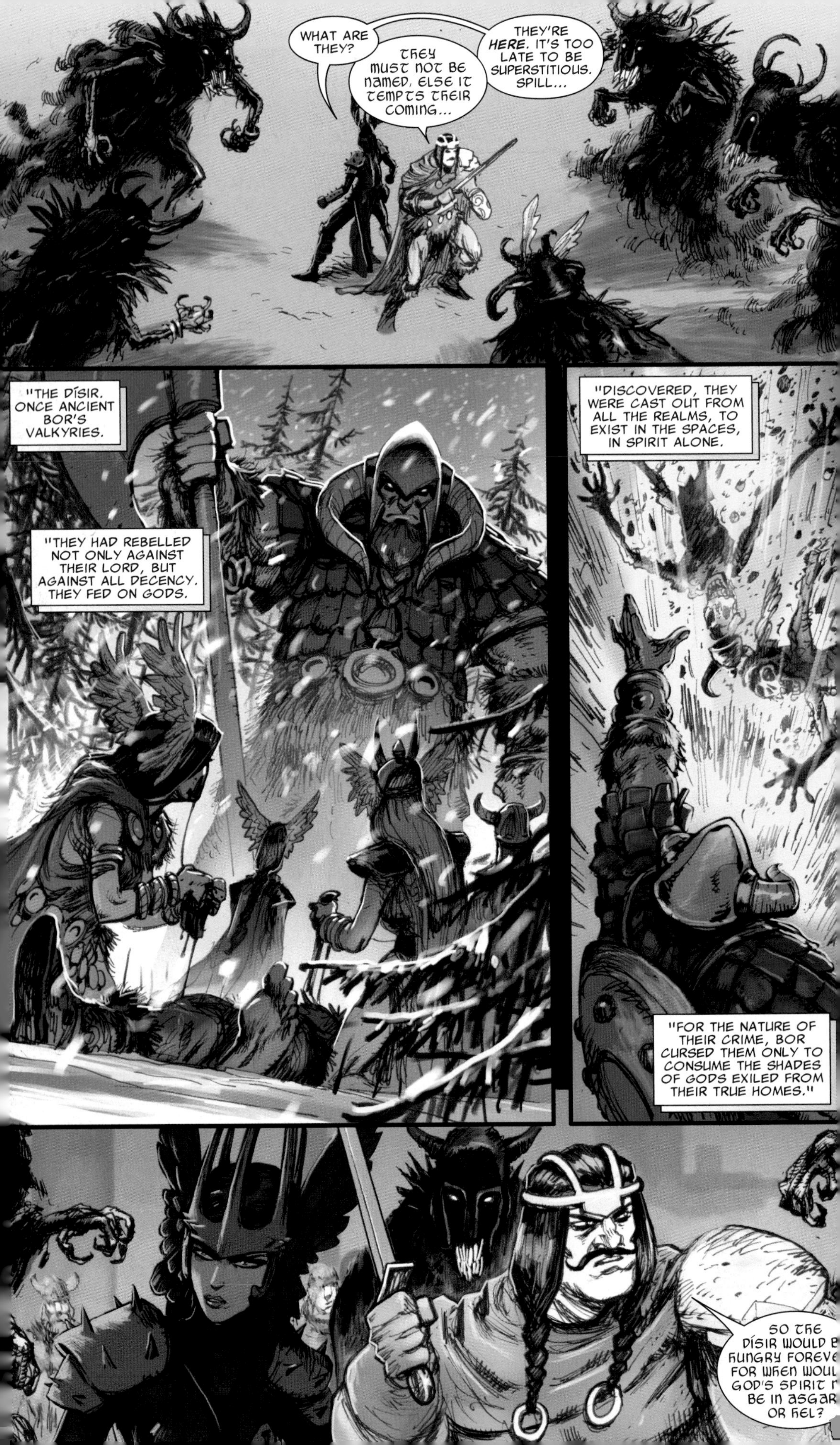
WHAT ARE THEY?
THEY MUST NOT BE NAMED, ELSE IT TEMPTS THEIR COMING...
THEY'RE *HERE*. IT'S TOO LATE TO BE SUPERSTITIOUS. SPILL...
"THE DÍSIR. ONCE ANCIENT BOR'S VALKYRIES.
"THEY HAD REBELLED NOT ONLY AGAINST THEIR LORD, BUT AGAINST ALL DECENCY. THEY FED ON GODS.
"DISCOVERED, THEY WERE CAST OUT FROM ALL THE REALMS, TO EXIST IN THE SPACES, IN SPIRIT ALONE.
"FOR THE NATURE OF THEIR CRIME, BOR CURSED THEM ONLY TO CONSUME THE SHADES OF GODS EXILED FROM THEIR TRUE HOMES."

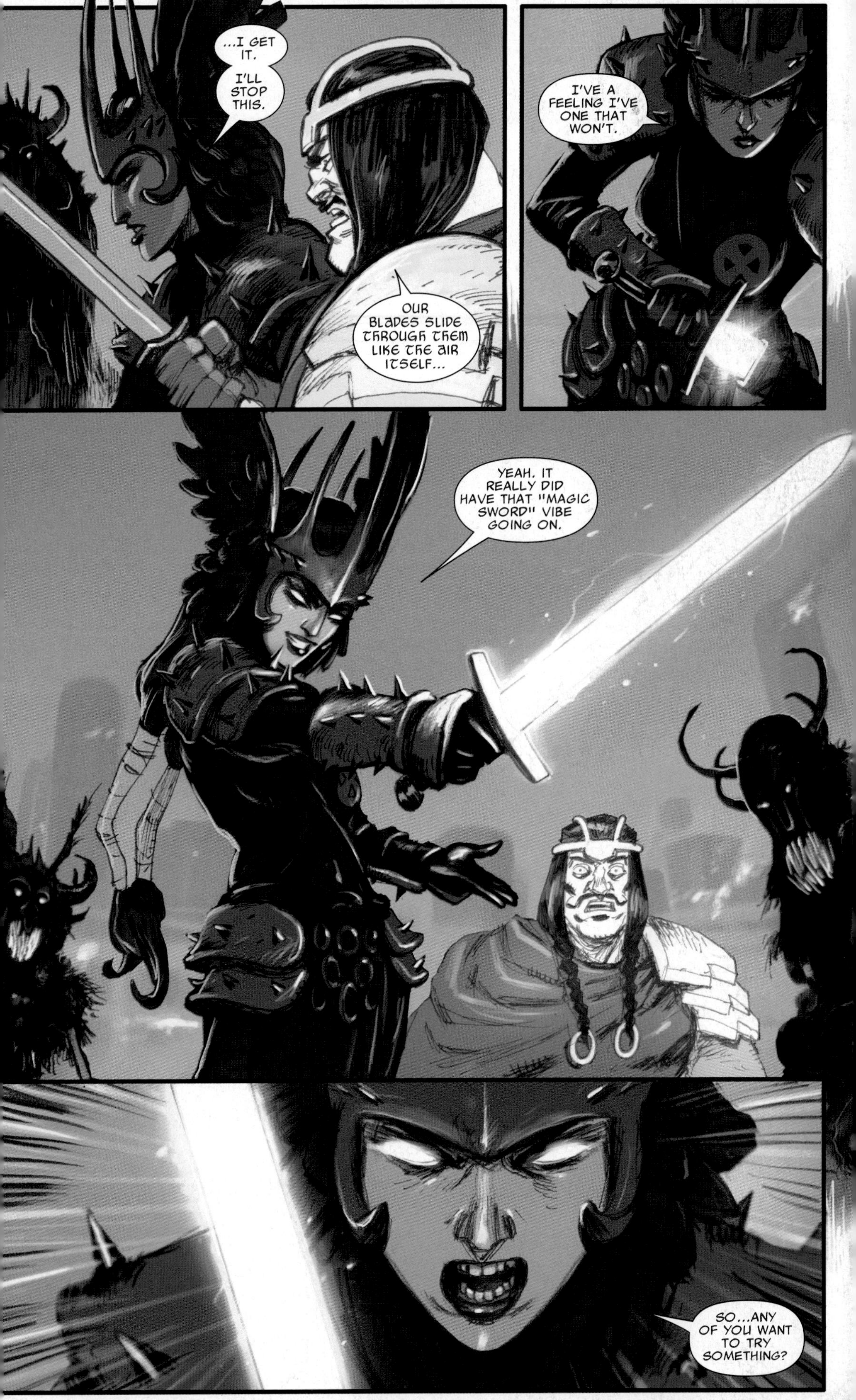
...I GET IT.
I'LL STOP THIS.
OUR BLADES SLIDE THROUGH THEM LIKE THE AIR ITSELF...
I'VE A FEELING I'VE ONE THAT WON'T.
YEAH. IT REALLY DID HAVE THAT "MAGIC SWORD" VIBE GOING ON.
SO...ANY OF YOU WANT TO TRY SOMETHING?

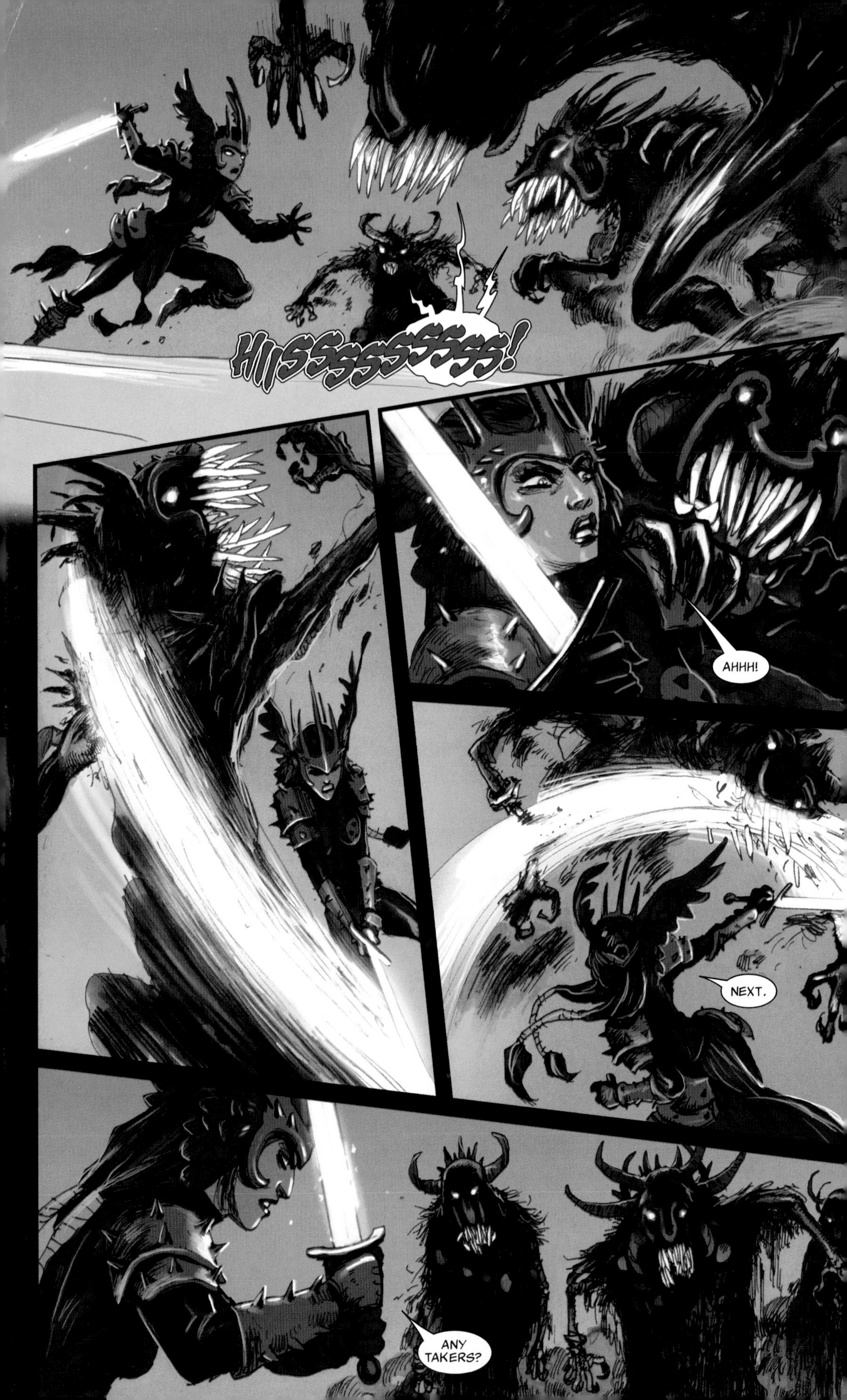
HIISSSSSSSSS!
AHHH!
NEXT.
ANY TAKERS?

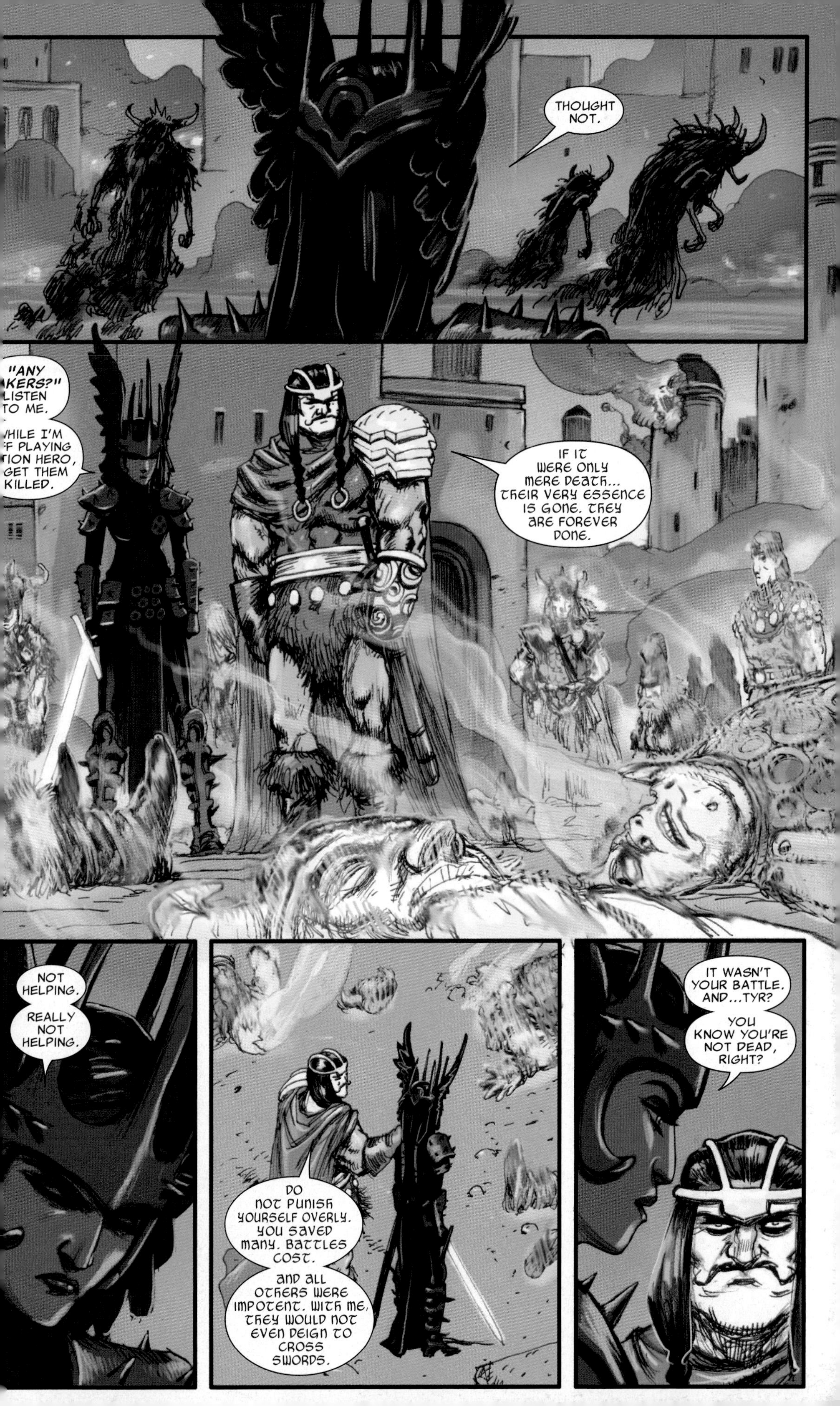
THOUGHT NOT.
"ANY
KERS?" LISTEN TO ME.
WHILE I'M F PLAYING TION HERO, GET THEM KILLED.
IF IT WERE ONLY MERE DEATH... THEIR VERY ESSENCE IS GONE. THEY ARE FOREVER DONE.
NOT HELPING.
REALLY NOT HELPING.
DO NOT PUNISH YOURSELF OVERLY. YOU SAVED MANY. BATTLES COST.
AND ALL OTHERS WERE IMPOTENT. WITH ME, THEY WOULD NOT EVEN DEIGN TO CROSS SWORDS.
IT WASN'T YOUR BATTLE. AND...TYR?
YOU KNOW YOU'RE NOT DEAD, RIGHT?

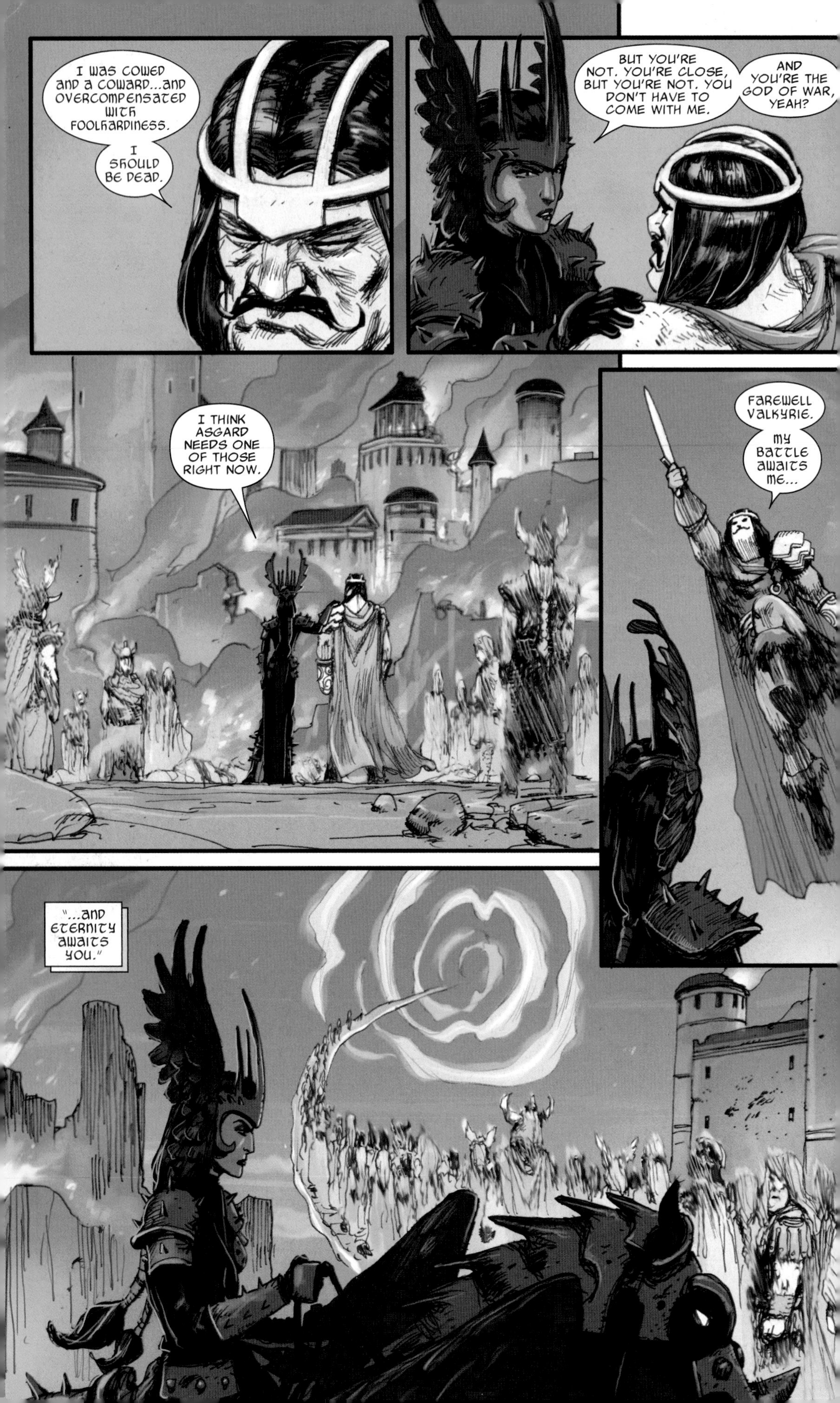
I WAS COWED AND A COWARD...AND OVERCOMPENSATED WITH FOOLHARDINESS.
I SHOULD BE DEAD.
BUT YOU'RE NOT. YOU'RE CLOSE, BUT YOU'RE NOT. YOU DON'T HAVE TO COME WITH ME.
AND YOU'RE THE GOD OF WAR, YEAH?
I THINK ASGARD NEEDS ONE OF THOSE RIGHT NOW.
FAREWELL VALKYRIE.
MY BATTLE AWAITS ME...
"...AND ETERNITY AWAITS YOU."

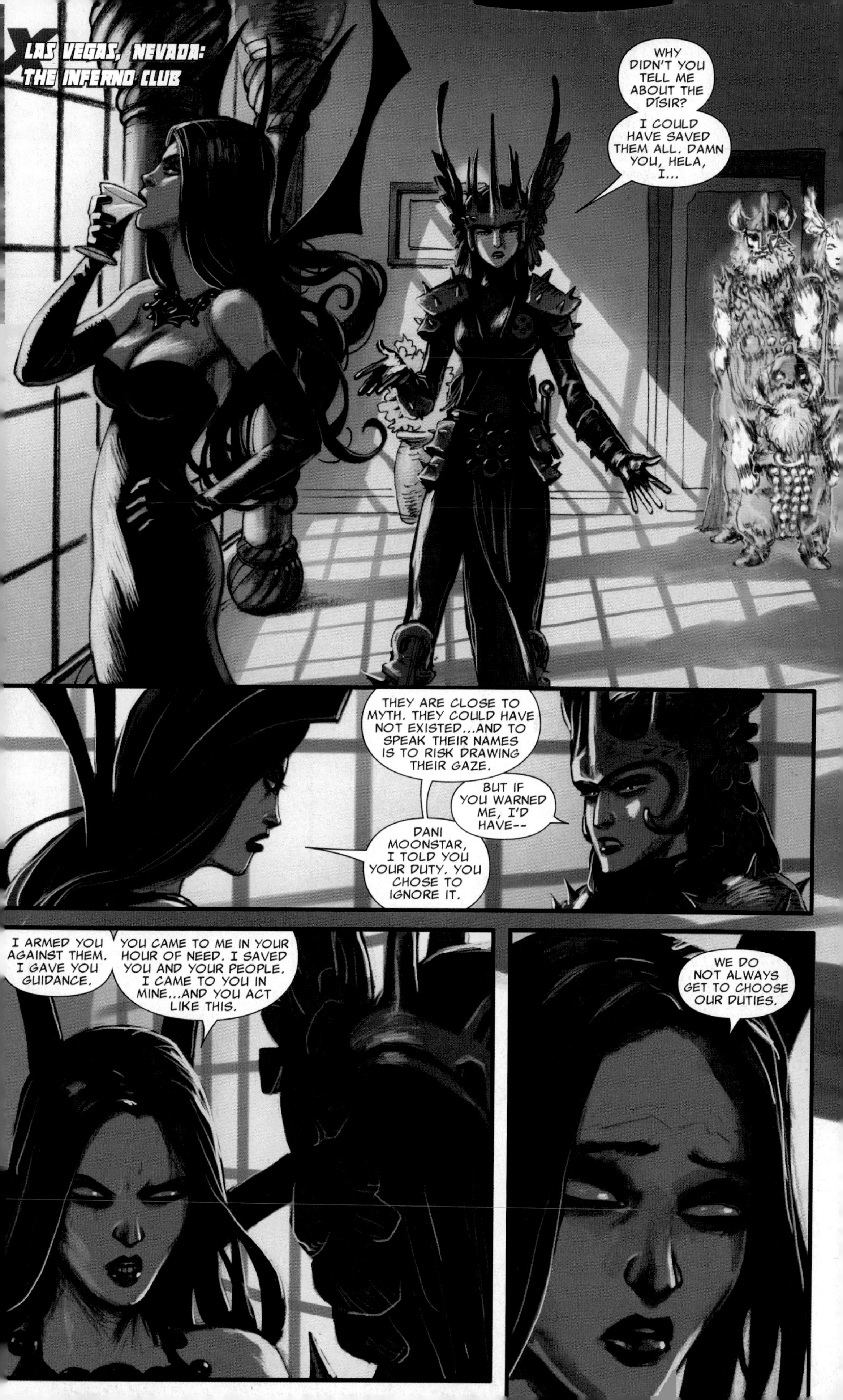
LAS VEGAS, NEVADA: THE INFERNO CLUB
WHY DIDN'T YOU TELL ME ABOUT THE DÍSIR?
I COULD HAVE SAVED THEM ALL. DAMN YOU, HELA, I...
THEY ARE CLOSE TO MYTH. THEY COULD HAVE NOT EXISTED...AND TO SPEAK THEIR NAMES IS TO RISK DRAWING THEIR GAZE.
BUT IF YOU WARNED ME, I'D HAVE--
DANI MOONSTAR, I TOLD YOU YOUR DUTY. YOU CHOSE TO IGNORE IT.
I ARMED YOU AGAINST THEM. I GAVE YOU GUIDANCE.
YOU CAME TO ME IN YOUR HOUR OF NEED. I SAVED YOU AND YOUR PEOPLE. I CAME TO YOU IN MINE...AND YOU ACT LIKE THIS.
WE DO NOT ALWAYS GET TO CHOOSE OUR DUTIES.

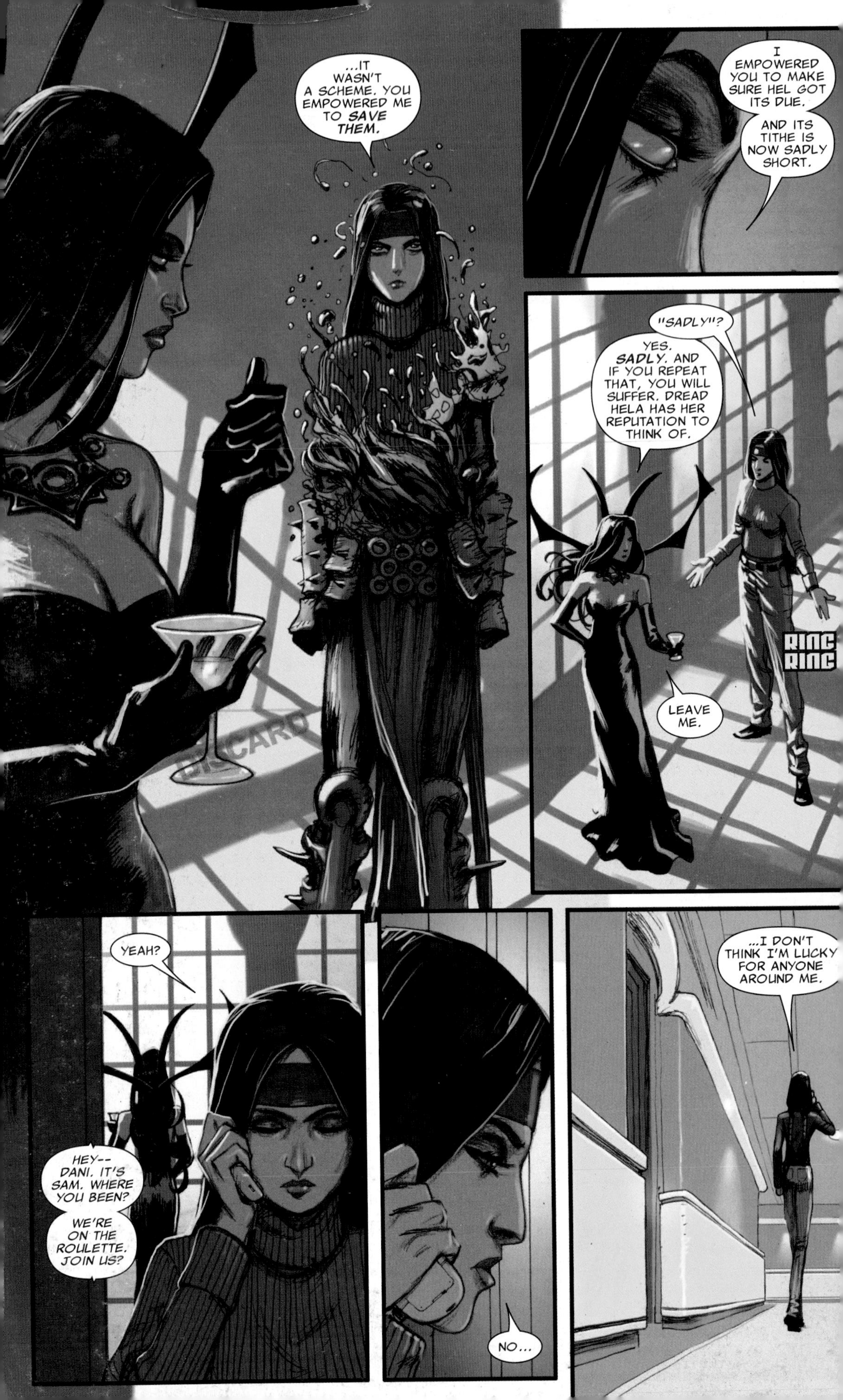

...IT WASN'T A SCHEME. YOU EMPOWERED ME TO SAVE THEM.
I EMPOWERED YOU TO MAKE SURE HEL GOT ITS DUE.
AND ITS TITHE IS NOW SADLY SHORT.
"SADLY"?
YES. SADLY. AND IF YOU REPEAT THAT, YOU WILL SUFFER. DREAD HELA HAS HER REPUTATION TO THINK OF.
RING RING
LEAVE ME.
YEAH?
HEY-- DANI. IT'S SAM. WHERE YOU BEEN?
WE'RE ON THE ROULETTE. JOIN US?
NO...
...I DON'T THINK I'M LUCKY FOR ANYONE AROUND ME.